General Editor Alastair Service

THE BUILDINGS OF BRITAIN
TUDOR AND
JACOBEAN

Malcolm Airs, the Conservation Officer for South Oxfordshire District Council, is the author of *The Making of the English Country House, 1500–1640* (1975) and was Architectural Editor of *The Survey of London* (1973–4).

The Series Editor, Alastair Service, is the author of *Edwardian Architecture* (1977), *The Architects of London: 1066 to the Present Day* (1979), *A Guide to the Megaliths of Europe* (1979, paperback 1981), and other books. He is a Committee Member of the Victorian Society.

Uniform with this volume in the series *The Buildings of Britain*:

REGENCY
David Watkin

Titles in preparation:
ANGLO-SAXON AND NORMAN
MEDIEVAL AND GOTHIC
STUART AND BAROQUE
GEORGIAN
VICTORIAN
TWENTIETH CENTURY

General Editor Alastair Service

THE BUILDINGS OF BRITAIN
TUDOR AND JACOBEAN

A Guide and Gazetteer

MALCOLM AIRS

Barrie & Jenkins

London   Melbourne   Sydney   Auckland   Johannesburg

To Megan in celebration of ten happy years

Barrie & Jenkins Ltd
An imprint of the Hutchinson Publishing Group
17–19 Conway Street, London W1P 6JD

Hutchinson Group (Australia) Pty Ltd
30–32 Cremorne Street, Richmond South, Victoria 3121
PO Box 151, Broadway, New South Wales 2007

Hutchinson Group (NZ) Ltd
32–34 View Road, PO Box 40–086, Glenfield, Auckland 10

Hutchinson Group (SA) (Pty) Ltd
PO Box 337, Bergvlei 2012, South Africa

First published 1982

For illustration copyrights, see Illustration Acknowledgements

Set in 10/12pt Goudy Old Style
by V & M Graphics Ltd, Aylesbury, Bucks
Printed in Great Britain by Fletcher & Son Ltd, Norwich

British Library Cataloguing in Publication Data
Airs, Malcolm
    Tudor and Jacobean: 1500–1640.—(The Buildings of Britain)
    1. Architecture, Tudor—Guide-books
    2. Architecture, Jacobean—Guide-books
    I. Title   II. Series
    724'.1   NA965
ISBN 0 09 147830 8 (cased)
ISBN 0 09 147831 6 (paper)

CONTENTS

AUTHOR'S ACKNOWLEDGEMENTS

A book of this nature could never have been written in the time available to me without the unstinting help and encouragement of many friends. In Scotland, not only did Anne Riches provide me with generous hospitality and the benefit of her knowledge but she also lent me books from her library, helped me wrestle with unfamiliar architectural terms, tracked down difficult photographs, and capped it all by her immaculately smooth driving.

In Wales I have been constantly enlightened by my expeditions over the years with Edward Parry and he valiantly undertook the initial research into the literature of the Principality. Edward Hubbard very kindly let me read parts of the text of his forthcoming volume on Clwyd in *The Buildings of Wales* series and my own entries for that county have undoubtedly benefited from his insight.

My principal mentor and occasional travelling companion in England has been Anthony Quiney and to him I owe a very special debt. Our dialogue on all aspects of architectural history has provided me with constant stimulation. Without it I would never have tackled this project. When I had completed it, he carefully and speedily improved the text and travelled extensively to ensure that it was adequately illustrated.

Others who have generously assisted me in specific ways during the writing of the book include Frank Kelsall, Robert Weston, John Ashdown, Roddy and Mary Smith, Chris Tyson, and Mike Price. Roger Mant selflessly relieved me of many time-consuming burdens during its compilation. I am grateful to Peter Leach, John Newman, John Summerson, Howard Colvin, Eric Mercer, Edward Hubbard and Emil Godfrey for discussions on particular aspects of the period.

The hospitality of the Hills of Redcar and the Parrys of Aberhafesp sustained me on my field trips and provided a welcome antidote to some of the landladies that I encountered. The domestic support of Megan Parry will never be repaid adequately. In addition to typing the text beautifully, she continued to ask me thought-provoking questions and to compose the most stunning photographs.

Finally, without the heroic achievement of Sir Nikolaus Pevsner this book could never have been written.

Malcolm Airs

September 1981   Dorchester-on-Thames

INTRODUCTION

The period between the Wars of the Roses and the Civil War saw the beginnings of the creation of the modern British nation. It was a momentous era crowded with profound changes and crowned with enduring achievements. During the period the separate kingdoms of England, Wales and Scotland were united under a single crown and an absolute state was established which, by the standards of the time, was notable for the efficiency with which it was administered. The established religion was irrevocably overthrown and the enormous fabric of the monasteries was dissolved. Partly as a result of these actions, the emergent nation stood alone for much of the period, isolated from the rest of Europe and forced to divert its precious resources into the creation of a navy capable of handsomely defending its sovereignty. An expanding population and a staggering rise in food prices stimulated further social change and ensured that by the end of the sixteenth century the medieval way of life was well and truly ended.

Parallel with these changes was a great expansion in British industry, agriculture and trade. The colonisation of the New World had begun and the arts, particularly poetry and the theatre, flourished as never before. It is against this background that the architecture of the period must be seen and its qualities recognised. In response to the political circumstances of the time, British architecture in the sixteenth century pursued its own course, independent of the Classical spirit which overwhelmed the rest of Europe. In the process it created its own indigenous styles which were fully as exciting and inventive as the other cultural achievements of the late Elizabethan and Stuart courts. The elements of this exhilarating story, both in the town and in the countryside, at Court and in the farmhouse, are told in the following pages, and the principal surviving monuments are listed in the gazetteer.

The most important architectural legacy of the age was the way in which radically changed social circumstances led to new domestic requirements which stimulated imaginative experiments in planning and massing. This forms the principal theme of the book and is in contrast to the dogged conservatism of the Church, the Law, and the Universities. Limitations of space have prevented any coherent treatment of the more specialised industrial and defensive buildings of the period and architectural decoration and fittings are only briefly considered. Many of the farmhouses discussed in Chapter 5 have been greatly altered so that their significant features are now apparent only to the specialist. As they are often working farms and difficult of access, they have not been noted separately in the gazetteer. The interested reader is referred to J. R. Armstrong's book listed in the bibliography for those smaller houses which are open to the public.

Within the confines of the gazetteer it would clearly be impossible to list every single surviving building of the period. What it contains is my own personal choice of the most significant and interesting buildings spread over the widest geographical area. I would welcome suggestions from readers for inclusion in any future editions.

Burghley House, Cambridgeshire, c.1550–87. William Cecil's important house which influenced the changing taste from Classical to Gothic

CLIENTS AND CRAFTSMEN

Every man almost is a builder and he that hath bought any small parcel of ground, be it never so little, will not be quiet till he have pulled down the old house (if any were there standing) and set up a new after his own devise.

W hen William Harrison made this observation in 1577, many parts of England, Wales and Scotland were in the midst of a domestic building boom which was to continue unabated to the eve of the Civil War. The surviving evidence for such unprecedented architectural activity is visible to the casual observer in unusual abundance, and for every building which still remains the historian is aware of many others which have long disappeared. In general, it was the upper echelons of society, the nobility and the gentry and the wealthy commercial magnates, who inspired and partici-pated in the boom. In certain parts of England and Wales, however, the characteristic regional architecture of the sixteenth and seventeenth centuries is as much a product of the yeoman and the smaller merchant as of the lord of the manor, and their important contribution should be recognised.

Compton Wynyates, Warwickshire; early sixteenth century. The most complete surviving example of an early Tudor moated courtyard house, built without any thought for contrived symmetry

Indeed, in the prosperous south-east, especially in Kent, the overall impression in the first half of the sixteenth century is that this class more than any other was monopolising the services of the local building crafts. The innumerable brick manor houses in the stone-less areas of eastern England, the wealth of buildings in the stone belts from Dorset in the south to Derbyshire in the north, and the flamboyant timber-framed houses of the west Midlands, the Welsh marches and the north-west, testify to an energetic activity by the gentry in the period from the accession of Elizabeth in 1558 until well into the seventeenth century. In the further north, beyond the

Borders, there was a flowering of the tower-house of the Scottish lairds and gentry in the same period. It is only in the troubled areas of northern England before the union of the thrones in 1603, and in the harsh soils of Cornwall, western Wales, and highland Scotland, that evidence for sixteenth-century building becomes hard to find.

By contrast with earlier periods, the vast majority of the surviving buildings from the sixteenth century are purely domestic. For the first time it is possible to write a history based on standing structures of the housing of the middling ranks of society as well as the nobility. Public and educational buildings also begin to assume a greater significance as the architectural importance of devotional building rapidly declines. The details of this picture are sketched in the succeeding chapters, but first it is necessary to examine the circumstances which led not only to such an extraordinary amount of building but also to what was a unique British contribution to European architectural culture.

In the countryside of England and parts of Wales there were a number of powerful influences at work to stimulate new building of houses, although the interrelationship between them is far more complex than their mere recital can adequately convey. The most important influence, and the one that underlies all the others, occurred at the end of the fifteenth century, although it was a generation or so before its architectural consequences were felt to the full. The Battle of

Pitchford Hall, Shropshire. A timber-framed house extended in the sixteenth and early seventeenth centuries from a fifteenth century core, but easily unified by the decorative pattern of its framework

Bosworth Field in 1485, which heralded the end of the Wars of the Roses and the accession to the throne of Henry Tudor, ushered in an era of uneasy peace which gradually strengthened in the course of the sixteenth century. Those in the forefront of public life were able to concentrate their energies and their finances on ceremonial display rather than armed conflict. Moreover, as a Welshman by descent, Henry VII was able to achieve the assimilation of the Principality into the English state more easily than might otherwise have been the case. The union was consolidated by the Acts of 1536 and 1542 which extended English law throughout the country, abolished the independent jurisdictions of the Marcher lordships, and encouraged the growth of Welsh agriculture and commerce by opening up free access to the English market.

The house of Tudor firmly wedded the general course of Welsh polite architecture to the broad trends emanating from

Gayton Manor House, Northamptonshire, c.1570. The conceit of a Greek cross plan at manor house level, still with arched lights to the windows

the English Court. In Scotland in the first half of the sixteenth century, events took a very different turn. With the notable exception of houses such as Craig Castle and Earlshall, few tower-houses of any consequence were built from the late fifteenth century until after the Scottish Reformation of 1560. As Stewart Cruden has described it:

The impetus to building flagged. It died with the medieval chivalry of Scotland at Flodden in 1513. Then all Scotland was in mourning. The lost generation could not build. Hertford invaded for Henry VIII in 1540, and the following years of the Reformation were not propitious. The continuation of the tower-house tradition was thus interrupted for some 80 years.

When Mary Queen of Scots returned from France in 1561 to rule over a Protestant Scotland, it marked the beginning of a remarkable late flowering of the traditional Scottish house, culminating in the undoubted masterpiece of Craigievar, completed by 1626.

In both England and Wales the establishment of a strong Tudor state was buttressed by the creation of new administrative posts within the government and in the shires, and many of these posts were deliberately filled by new men untainted by the political and dynastic rivalries of the old-established families. They were lawyers and men of proven administrative talents who owed their positions of new eminence to the patronage of the state and thus had a vested interest in maintaining its hard-won supremacy. Such men were handsomely rewarded for their allegiance and generated their own demand to be suitably housed in accordance with the proper status that their new-found wealth and power required. The Bacon family is perhaps the prime example of this group, rising from the status of yeoman farmers to the Lord Keepership of England within the space of two generations, and acquiring or building something like half a dozen new houses of increasing splendour in the process. The dissolution of the monasteries in the late 1530s released vast numbers of potential building sites, providing the Crown with a timely opportunity to satisfy the housing demands of these men while at the same time tying them more closely to the policies of the state. Sir Nicholas Bacon's first country house, for example, was built at Redgrave in Suffolk on the site of a hunting lodge of the Abbots of Bury St Edmunds, which he acquired in 1545 when he was Solicitor of the Court of Augmentation. Large numbers of other new houses of the

Audley End, Essex; begun 1603. The surviving hall range of the Earl of Suffolk's enormous double-courtyard house. The twin porches provided a separate entrance for the King and Queen

sixteenth and early seventeenth centuries, including such major monuments as Syon House, Longleat and Audley End, were built on former monastic sites and, wherever possible, this provenance has been noted in the gazetteer.

In addition to the creation of a whole new class of country house builders, the growing prospects of lasting domestic peace meant that the function of the great house itself was gradually changing through the sixteenth century in ways that were to have a strong influence on its architectural development. In the first place, in most of England and Wales, it was no longer necessary, or indeed politic, to build fortified houses which could withstand some form of siege or attack. Such an ambition, particularly in the uncertain times at the beginning of the century, could be construed as a provocative threat to the Crown, and it is not without significance that the construction of Thornbury Castle formed a specific part of the indictment that led to the execution of the Duke of Buckingham in 1521.

Secondly, in the sixteenth century there was no longer a compulsion to build great houses as a centre of economic activity on a large estate, for the major landowners came to rely increasingly on income from rents rather than direct farming of the demesne as the foundation of their wealth. They were therefore free to build wherever they chose and many new houses were constructed on sites selected for reasons of convenience or beauty and dependent for sustenance on the owners' estates elsewhere in the country. Theobalds, Lord Burghley's now demolished Hertfordshire mansion, was conveniently placed for easy access to the Court and had 'neither lordship nor tenants nor so much as provision of fuel', as Bishop Goodman noted.

A further diminution of the medieval way of life that was to have architectural consequences was a gradual decrease in the size of the household that a magnate considered it proper to surround himself with and to accommodate in his house. As the Tudors slowly substituted the rule of law for the local power politics of noble families, the bands of retainers and lesser families owing allegiance became increasingly anachronistic as an aspect of everyday life and the expense of housing them and travelling in state with them became more of a burden than a necessary display of power and status. Smaller permanent households meant that all but the most ambitious could build smaller houses which in turn were more suited to the prevailing architectural disciplines of order and proportion.

Besides encouraging the building of new houses, the net effect of these developments during the sixteenth century was to render obsolete and visibly out of date the traditional houses and castles which previously had satisfied the needs of many generations of established families. Throughout the century there was a clear stimulus to take advantage of the changed circumstances and to create better standards of comfort, privacy, light and sanitation. The glittering lantern-like glazed walls of a house like Hardwick Hall are an exhilarating symbol of this freedom from medieval architectural repression, and it is no mere coincidence that the flushing water-closet was invented by Sir William Harrington in those heady years of the late sixteenth century.

Indeed, freedom from cultural restraint and a restless pursuit of personal and intellectual pleasure shine through as abiding aspects of late sixteenth-century society, perhaps in compensation for the restrictions imposed on political freedom by the creation of an absolute state. 'Delight' was a word much used by contemporaries, and it expressed perfectly the response that was expected from the constant experimentation in planning and applied decoration which characterise many of the buildings of the period. Few of their creators were attracted to the sort of intellectual discipline that was implied by the rules of Classical architecture, and it is a fundamental mistake to see British architecture of the sixteenth century in terms of a failure to adopt the canons of Renaissance design laid down in Italy and France. This is a theme which undoubtedly demands consideration, but it is only a minor part of the exciting story which culminated with both England and Scotland creating their own unique styles, particularly in country house architecture, with a vigour which often seems to be lacking in continental Europe.

For many of the builders, their houses were not simply places in which to live in the appropriate degree of style demanded by their positions in society. They were also status symbols and objects of intense social rivalry which could publicly demonstrate their prosperity, wit and modernity. Above all, it is impossible not to feel that many of them were consciously intended to be fun. The cultured contemporary mind delighted in anything that was strange or curious, particularly if it were later revealed to have a hidden meaning, and this delight enthusiastically spilled over into almost every aspect of public and domestic life including paintings, literature, buildings, correspondence and even on occasion the presentation of food. The expressions of this cerebral sport were known as 'devices' and were defined by Geoffrey Whitney in a popular book published in 1586 as 'something obscure to be perceived at the first, whereby when with further consideration it is understood, it may the greater delight the beholder'. For a gentleman it was far more important and seemly that he should understand the clues to these exclusive crossword puzzles than that he should be learned in a bookish sense, and, indeed, at the end of the sixteenth century George Bruce copied the engravings with their mottoes from Whitney's book as part of the painted decoration in the new range that he added to his house at Culross, supposedly in anticipation of a royal visit.

The architectural manifestation of the device is often found in the lodges and other small buildings which adorned an estate. The best-known of them all is the tiny lodge which Sir Thomas Tresham constructed between 28 July 1594 and 24 September 1597 on his estate at Rushton, Northampton-shire, to house his warrener. Built after his conversion to Roman Catholicism, the Triangular Lodge is nothing less than a defiant public celebration of the Holy Trinity and the doctrine of the Mass with almost every stone pregnant with allegorical meaning. Each of its three sides is thirty-three and a third feet long, or a third of a hundred feet. It is three storeys high with three gables on each side and three windows composed of multiples of three on each storey. The symbols and inscriptions on each side refer to one of the persons of the Trinity and each inscription is composed of exactly thirty-three letters. Over the doorway is the text *TRES TESTI-MONIUM DANT*, which, with characteristic ambiguity, can be read as both 'There are three that bear witness' from the first epistle of St John (the doctrine of the Holy Trinity) and 'The Treshams bear witness'. No doubt his wretched warrener felt uncomfortably embarrassed by this blatant display, but it must have afforded Tresham considerable satisfaction during his periods of imprisonment for his faith.

It was comparatively cheap to use such minor buildings for the boldest displays of wit, but country houses themselves were not immune from the same spirit. Even if the bizarre house based on his initials that John Thorpe designed for himself and entitled

> These 2 letters I and T
> (being) joined together as you see
> Is meet for a dwelling house for me

was never likely to be built, there are a significant number of surviving examples of both architectural drawings and completed houses which can be shown to have been conceived or recognised as 'devices' in one form or another. Mostly, as might be expected when the wit had to be tempered by domestic necessity, they are simple exercises on various geometrical figures, such as the plans based on circles,

Opposite: Triangular Lodge, Rushton, Northamptonshire, 1594–7. A perfect Elizabethan conceit symbolising the Holy Trinity and the doctrine of the Mass and publicly proclaiming Sir Thomas Tresham's Roman Catholicism

Below: Lyveden New Build, Northamptonshire, 1604. Tresham's other allegorical lodge, symbolising the Passion, with sophisticated architectural details supplied from London by Robert Stickles

triangles and Greek crosses in the Thorpe and Smythson collections and such extant houses as Stiffkey Hall, Hardwick Hall and Longford Castle, or the smaller Y-planned houses of Newhouse Farm, Goodrich, or the similarly named New-house at Redlynch, Whiteparish, in Wiltshire. Once the effort of looking at them with sixteenth-century eyes has been made, it is not too difficult to identify them; with other buildings, however, the mental gulf is too great and it is only by the chance survival of documentary evidence that we can see them as their creators intended or in the way that their contemporaries responded. It comes as some surprise, for example, to read in John Strode's diary an explanation for the E-shaped plan that he chose for Chantmarle House, Dorset, in 1612: 'It is built in the form of the letter E, for Emmanuel: that is, our Lord in Heaven.' Visible confirmation is provided by the word Emmanuel, beautifully carved above the entrance. The belief that all E-planned houses were intended as a tribute to Queen Elizabeth, whether or not it is true in other cases, is itself nothing more than an implicit acceptance of the idea of the architectural 'device'.

Newhouse Farm, Goodrich, Hereford and Worcester, 1636. Y-planned parsonage house built for the Rev. Thomas Smith, possibly as an allegory on the Trinity

The underlying assumption behind such expensive displays of ingenuity is that your peers would be as passionately interested in the novelty of your buildings as you

Newhouse,
Whiteparish,
Wiltshire, c.1619.
Y-planned hunting
lodge for Sir
Thomas Gorges
whose principal
house was the
triangular
Longford Castle

yourself were, and it is abundantly clear that in the upper ranks of society, at least, architecture was a common subject for enthusiastic discussion. James Cleland in *The Institution of a Young Noble Man* (1607) considered that a knowledge of the principles of architecture was an essential part of a gentleman's education and the surviving correspondence of the period is scattered with references to building. The fulsome letters praising the cleverness of their houses that Burghley and Sir Christopher Hatton wrote to each other are well enough known, but there are many others, ranging from the ingratiating through the practical to the brutally honest, which enliven the study of the subject and help to imbue the surviving monuments with human sentiments. Sir Nicholas Bacon, for example, clearly felt that Sir William Cecil had gone too far in striving for symmetry at his newly built London house. He wrote to him in 1560 to tell him that he had placed a privy 'too near the lodging, too near an oven, and too near a little larder', adding 'I think you had been better to have offended your eye outward than your nose inward.'

21

In the evolving circumstances of the Tudor style of government with its insistence on the attendance at Court of any nobleman anxious to secure the patronage which alone could guarantee his wealth and power, many a tedious waiting hour must have been spent in talk of building and architecture. Who was building the longest gallery and who was creating the prettiest ceiling in their great chamber seem to have been questions which evoked as much curiosity as the latest gossip about dress or the theatre in the anterooms and presence chambers at Whitehall or St James's. When the courtiers and officials returned to their country estates, they lost no time in putting the information that they had gleaned to good effect on their own buildings. Ideas of fashionable design and knowledge of exceptional craftsmen seem to have circulated freely in this way, so that it is safe to assume that Lord Herbert, for example, first heard of the Hertfordshire carpenter, John Scampion, in London when he was attending at Court and it was there that he recruited him to travel to Wales and to design a new building for Montgomery Castle. Certainly, the owners of the great country houses were just as interested in the skills of each other's craftsmen as they were in the devices that they created. Thus, hearing of his excellent workmanship, Sir William Cavendish wrote to Sir John Thynne asking for the loan of a 'cunning plasterer' when he had finished at Longleat, and Sir Edward Pytts recruited John Bentley in the seventeenth century from Oxford for his new house in Worcestershire largely because Bentley had 'wrought the new addition to Sir Thomas Bodley his famous library'.

Such was the demand for skilful craftsmen that Sir Edward Hext wrote with evident relief in 1610 after he had secured a contract with the mason William Arnold to build Wadham College, Oxford: 'If I had not tied him fast to this business we should hardly keep him; he is so wonderfully sought being indeed the absolutest and honestest workman in England.' It was not simply a shortage of men of the highest skills at a time of unprecedented building activity that caused such competition for established craftsmen. It was also the ancilliary skills in drawing and supervision, their ability to render accounts and to administrate other trades than their own, and the knowledge of materials and supplies that they brought with them, that made them 'so wonderfully sought'. In many ways they were the key figures of the entire building and design process of the period. They were not architects in any modern sense, but, in view of the other demands on their employers' time and the rigidly ordered concepts of what it was proper for a gentleman to involve himself with, the craftsman-cum-administrator was just as influential as his client regarding the finished appearance of many of the country houses of the sixteenth and early seventeenth centuries.

Undoubtedly this is one of the main reasons why many of the motifs of Classical architecture, such as columns and pediments, were adopted in Britain during the sixteenth century as decorative features, with little or no understanding of the logic and grammar behind them. The novelty-conscious courtier-classes saw them as fashionable conceits to be

A doorway from *Architectura* by Wendel Dietterlin (plate 67 from the second edition of 1598). Based on the Classical Doric order, this sort of elaborate decoration had great appeal for contemporary British taste

23

discarded for other modish forms of decoration as fashions changed. This is well illustrated by Lord Burghley's house near Stamford which was begun in the 1550s as a Classical building in the idiom briefly popularised by the Duke of Somerset, but which, by the time of its completion in the late 1580s, had adopted the whimsical details of the Gothic revival which Sir Francis Willoughby had initiated at Wollaton Hall. By the same token, when the fully developed Renaissance finally arrived in England with the Queen's House at Greenwich early in the following century, contemporaries saw it as nothing more than 'some curious device of Inigo Jones'; another fad which would give pleasure enough until it was superseded by something else – which, indeed, it was.

As a fashion, the courtier-builders were able to hand their craftsmen-designers illustrations from the more popular architectural books of the day to show them the sort of thing that they wanted, and their craftsmen would duly oblige by copying or adapting them. The libraries of men such as Sir Thomas Tresham, Sir Thomas Smith, Lord Burghley and the Earl of Northumberland, are known to have contained copies of John Shute's *The First and Chief Groundes of Architecture* (1563), the books of engravings by Wendel Dietterlin and Vredeman de Vries, and the highly influential illustrated edition of Serlio's *Architettura* (1566), and drawings based on these and other contemporary books can be found in the notebooks of both the Smythsons and John Thorpe. Such eclectic copying from published examples was hardly likely to foster in the craftsmen a true understanding of the philosophical basis of Classical architecture. It simply expanded their repertoire of 'curious devices'. The essential means to a true understanding were book learning and direct contact with Europe, but both these sources of inspiration were largely denied to the craftsman class.

Intellectual commitment to the Renaissance remained the province of the courtier class which alone had the necessary leisure, education and motivation to maintain a link with the European literary and cultural sources of the movement. Only a very few men from that class, however, were prepared to devote themselves to the rigorous discipline that the pursuit of such an ideal implied. They might admire the logic and the proportional order of the Classical 'device' but, ultimately, with a few notable exceptions, they were of the same mind as Francis Bacon that 'houses are built to live in, and not to look on: therefore let use be preferred before uniformity, except where both may be had. Leave the goodly fabrics of houses for beauty only to the enchanted palaces of the poets, who build them with small cost.' Consequently, the owners entrusted their craftsmen with a degree of freedom in the execution of design which would have been unthinkable by the latter part of the seventeenth century. Provided that the accommodation satisfied the particular needs of the owner and was sufficiently grand to match his social status, and provided that the external appearance conformed with the view that he wished to present to the world, the owner was often content to leave the details to his principal artisan, confident, for example, that someone like Robert Smythson who had done such a competent job for Sir John Thynne at Longleat or Sir Francis Willoughby at Wollaton would be unlikely to let him down.

This explains why men such as Smythson travelled such long distances in their working careers when the majority of their class were relatively static, and it also helps to account for the regional spread of architectural ideas at the same time. These did not emanate simply from the gossip at Court, but also travelled the country in the notebooks and the heads of the craftsmen who executed them. Recent research has helped to re-establish the importance for sixteenth- and early seventeenth-century design of such craftsmen as the Smyth-

Condover Hall, Shropshire, 1586–98; Walter Hancock principal mason. The flamboyant projecting porch and the disciplined arrangement of gables, windows and chimneystacks are characteristic of the best houses of the period

sons, the Grumbolds and the Thorpes in England, and the Bells in Scotland; and there are many others of whose existence we are only dimly aware, but whose influence was just as significant. Such men as the Shropshire mason Walter Hancock, of whom it was recorded at the time of his death in 1599 that he was skilful 'in the art of masonry, in setting of plots for buildings and performing of the same, engraving in alabaster and other stone or plaster, and diverse other gifts that belong to that art as doth appear by his works which may be seen in diverse parts of England and Wales; most sumptuous buildings, most stately tombs, most curious pictures.' We know a little of Hancock's work, but not enough to assess properly the validity of such a fulsome obituary. We know, for example, that he made the monument to Richard Herbert in Montgomery Church, that he almost certainly designed the Market Hall in Shrewsbury, and that he worked as the principal mason at Condover Hall in Shropshire. There is also the possibility that he was responsible for the few fragments that survive of Sir Francis Newport's houses at High Ercall and Eyton-on-Severn in the same county. From what we can see, he appears to have been a first-class provincial mason of no more than local repute, but his work is far more characteristic of the mainstream of English and Welsh architecture of the time than the work of those who were responsible for the more obviously significant buildings such as Longleat or Hardwick Hall. In the final analysis, it is just as important to recognise the contribution of these craftsmen to the first flowering of the larger British house as it is to dissect the intellectual motives of the men who employed them.

2

ROYAL BUILDINGS

Royal building in both England and Scotland followed a very uneven pattern during the course of the sixteenth and early seventeenth centuries, with frenetic periods of new building alternating with long spells of inactivity. No new royal building of any consequence was erected in Wales in the entire period; in England, however, most of the outstanding buildings of the first half of the sixteenth century were the work of the Crown, which, again, in the early part of the seventeenth century, was responsible for a group of significant buildings which have fascinated the minds of architectural historians ever since. In the very different circumstances of Scotland, work of the highest European quality in the 1530s and the 1590s contrasts starkly with the barren years between.

The establishment of a secure throne occupied most of the early years of Henry VII after Bosworth and it was only towards the end of his reign that he was able to turn his attention to the pleasures of building. Of his palace at Richmond, commenced in 1497, only a gateway bearing his coat of arms and a few brick fragments survive, but it is known from drawings to have been a large double-courtyard structure with a multitude of towers and turrets. Nothing now remains of the buildings that he erected at his other London palace in Greenwich and it is principally as a builder of several works of an ecclesiastical nature that he now demands our attention. Some of them, such as St George's Chapel, Windsor, and King's College Chapel, Cambridge, were only the continuation of works that others had started and which were not to be completed until the reign of Henry VIII. Others were new foundations and bear testimony to the last gasp of medieval regal piety, which was to begin to expire with Henry himself and to be extinguished finally by his son within the space of three decades. Like his domestic palaces, the monastery that he founded at Richmond in 1501, the almshouses in Westminster, and the enormous Savoy Hospital to provide overnight accommodation for a hundred poor people at Charing Cross, have all disappeared; but the magnificently vaulted and lavishly decorated chapel which he caused to be added to Westminster Abbey as a monument to house the body of his uncle, Henry VI, still survives in all its splendour. Begun in 1503, it was completed in 1512, three years after his death. For all its beauty, it must be considered a backward-looking building signifying the final flowering of the Middle Ages rather than pointing the way forward to what was to come, and so it falls outside the main themes of this volume.

Henry VII's Chapel, Westminster Abbey, 1503–12. The magnificently vaulted ceiling of the most flamboyant of all English late Gothic ecclesiastical buildings

In the event, Henry VI's tomb remained at Windsor and the principal significance of the project for our purposes is the tomb of Henry VII which Henry VIII commissioned in 1512 from Pietro Torrigiano, the Florentine sculptor, and set up behind the altar at the east end of the chapel. This astonishing work in black and white marble, with gilded decoration in the finest Italian quattrocento style contrasting sharply with the Gothic architecture of its setting, could not have marked more completely the change in taste from one age to another. It was the first example of Renaissance art to appear in the kingdom and it must have seemed to indicate the inevitable decorative style to accompany the young Henry VIII's image as a Renaissance Prince. Perhaps if the links with the Continent had remained open this would ultimately have been so, but the political events which served to isolate England from the cultural forces of Catholic Europe prevented it and no work of art comparable to the quality of Torrigiano's tomb was to appear in London for another hundred years or so.

In the early years of his reign, Henry VIII built little that has survived, and it was only with the downfall of Wolsey in 1529 that his appetite for building became truly voracious. It has been reckoned that at the time of his death in 1547 he had more than forty houses at his disposal in various parts of the country, many of which had consumed large sums in maintenance and new building. The most important survivor of this burst of building activity is Hampton Court which, despite the later additions of Wren and others, still presents an almost complete picture of the scale and appearance of a Tudor palace.

Hampton Court was begun in 1515 for Cardinal Wolsey and was already a double-courtyard house of great size and opulence when Wolsey deemed it expedient to make it over to the King ten years later. He continued to live there, however, and it was only with his ultimate fall from grace in 1529 that Henry took possession. There is no doubt that one of the tactical errors which alienated the Monarch from his Cardinal was that the latter had flagrantly built himself a house which far exceeded the splendour of any of the contemporary royal palaces, but Henry soon set to work to eradicate the memory of this intolerable slight. Within a few years he had added two projecting wings to Wolsey's entrance front, built the magnificent Great Hall and remodelled the other ranges round the Clock Court, extended the plan to the east by the addition of a further courtyard now occupied by Fountain Court,

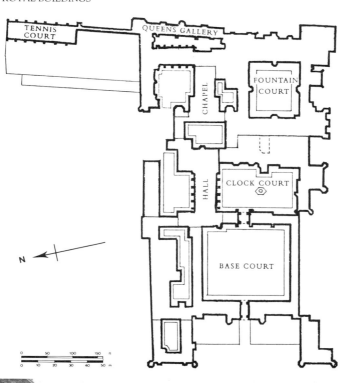

Left: Hampton Court Palace, Richmond upon Thames. The shaded areas indicate the additions made by Henry VIII in transforming Wolsey's large courtyard house into a royal palace. Note particularly the symmetrical effect on the entrance elevation of the two western projections

Below left: Great Hall of Hampton Court, built 1531–6 for Henry VIII to replace Wolsey's more modest hall. Despite its grandeur it is still in the medieval tradition with an open hearth and Gothic windows

Medallion of Emperor Hadrian at Hampton Court by Giovanni da Maiano, 1521, for Cardinal Wolsey; with its theme and Classical decoration, one of the earliest examples of the Renaissance in England

and created two smaller courtyards to the north by building around Wolsey's Chapel and his own hall.

Wolsey's London house of York Place also came to Henry and between 1530 and 1536, when the work at Hampton Court was at its height, he greatly extended it over some 23 acres to form his new palace of Whitehall. Apart from the cellars, nothing now survives, but the gatehouse and chapel remain from Henry's other London palace, a short walk away at St James's, built between 1532 and 1540. These fragments reinforce the impression gained from Hampton of a palace-cum-castle Court style with their late gothic detail and considerable emphasis on an imposing gate-house flanked by octagonal towers. Apart from the symmetry of the west front and the pendants of the hall roof, all the features at Hampton Court which could be considered to be advanced, such as the terracotta roundels of the heads of Roman Emperors by Giovanni da Maiano and the decoration of Wolsey's closet, predate its transformation into a royal palace.

In the field of defence, however, there was no room for conservatism. The increasing efficiency of artillery warfare had stimulated the rapid evolution of radically new types of fortifications in Italy and Germany in the early years of the

sixteenth century, and when an invasion from Catholic Europe seemed imminent in 1538, Henry responded with a crash programme of castle building which incorporated many of the most up-to-date defensive features. Within the space of a few years a string of small fortresses had been constructed along the south coast from Gravesend in the east to Pendennis and St Mawes in the west. Many of them still remain as an impressive architectural testament to England's isolated position in the years after the break with Rome.

The contradictions which were inherent in Henry as a man were given full architectural expression in his last great palace of Nonsuch in Surrey, begun in 1538 shortly after the revenue from the dissolved monasteries put him in a position where he could indulge his grandiose fantasies without restraint. As a double-courtyard house with the state apartments placed in the inner courtyard entered through a gate-house, the plan superficially resembled a more disciplined version of Henry's earlier palaces. The elevations and the opulence of the applied decoration were something else, and it was these which so impressed contemporaries and have tantalised historians ever since the palace was demolished in the late seventeenth century. The lower part of the building was of stone, but the upper part was timber-framed 'richly adorned and set forth and garnished with a variety of pictures and other antick forms of excellent art and workmanship', according to a survey of 1650. Various foreign craftsmen, such as Nicholas Belin of Modena, who had worked at Fontainebleau, William Cure of Amsterdam and Giles Gering, were recruited to execute the decorative work which included life-size plaster statues and patterned slate-hanging of the highest quality. Judging from

Camber Castle, Rye, East Sussex, c.1540. One of Henry VIII's south coast castles with a characteristic low profile and symmetrical plan the famous drawing of the garden front by Hoefnagel, Nonsuch with its careful symmetry, its octagonal corner towers and its battlemented parapets resembled nothing so much as the fantasy castles of the later sixteenth century. Whether the details of the decoration equally influenced Elizabethan and Jacobean architecture, as Sir John Summerson has plausibly suggested, will have to wait until the excavation reports, so eagerly awaited for the last twenty years, are finally published.

What seems certain is that Henry was consciously motivated in his ambitions for Nonsuch by a deep personal rivalry with François I of France which had its origins as far back as their historic meeting at the Field of Cloth of Gold in June 1520. Nonsuch was Henry's belated riposte to the Chambord of François, but the influence of the French Court had already penetrated north of the border and in far greater depth a short while before. The 1530s in Scotland was a period of royal building fully comparable with the strenuous efforts of the English Office of Works. As with Henry, the early architectural excursions of James V were firmly rooted in native building traditions. In developing the quadrangular form and reorientating the entrance of Linlithgow Palace in about 1535 he exhibited nothing remarkable in architectural treatment, while the apartments that he built at Holyrood Palace in Edinburgh between 1529 and 1532 were forbid-

Nonsuch Palace, Surrey; begun 1538, demolished 1687. The lively skyline of the symmetrical garden front gives a tantalising impression of Henry VIII's most opulent palace

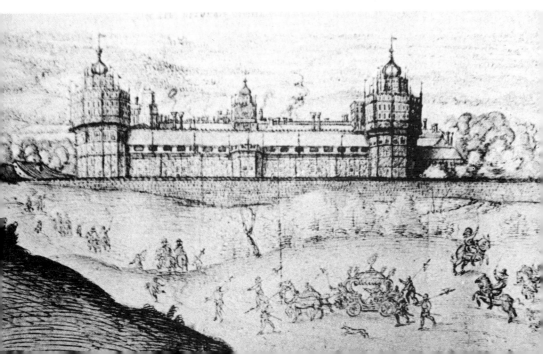

dingly medieval in their tower form. In 1537, however, James was at the French Court seeking to revive the Franco-Scottish alliance by marriage to Magdalene, the daughter of François. When she died shortly after her arrival in Scotland, James returned to secure the hand of Mary of Lorraine, another, adopted, daughter of the French King. Not only did these visits bring James into direct contact with the distinctive culture of the French Court, but he was also able to recruit French craftsmen into the Scottish Works with immediate results that briefly were to revolutionise Scottish architecture.

Between 1537 and 1541, Falkland Palace was extensively remodelled with courtyard façades incorporating attached Classical columns, regular fenestration and stone medallion busts, clearly derived from France. The work is of the very highest quality and Mark Girouard has described it as 'a display of early Renaissance architecture without parallel in the British Isles'. If this alone had been the architectural harvest of the renewal of the 'Auld Alliance', it would have been remarkable enough, but between 1540 and 1542, James embarked upon an ambitious scheme of new building at Stirling Castle where he created a new set of royal apartments around a small courtyard. Whereas at Falkland the decorative emphasis had been on the courtyard elevations and had shown

Stirling Castle,
Central Region.
Below: Carved oak
ceiling medallion
of a man in
armour from the
King's presence
chamber. As the
illustrations on
pages 31 and 154
show, such motifs
were a popular
theme of early
Renaissance
decoration
Bottom: The
Palace, 1540–2.
Stirling is a more
mannered and
eclectic
composition than
Falkland but
imbued with
similar French
influence

disciplined restraint, at Stirling all the external façades were covered with a profusion of carving and sculpture which compensates delightfully for the fortress-like surroundings and the dourness of the grey stone. Semicircular niches with cusped tracery contain strange baluster shafts supporting sculptured figures. These alternate with the large iron-barred windows adorned with carved heads. There is an enriched cornice above with further figures on pedestals interspersed with elongated crenellations.

The royal apartments were on the first floor with the King's rooms occupying the northern range and a complementary set for the Queen in the southern range. The ceiling of the King's presence chamber was decorated with a scheme of wooden medallions of a similar inspiration to Wolsey's terracotta roundels at Hampton Court and the stone medallions on the courtyard elevation of the south range of Falkland.

Such opulent and revolutionary architecture, derived from foreign examples and partly executed by foreign craftsmen, did not survive the monarch who inspired it and had no lasting effect on the development of Scottish architecture. When the Scottish nobles came to build again in the decades after 1560, they reverted to their native style just as though Falkland and Stirling had never been. The works that Regent Morton put in hand at Edinburgh Castle in 1574, principally the Portcullis Gate and the Half Moon Battery, were primarily defensive and provided little opportunity for architectural display. In 1594, James VI, who had himself been baptised at Stirling, chose the same venue for the baptism of his eldest son, Prince Frederick Henry. The occasion was used as an opportunity to demonstrate the dignity and splendour of the Scottish Court and a new Chapel Royal was built within the confines of the castle for the ceremony. The simple Classical building, with plain arched lights under semicircular heads and a central porch flanked by coupled columns, betrays its ancestry only by the use of crow-stepped gables. Again, the sophisticated taste of a Scottish monarch was demonstrated and, again, it had little influence on the taste of his subjects. Within a decade the thrones of Scotland and England had been united and the Scottish Court had moved south to reassemble in London.

There was to be no further royal building in Scotland until well into the seventeenth century when the brief return visit of James in 1617 inspired the refurbishment of the ruined northern quarter of Linlithgow Palace on a double-pile plan

and the remodelling of the King's lodging at Edinburgh Castle. The redecoration of the Chapel Royal at Falkland Palace in 1633 marked the first northern journey of Charles I. There were no architectural works to celebrate his second hurried return in 1641.

Newly crowned as James I of England, James VI found that there had been little royal building in his new kingdom since the death of Henry VIII. Henry had bequeathed Edward VI, his sickly infant son, exhausted coffers and a sufficiency of royal palaces. The troubled reign of Philip and Mary was hardly propitious for an overt demonstration of princely extravagance and by the time that Elizabeth had acceded to the throne, the initiative in ostentatious building had passed into the hands – and dug deep into the pockets – of her noble subjects. This seems to have suited the parsimonious ways of the new Queen and the story of her reign, where the building of large-scale houses is concerned, is largely one of aristocratic rivalry to provide suitably grand accommodation to house her on her stately summer Progresses around the country. It is a story which is told more fully in the following chapter.

Such an arrangement, whereby not only the capital costs of building but also the considerable expense of entertaining the Court when they were present devolved upon the host, had obvious financial advantages for an indigent monarch, and James enthusiastically adopted the custom. Indeed, if anything, the Progress became more lavish and extravagant

Stirling Castle, Central Region. Chapel Royal, 1594. Built for the baptism of Prince Frederick Henry in a remarkable restrained Classical form under James than it had been under Elizabeth. Royal patronage demanded selfless generosity on the part of those who hoped to benefit from it, but one is still left breathless at the way that James acquired the only new palace of the early years of his reign. Theobalds, Lord Burghley's country mansion near Cheshunt, 'begun by me with a mean measure but increased by occasion of her Majesty's often coming', had been a favourite house of Elizabeth and James found it equally attractive. So much so, indeed, that in 1607 the Earl of Salisbury, who had succeeded on the death of his father, found it prudent to offer the house and parks to the King. He received seventeen royal manors in exchange for his generosity but, nevertheless, the cost of building a replacement house at Hatfield over the next five years nearly bankrupted the Cecil family fortunes.

Whether the Stuarts brought a predilection for Classical architecture south with them, or whether they merely responded to the extraordinary talents of the man who arranged their beloved masques and who was appointed Surveyor of Works to Prince Henry in 1610, must remain an unanswerable question. But no matter what the truth might be, there can be little doubt that the architectural achievement of both James and Charles I is inextricably associated with the buildings that Inigo Jones designed for them. Prince Henry died of typhoid fever in September 1612 and exactly three years later Jones entered into office as Surveyor of the King's Works. It was a timely moment. For the first time for over fifty years the Crown had assumed its self-appointed role as leader in the building world. The Office of Works might have functioned under Elizabeth on a budget of no more than £4,000 a year but once James had established himself on the throne a very different attitude was brought to bear. In the three years following 1607 more than £73,000 was spent on building. A spirit of extravagant royal building was once more abroad in the land, but the circumstances of early seventeenth-century society were very different from those surrounding the Court of Henry VIII.

All the evidence that we have suggests that Jones imposed his own rigorous canons of architectural design on all the projects that emerged from the Works during his long tenure of the Surveyorship. Unfortunately, the major buildings at Newmarket and Somerset House, and the alterations to Oatlands, Whitehall and Theobalds have all been destroyed. The three small buildings that have survived are of such exquisite beauty that they create the immediate illusion of rendering the remainder of contemporary architecture provincial or vulgar by comparison. It is a dangerous illusion, but one that is difficult to avoid when faced with such modular perfection and Classical reserve.

The Queen's House at Greenwich was begun in 1616, left unfinished at her death in 1619, and completed between 1629 and 1635. This 'curious device of Inigo Jones' originally consisted of an elongated rectangular building within the palace grounds and a similar block in Greenwich Park linked by a bridge over the main London-to-Dover road, the whole being encompassed within a square ground plan. The effect, with its fine ashlar and rusticated ground storey, its balustraded parapet and first floor loggia, and the studied relationship of solids to voids, is of an Italian villa translated to the banks of the Thames. It was quite unlike anything that had been built in Britain before.

In 1619, Jones designed a Banqueting House in Whitehall to replace an earlier one with which he had also been associated and which had been destroyed by fire. Work

The Queen's House, Greenwich, 1616–19 and 1629–37. The beautifully proportioned south front of the Palladian villa designed by Inigo Jones and dismissed by John Chamberlain as 'some curious device'

commenced in June and was completed in 1622. Comprising a grand double-cube saloon for the presentation of masques and for formal receptions, the elevations were based on a lavishly decorated Palladian town house. The third of Jones's surviving royal buildings is the chapel of St James's Palace, begun in 1623 for the Catholic Spanish Infanta, at that date the intended bride of Prince Charles, and completed in 1627 for his Queen, Henrietta Maria. Again the interior was designed on the theme of a double-cube, this time with a coffered ceiling and lit by a Venetian window at the east end. The narrow entrance front is crowned by a heavy pediment of suitable temple-like proportions.

All three buildings were commissioned during the reign of James I. Under Charles, Jones was heavily engaged at Somerset House and elsewhere, culminating in the production of a series of grandiose designs for the total rebuilding of Whitehall Palace in the late 1630s. There was never any likelihood that the money could be found for such an ambitious scheme. The growing isolation of the Crown from an increasingly influential section of the community was about to become an irrevocable breach which was eventually to cost Charles his head. Nothing was to symbolise this gulf between Court and country with greater clarity than the failure of the architectural preferences of the circle surrounding both Stuart kings to find anything other than a faint echo in the rest of the kingdom. The shade of Inigo Jones had to wait for another hundred years after the Queen's House before it was properly honoured, or even understood.

3

THE
COURTIER HOUSE

The forces that stimulated the vast increase in domestic building described in Chapter 1 only gathered momentum as the Tudor settlement strengthened. There was no clear break with the architecture of the immediate medieval past. In the early years of the sixteenth century the accommodation required by the great noble household differed little in kind or degree from that of the past century or more. A large hall, complete with a decorated screen at one end and a raised high table at the other, was still the formal centre of the house, even if its everyday function as the setting for the ceremonial dining of the head of the house had been superseded by the great chamber. Spacious kitchens with separate buttery and pantry were necessary adjuncts to the hall, and a chapel for daily devotions provided for the spiritual needs of the household. During the course of the sixteenth century the hall declined in importance, the private chapel became less essential, and the size of the household gradually diminished. The functions of the various apartments became more closely defined as specialised chambers for eating, sleeping, public show and private retreat, and they were joined by new areas often set aside for pleasure and display such as the long gallery and the banqueting hall.

As Mark Girouard has demonstrated in *Life in the English Country House*, the effects of these changes should not be exaggerated. To a large extent, the architectural development of the courtier house from the beginning of the sixteenth century into the seventeenth century is concerned with experiments in the disposition of these rooms in the interests of architectural effect rather than with any radical rethinking of the accommodation that the house should provide. The royal palaces of Henry VII and Henry VIII continued the medieval tradition of houses arranged around several court-yards with the principal outward show concentrated on a prominently emphasised gate-house entrance and a series of symbolically defensive towers. The opulent glazing and the lavishly carved decoration were reserved for those whose business took them through the gate-house and into the courtyards beyond. The somewhat forbidding exterior must have been deliberately contrived as a public demonstration of power and strength. Appreciation of the owner's taste was the preserve of a more exclusive audience.

All these features were present to a greater or lesser extent in the houses built by the most prominent subjects of Henry VIII. Hampton Court, as begun by Wolsey in 1515, was already a double-courtyard house with a central gate-tower before it passed to Henry VIII in 1525. Thornbury Castle, begun in 1511, and left unfinished at the execution of the Duke of Buckingham in 1521, was conceived on an even grander scale, with three courtyards, a symmetrically placed gate-house between two massive octagonal towers, and a group of astonishingly lavish, projecting bay windows overlooking the enclosed Privy Garden which contrast sharply with the comparative austerity of the fenestration to the inner court. Thornbury is a stone-built house, but the chimneystacks are constructed of decorated brickwork. Brick, as used by both

Thornbury Castle, Avon, c.1511–21. The largest courtier house of the period, with the massive octagonal corner towers and the delicately glazed bay windows providing a telling contrast between the demands of defence and luxury

41

Henry VII and Henry VIII, was still a potent status symbol even in those areas where good building stone was abundant. It was used by Wolsey for Hampton Court and, in combination with stone, by Sir David Owen and Sir William Fitzwilliam, the successive builders of Cowdray House in Sussex. Most of the other large mansions of the period, such as the Earl of Southampton's Titchfield Place and the Countess of Salisbury's Warblington Castle, both now surviving only as ruins in the Hampshire countryside, give prominent display to their brickwork.

Perhaps the most complete surviving example of an early Tudor great courtyard house is Compton Wynyates in Warwickshire. Built of brick with stone dressings and timber-framing in the gables, it is the work of Sir William Compton, favourite and companion of the young Henry VIII. It now comprises a single courtyard surrounded by a filled-in moat, but it is possible that a kitchen court originally existed beyond the hall where the eighteenth-century range now

Right: Compton Wynyates, Warwickshire. A courtyard plan in the established medieval tradition. Protected by a gate-tower, the residential court is dominated by the hall and its projecting bay window

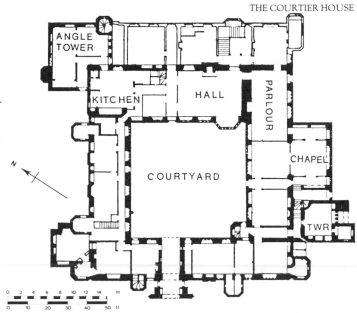

Hengrave Hall, Suffolk. *Left:* Entrance oriel, 1538. The advanced Classical putti and base mouldings of the window contrast with the conventional late-Perpendicular doorway

Left above: Detail

stands. The entrance through a buttressed and crenellated gate-tower is offset and leads directly across the courtyard to the screens-passage of the hall. The remaining kitchen is at the service end of the hall and doubtless there was another within the rebuilt north-eastern angle tower. The hall is lit by a canted bay window at the high-table end, beyond which is the parlour and the chapel attached to the southern range which also contains a high, battlemented residential tower. The lodgings for the remainder of the household were distributed around the northern and the western ranges.

Compton Wynyates was built early in the century and it exhibits a studied asymmetry about its entrance front which was soon to become old-fashioned. Hengrave Hall in Suffolk, begun in 1525 for Sir Thomas Kytson, has been greatly reduced in size and the eighteenth-century remodelling of the east side of the front range effectively disguises the ingenious manipulation of the plan, which originally produced a balanced symmetry to either side of the entrance, the latter being offset, as at Compton Wynyates, in relation to the courtyard behind. The courtyard at Hengrave Hall was provided with the hitherto unprecedented feature of a corridor running around three sides and giving entry to the hall, but in all other respects the plan was a conventional one with an outer court (now demolished), the hall lit by a bay window on the far side of the inner court, and the kitchens in an irregular group of buildings to the east.

43

The symmetry about the entrance to the main court at Hengrave is a curious affair, created, one cannot help feeling, as a talking-point rather like the later Elizabethan 'device'. Indeed, it was in this way that the decorative motifs of the Renaissance, introduced by Henry VIII with his appointment of Torrigiano in 1512 to design a fitting memorial to his father, appealed to the more sophisticated men of the day. Cardinal Wolsey, with his broad European horizons, hired his own Italian craftsmen to provide him with terracotta medallions and a coat of arms, but they were simply dotted about his traditionally designed house at Hampton Court. Similarly, Sir Richard Weston, who had accompanied Henry VIII to the Field of Cloth of Gold in 1520 where he would have seen at first-hand the new influences on the French Court, decorated his courtyard house at Sutton Place, begun in about 1522, with terracotta panels of naked putti of pure Italian inspiration, but they are interspersed with windows, doorways and parapets cusped and moulded in the conventional late-Perpendicular manner.

The contemporary terracotta decoration of Lord Marney's soaring gate-house at Layer Marney is more full-blooded with candelabra and scrolls decorating the principal windows and a parapet capped by dolphin supporters to semicircular panels. But even here, the form of the building is thoroughly traditional and other decorative motifs remain Gothic in character. The mansion which would have accompanied the gate-house was never completed and it is possible that, had he lived, Lord Marney would have carried through his early

Layer Marney Towers, Essex, c.1520. The brick gate-house of Lord Marney's uncompleted mansion with Early Renaissance terracotta decoration

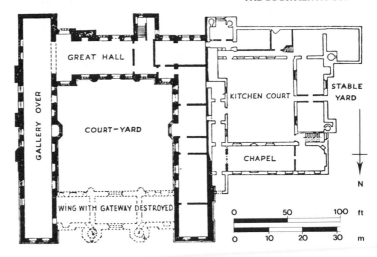

Sutton Place, Surrey. The deliberate symmetry of the courtyard elevations, with a central entrance to the hall and balanced fenestration throughout, contrasts with the more casual arrangement of the external elevations

Renaissance theme in a more consistent manner. However, the limited ambitions of his contemporaries suggest otherwise. As late as 1538, when Kytson was converted to the 'Antique' (as these Classically derived decorative forms were called) and added a charming oriel window over the entrance to Hengrave, it is only the fat little putti and the base mouldings which dress up its essentially retrospective character.

Apart from its fashionable decoration, there was another aspect of Sir Richard Weston's house at Sutton that was to be of more lasting significance. All the courtyard elevations and the principal external elevation of the gate-house range were totally and consistently symmetrical with a thoroughness of purpose unprecedented in the domestic architecture of the times. Even the hall range, where the historic emphasis on distinguishing the important high-table end by a large projecting bay window conflicted with the concept, symmetry was achieved by the deceit of placing a matching projecting bay at the opposite end of the façade where the generous expanse of its glazing belied the insignificance of the rooms behind. Of itself, symmetry was not alien to native architectural traditions, but the obsessive pursuit of symmetry at the expense of convenience must be seen as the principal influence of the Renaissance on later Tudor architecture. The discipline of proportion and balance, in Cecil's words of 'each part answerable to other to allure liking', proved to be more enduring than any allegiance to Classical decoration.

With the death of Henry VIII in 1547, the initiative in ostentatious building temporarily passed to the Duke of

Somerset who, as Protector, ruled the country during the minority of Edward VI. His appetite for palace building was no less than that of the late monarch, but his tastes seem to have been considerably more refined, and for a brief period it appeared likely that the full panoply of Classical design would accompany the newly discovered courtier delight in symmetrical planning.

Somerset built himself two substantial courtyard mansions on the Thames at Isleworth and off the Strand, made preparations for a third, even grander mansion at Great Bedwyn in Wiltshire, and carried out less extensive works at his other houses at Banbury, Odiham and Reading. Of these, only the refaced Syon House at Isleworth survives, but Old Somerset House is sufficiently documented in the drawings of John Thorpe to justify the conviction of Sir John Summerson that it 'was probably the first deliberate attempt to build in England a front composed altogether in the Classical taste'. The Strand front was symmetrically composed with a central three-storey gate-house adorned with superimposed orders flanked by two-storeyed ranges which terminated in shallow projecting bays set slightly in from the ends of the building. The windows were all pedimented with those in the bays being doubled and decorated with columns. The crowning balustrade deliberately hid the form of the roof behind. Given the tenor of contemporary European culture, it should have exercised a crucial influence on the future course of English and Welsh architecture but, like the earlier buildings of James V at Falkland and Stirling in Scotland, it failed to make any lasting impact.

Somerset's brief period of power was of too short a duration for the founding of any general school of taste, and his fall and execution were reasons enough to dissuade any wavering courtier from following his architectural example. But proof that the design of Somerset House stemmed from a deep commitment to the canons of Classical architecture as reinterpreted by the Italian and French Renaissance, rather than a mere passing interest in the trappings of its decoration, is provided by the activities of a number of men who were all closely associated with Somerset during his years of influence.

One of these, Sir William Sharington, who had served Thomas Lord Seymour, Somerset's brother, introduced a number of Classical features to the mansion that he was creating at Lacock in the late 1540s from the dissolved nunnery he had acquired in 1540. The precise date of

Sharington's work is not known, but he died in 1553. It includes a polygonal banqueting tower with a balustraded top containing two polygonal stone tables of exquisite design. Sharington's death closely followed Somerset's more abrupt end. The younger members of his circle who managed to survive his fall with their heads still intact were forced to retire from public life until the dangers of association with him had been spent.

Sir John Thynne, who had been Somerset's steward with overall responsibility for the supervision of his building work, spent the next thirty years restlessly perfecting his own house at Longleat which he had commenced in 1546. The final version, conceived after a disastrous fire in 1567, owed much to the design of Somerset House but, as one could expect after almost two decades of further gestation, it is a far more accomplished work. Like many of the large houses that had preceded it, Longleat was built around a double courtyard, but unlike them its architectural display is concentrated on its outward elevations. All four fronts are symmetrical and are so disciplined in the details of their design that this could easily be mistaken for a building of 150 years later. Sir Nikolaus Pevsner has called it 'a milestone in English sixteenth-century architecture', but it was placed on a very isolated road.

Longleat House, Wiltshire, 1567–80. The outward-looking symmetrical elevations with their disciplined Classical detailing are the perfect expression of the abortive architectural movement associated with the Duke of Somerset

Hill Hall, Theydon Mount, Essex, c.1575. Courtyard elevation showing the superimposed Classical orders employed by Sir Thomas Smith

So too were the buildings of Somerset's other protégés and servants. Hill Hall in Essex, where Sir Thomas Smith boldly employed two orders of attached columns on his courtyard elevations, had no immediate successors, while the gates of Humility, Virtue and Honour designed by Dr Caius, physician to Edward VI during the Protectorate, for his own foundation stand alone among the late sixteenth-century college architecture of Cambridge. Only William Cecil, later Lord Burghley, provides the essential link between the 'momentary High Renaissance' of Somerset and the excitement of the Elizabethan Court. Having diplomatically survived the tricky years of Mary's reign after his exposed public service as secretary to the discredited Somerset and Secretary of State under his shortlived successor Northumberland, Cecil emerged under Elizabeth as the chief minister of the Crown and remained the most influential man in the land until almost the end of her reign.

During the years of exile from the Court, Cecil had started to build a house at Burghley, near Stamford, in a similar style to the houses of the other members of the Somerset circle. From its modest Classical beginnings, Burghley House was to grow in size as its builder grew in political influence, and its changing appearance from discreet reticence to flamboyant exuberance came to express perfectly the architectural taste of the time. There is sufficient evidence from letters and other surviving documents that Cecil, and his son after him, was to influence much of that changing taste, from a delight in the excesses of Flemish ornament to the patriotic flirtation with England's Gothic past symbolised by the hammerbeam hall roof and the final turreted and bay-windowed form in which Burghley House ultimately emerged in the 1570s and 1580s.

Burghley, as it developed, was a large house, but Theobalds, where Cecil started building in 1564, was gigantic. By the date of its completion in 1585, it extended across five courtyards with massive three-storeyed towers capped by ogee-roofed turrets breaking the skyline. Its accommodation was far in excess of anything that a private citizen, no matter how powerful, could require. However, by the time of its final enlargement, it was no longer simply the residence of a private citizen. It was more of a royal palace for the occasional use of the monarch whenever she should choose.

Gate of Virtue, Gonville and Caius College, Cambridge, 1567. Designed in a scholarly Classical style by Dr Caius as part of a sequence of gateways symbolising the progress of the student through the college

Elizabeth built no palaces of her own. She capitalised on the cult of sovereignty, which had been deliberately fostered to bolster her initially weak position on the throne, to encourage her noble subjects to build on a scale which in the past would have been seen as a dynastic threat. Buckingham's execution in 1521 must still have been a potent memory, but the ostentatious builder was now firmly harnessed to the throne. Every summer she went on a Progress, moving with a large retinue from house to house of her principal subjects. Her recorded comments on the meanness of the accommodation provided for her by Bacon at Gorhambury and even Cecil at Theobalds were not lost either on the recipients, who extended their houses accordingly, or on the other ambitious men who surrounded her. If they wished to reap the rewards of office and patronage, they must be prepared to speculate by building on a scale appropriate to the proper entertainment of the ultimate source of such rewards. Cecil, who had been elevated to the title of Lord Burghley in 1571, made it perfectly clear when he wrote about their houses to Sir Christopher Hatton in 1579: 'God send us both long to enjoy her for whom we both meant to exceed our purses in these.'

Hatfield House, Hertfordshire, 1607–12. Robert Cecil's prodigy house on a compact E-plan with its architectural display open to public view

Burghley led the way with Theobalds, but other powerful courtiers were not far behind. The building of 'prodigy' houses – noble palaces of an awesome scale – continued through the reign of Elizabeth to reach its climax under James I. Apart from Burghley and Theobalds, the most notable examples in the sixteenth century are Sir Christopher Hatton's Holdenby House and Kirby Hall, both in Northamptonshire. Barely twenty-five miles separate these two enormous courtyard houses, yet building work was proceeding on both simultaneously. Theobalds having been sacrificed to the passing fancy of the King, the most important prodigy house to be built under James was again financed by a Cecil. Lord Salisbury, Burghley's son and his successor as chief minister of state, built Hatfield House between 1607 and 1612 on one of the royal manors granted to him in exchange for Theobalds. Like that much-lamented building, it was to have an immediate influence on the architectural taste of the Court. Not only did Sir Henry Hobart, the Lord Chief Justice, copy many of its striking decorative features for his mansion at Blickling, Norfolk, begun six years later, but he also recruited Salisbury's own surveyor, Robert Lyminge, to execute the work.

Left: Wollaton Hall, Notts, 1580–88. The height, compactness, emphasised projections, and fantasy-Gothic decoration are all recurrent themes of the period

Below: Kirby Hall, Northamptonshire. The hall range built after 1570 for Sir Humphrey Stafford. The giant order of pilasters and the contrived symmetry are

Classical motifs but the overall composition is unmistakeably English

Right: Ruperra Castle, Mid Glamorgan, 1626. Gentry sham castle on a similar plan to Lulworth. The roof line was orginally gabled. The traditional importance of the hall is still emphasised by the large window to the right of the porch

Blickling Hall was a double-courtyard house, like the most magnificent of all the Jacobean prodigy houses, Audley End, built for the first Earl of Suffolk between 1605 and 1614, but that concept which had governed the planning of all the largest houses from the Middle Ages onwards had been rendered out of date by the plan adopted for Hatfield House. By increasing the depth of the ranges so that they could accommodate two, and even three, sets of rooms side by side, Hatfield was built on a very compact plan which sacrificed nothing in the way of spacious apartments, but had the very positive advantage of opening all the expensive architectural display to immediate public view without the visual barrier of an entrance court.

In this, Hatfield was only reflecting a trend which had long been apparent in the less self-indulgent world of the relatively smaller house. As the glittering prodigy houses were growing more and more extended, there was a parallel move towards compactness among many of the houses that were being erected for some of the wealthiest men in the country. Given that this cannot be seen as a result of the restrictions imposed by a smaller purse, it must be accepted as a distinct preference for the subtle effects of architectural massing, the interplay of elevational recession and projection, and the crowning opportunity of a lively roof line that the combination of height and compactness encouraged. Symmetrical consistency was also rendered far more effective in the confines of

53

Left: Hardwick Hall, Derbyshire, 1590–97. The most attractive of all the late Elizabethan houses, with a richly modelled skyline and ascending importance of rooms announced by the increasing height of the windows

Below left: High Great Chamber, Hardwick Hall

Below: Plas-Teg, Hope, Clwyd, c.1610. Compact square plan, with extruded corner towers

a compact house than in the echoing courts of the prodigy house.

One of the threads of this trend can best be followed in the career of the mason and surveyor, Robert Smythson. Longleat, where he worked for Sir John Thynne from 1568 to 1580, despite being cloaked around the courtyards of the earlier houses on the site, exhibits perfectly all the qualities described above. Wollaton Hall, Sir Francis Willoughby's seat built by Smythson between 1580 and 1588, has the classic compact plan of a central block with four extruded corner towers which was to spread all over the country once the advantages of its symmetrical plan and the ability of its elevations to accept almost any style of decoration were appreciated. Similar fantasy castles soon followed Willoughby's example, such as Lulworth and Sherborne in Dorset and the more forbidding Ruperra in Glamorgan or Walworth in County Durham. But the plan was equally suited to the more **restrained setting of Sir John Trevor's Plas-Teg, built in the** early years of the seventeenth century in North Wales.

On the completion of Wollaton, Smythson moved on to find employment with Bess of Hardwick and her extended

family, and his influence, if not his hand, can be found in a large number of late sixteenth- and early seventeenth-century compact houses throughout the northern Midlands. Hardwick Hall itself, where the architectural handling of the mass and the impact of its fenestration are so masterly that the external decoration is hardly remembered, is quite properly the most celebrated of these houses but, in their own way, other examples of the genre, such as Barlborough Hall and Wootton Lodge, are almost as memorable.

Most of these houses were the principal residence of their builders, but the advantages of a tall rectangular plan as the setting for a private retreat and a more casual way of life also appealed to the same men who were building the prodigy houses. They all needed somewhere to escape from the pressures of the public life that the conventions of their position demanded of them when they were resident in their own mansions. A lodge with sufficient accommodation for essential servants and a few friends, preferably placed upon a hilltop, where it could command a good view of the surrounding countryside or the hunt, was the ideal solution. It was also a tempting opportunity for them to indulge their architectural whims on a small scale and to impress their friends with the cleverness of their conceits. In this, as in so many other areas of architectural taste, the Cecils seem to have become established arbiters.

Thomas Cecil, Lord Exeter, built himself a lodge in the form of a Greek cross with four slender towers in the re-entrant angles at Wothorpe 'to retire to out of the dust while his great house at Burghley was a-sweeping'. His brother, Robert Cecil, Lord Salisbury, built an arcadian miniature castle with tiny diamond-shaped lodges at Cranbourne in Dorset, and seems to have been consulted on a surprising number of similar projects that were mooted at the time. Thus Lord Bindon wrote to him in 1608 about Lulworth Castle:

If the little pile in Lulworth park shall prove pretty or worth the labour bestowed on the erecting of it, I will acknowledge as the truth is, that your lordship's powerful speech to me at Bindon, to have laid the first foundations of the pile in my mind.

It will be clear from the examples already given that many of these lodges took the theme of a castle or fort as their architectural inspiration. This is partly a product of the gate-house origins of the rectangular plan with corner towers as demonstrated at Kenilworth Castle in the 1560s and Tixall in

Cranborne Manor House, Dorset, 1608–11. Robert Cecil's arcadian private lodge on the site of a genuine medieval hunting lodge

Kenilworth Castle, Warwickshire. Gate-house, c.1563–71. The compact central block with corner towers provided the inspiration for many of the later lodges of the period

the 1570s. But the popularity of the theme is more closely connected with a romantic revival of chivalry in the later sixteenth century which was inextricably associated with the cult of sovereignty as personified by Elizabeth, the virgin Queen, whose honour and virtue were assiduously defended by the shining knights of her Court. In 1580 Sir Henry Lee devised the Accession Day Tilt and every year thereafter on 7 November, the anniversary of her accession, a full-scale tournament was held at which the Queen's Champion entered the lists on her behalf. Edmund Spenser's *Faerie Queen*, the first part of which was published in 1590, was the literary expression of this dramatic cult, and the lodges of Elizabeth's courtiers were its major architectural manifestation. The revival flourished under James I to reach a climax with the lodge to which Charles Cavendish retreated from his principal seat at Welbeck. Bolsover Castle, towering high above the surrounding countryside, is a perfect fantasy castle built on the ruins of a real medieval castle. In more ways than one it is the ultimate Jacobean conceit.

The cult of sovereignty and the concept of an architectural conceit almost certainly combined on occasion in that other thread of the trend towards compactness which was adopted at Hatfield, the E-planned house. This is so-called because of the resemblance of the plan, with its hall-range flanked by projecting wings and a slightly protruding central entrance, to the letter E. At a courtier level its popularity probably derived from the growing realisation that a man's status and power could be expressed to the world at large not only by the

Left: Tixall, Staffordshire, c.1574. A gate-house with corner towers, showing the Elizabethan delight in large areas of glazing

Below: Bolsover Castle, Derbyshire, 1612–21. The perfect expression of the Jacobean lodge as a fairy-tale castle

impregnable appearance of the blank walls and towering gate-house that shielded an inward-looking architectural display but also, far more satisfyingly, by throwing open his house so that the novelty or opulence of his decoration could be admired by all who passed and not just those who were admitted through the gate. In the single-courtyard house this effect was easily achieved by the simple expedient of removing the gate-house and its flanking ranges from the entrance to the court. Indeed, this is exactly what happened to Sutton Place in the eighteenth century, and to the uninitiated it is as though the gate-house wing had never existed, so used have we become to the open revelation of the principal elevations of the Tudor house.

Almost all the best-known examples of E-plan houses date from the second half of the century. In East Anglia the plan

seems to have been adopted as early as anywhere else with examples such as Melford Hall, Suffolk, for Sir William Cordell, dating from 1545. Castle Ashby in Northamptonshire was begun in 1574 for Lord Compton, although here a gate-house and screen were added in the seventeenth century, giving the house its present courtyard appearance. Montacute House in Somerset was begun in 1590 for Sir Edward Phelips. Welsh examples include St Fagans Castle of *c.* 1580 in the south and Plas Mawr, Conwy, built in phases between 1576 and 1595, for Robert Wynne in the north. At Trevalyn Hall, Clwyd, built for the Trevors, there is the unique conceit of two detached E-plan blocks set one behind the other. The principal block is dated 1576 and it is possible that the rear range was added in 1606, which is the date on the miniature lodge which separates them.

Left: Barrington Court, Somerset, 1552–64. A celebrated example of the E-plan. The central projecting porch leads into the screens passage of the hall and the bay window at the high end is balanced by the staircase turret in the other re-entrant angle

Below: This view of the rear elevation shows Barrington Court's symmetry of design interrupted by the added emphasis given to the hall chimneystack and fenestration

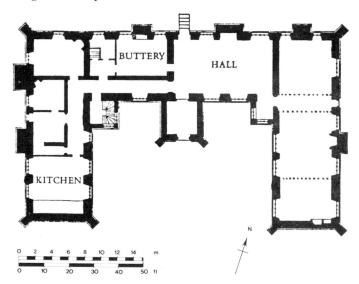

Right: St Fagans Castle, South Glamorgan; begun c.1580. An austere E-plan house where the only decoration is provided by the symmetry of the gables and the fenestration

Above: Plas Mawr, Conwy, Gwynedd, 1576–95. Courtyard elevation showing the casual asymmetry of the towers in the re-entrant angles and the decorative effect of the stepped-gable motif

It was a basic plan that was admirably capable of being adapted to display all the various changes that architectural fashion dictated throughout the period. Classical references could be supplied by the provision of pediments to the windows, as at Trevalyn and in most of the E-plan houses in **Norfolk and Suffolk, and by the use of columns or pilasters** flanking the entrance doors. Gothic allusions could be made in other decorative features, such as the tiny tourelles which take the place of pinnacles at the ends of the wings at Ingestre Hall, Staffordshire. Gables could be employed to underline the symmetry and as a vehicle for the Dutch fashions which were popular in the early seventeenth century. Their presence produced a lively roof line, their absence deliberately emphasised the mass and height of the rest of the building. Any accommodation which was sacrificed by not providing a gate-house range could be recovered by increasing the height of the main house to dramatic effect. The emphasis which had traditionally been provided by the gate-tower could be reproduced on the central frontispiece of the house itself, either by a lavish display of decoration or by projecting it for an extra storey above the roof. That new status symbol, the long gallery, could occupy the full length of one of the wings or enjoy a commanding position at the top of the main block with views out across the estate from windows placed at either end.

Above all else, the E-plan and its derivatives gave full reign to the Elizabethan delight in manipulating the planes of walls so that they present a constant progression of projection and recession, all within an ordered symmetrical framework. If tradition still demanded that the central entrance should lead into the screens-passage at one end of the hall, then the sharp angle between the projecting wing and the high end of the main block could be enlivened by the bay window to the hall, matched by a similar projection at the other end to house the staircase. Canted, semicircular or rectangular bays could project from the ends of the wings, and this device could also be used to break up the expanse of their inner elevations.

The most subtle interplay of planes was achieved when the wings did not dominate the whole by projecting too far. Towards the end of the sixteenth century this was producing a

Castle Ashby, Northamptonshire; begun 1574. Large E-plan house with the courtyard closed by a Classical screen of c.1634. The lettered balustrade reflects an early seventeenth-century fashion

refinement on the E-plan, whereby the wings were projected to the rear of the hall block as well as on a reduced scale to the front, rather like a letter H. It can be seen in several buildings of the 1590s, such as Doddington Hall, Lincolnshire, and Condover Hall in Shropshire. By the early seventeenth century this had become a popular Court plan. Apart from its more pleasing visual form it offered significant advantages in terms of circulation and cost. The centre of the wings could now be placed adjacent to the staircases in the main block, reducing the inconvenience of long corridors or intercommunicating rooms throughout their length, and the more compact carcass of the house diminished the amount of walling necessary for its construction. By 1606, when Sir

Charlton House, Greenwich, c.1607–12. The epitome of the symmetrical H-plan, with the decorative emphasis concentrated on the central porch and canted bays terminating the wings

Plan of second-floor level showing the double-pile central block and the long gallery occupying the full length of the north wing.

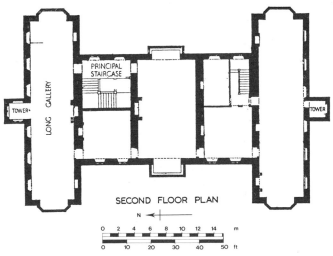

PRINCIPAL STAIRCASE

LONG GALLERY

TOWER

TOWER

SECOND FLOOR PLAN

N

0 2 4 6 8 10 12 14 m

0 10 20 30 40 50 ft

Walter Cope built Holland House at Kensington, the trend towards compactness had already resulted in the doubling of the width of the hall block. Sir Adam Newton's house on the other side of London at Charlton, built between 1607 and 1612, pursued the possibilities of the H-plan to its limits with a double-width hall range flanked by single-width wings arranged in such a way that the potential for symmetry at both front and rear was manifest. Charlton House completes the link between the compact houses of the 'Smythson School' and the houses deriving from the E-plan. The way forward was clear to the double-pile houses of Sir Roger Pratt's generation after the Civil War.

The political and economic circumstances of Scotland during the sixteenth century were so different from England and Wales that architectural comparisons become too complex to be dealt with here. The tower-houses, discussed in the following chapter, fortuitously exhibit similar qualities of compactness, but neither Scottish wealth nor the loyalty of its nobility permitted anything like the English prodigy house. If the double palace that Earl Patrick Stewart built in Kirkwall, Orkney, around 1600, was the nearest equivalent, it sprang from very different motives and merely emphasises the isolation of the northern part of the Scottish kingdom. The blood that the Scottish nobility continued to spill among themselves and the periodic incursions of the English inevitably restricted the architectural choices that they could

Earl's Palace, Kirkwall, Orkney, c.1600. A Scottish prodigy house still in the feudal tradition

make in the first half of the sixteenth century. Consequently, it is not surprising that the important buildings of the period, such as Lord Ruthven's range at Dirleton, Sir James Hamilton's work at Craignethan, and the reconstruction of Craigmillar, should all have taken place behind the fortified curtain wall of an active castle.

Even in the period of comparative peace after 1560, the defensive potential of the new tower-houses underlined its fragile nature. Nevertheless, cultural contacts with Europe were freely available to the Scottish Court and they inspired a few nobles with ideas of considerable architectural sophistication, even if their achievements were on a comparatively small scale. Most extraordinary of all is the diamond-faceted façade above an open loggia that the Earl of Bothwell inserted in the courtyard of his essentially fifteenth-century castle at Crichton in the 1580s. It is a concept entirely without precedent in the British Isles, which can only be compared with the Palazzo dei Diamanti at Ferrara or the Casa de los Picos in Segovia

Lord Edzell's pleasance, constructed in 1604 to complement his fortified mansion of the 1580s, is a more easily appreciated creation. The formal walled garden with its tiny summer-house and matching bath-house seems to speak of the tranquillity that it was hoped the union of the crowns would bring. Indeed, it was a device that would have been understood with ease at the English Court. The walls are carved with representations culled from German engravings

Crichton Castle, Lothian Region. Courtyard elevation, 1580s. Remarkably Italianate diamond-faceted façade above an open loggia added to the Earl of Bothwell's medieval castle

of the cardinal virtues, the liberal arts, and the planetary deities, symbolising the builder's character, education and good fortune. All three sides are decorated with recesses to take flower-boxes which are arranged in a chequer pattern to represent the fess chequy of the Lindsay coat of arms. In all, particularly on a summer's day, it is a most attractive conceit.

The range that the Earl of Huntly added at Huntly Castle at about the same time is adorned with Renaissance detail, but it cannot disguise the essentially fortified nature of the complete building. The same comment must be applied to the new lodgings erected by the Earl of Nithsdale at Caerlaverock Castle in 1634. All these Scottish castles now lie in ruins and the contrast with their more peaceable English equivalents could not be more poignantly stated.

Edzell Castle, Tayside Region. The Pleasance, created in 1604 as a garden conceit symbolising the character, learning and destiny of the Lindsay family

4

THE GENTRY HOUSE

'G entry' is a familiar term with an imprecise meaning. It is used in this chapter to describe the houses of those men who were the most important individuals within their own communities, whether by virtue of their titles as lords of the manor or as a result of their wealth derived from trade, manufacturing, or the law. It covers a broad spectrum of society and the houses that these men built range in size from those which are almost comparable to the buildings of men with ambitions at Court to structures which are hardly distinguishable from the dwellings of the wealthy yeomen to be discussed in the next chapter. What is most noticeable about this conglomerate of diverse building, however, is the sheer numbers that can be dated to the sixteenth or early seventeenth centuries. Truly could Bishop Goodman, looking back on the reign of James I, comment that 'no Kingdom in this world spent so much in building as we did in his time'.

This statement, of course, cannot be applied to every part of England, Wales and Scotland with equal force. Unlike the courtier house which could be constructed wherever the builder wished to place it, the gentry house presents a regional distribution reflecting local conditions of economic prosperity and political calm. Thus the flourishing cloth trade in all its manifold branches from sheep-rearing to finished product was responsible for the marked concentrations of handsome manor houses in areas such as the Cotswolds, Northamptonshire and eastern England. Primary producers of food, benefiting from the Tudor price rise, created a similar architectural legacy on the rich agricultural lands of the southeast, the Midlands and parts of Wales. Conversely, the gentry house of the period is rarely encountered in large areas of western Wales and Scotland or northern England.

In the houses of the gentry a further regional variety related to the underlying geology of different areas can be seen. Building materials are heavy and bulky, and consequently were very expensive to transport over anything but a short distance. The navigable waterways of East Anglia meant that the excellent building stones of the Northamptonshire quarries were able to penetrate to a certain extent into Bedfordshire, Cambridgeshire, Norfolk and Suffolk, but in the main the gentry builder turned to those materials which were available in the immediate vicinity to fashion his new house. If he wanted stone windows to complement the brickwork of his walls and suitable free stone was not to be found locally, then he was quite prepared to seek another way of achieving the same effect. Many houses in eastern England, such as Eastbury House in Essex, have rendered windows masquerading as stone. As with so many things which ultimately derive from necessity, a positive virtue could be made of economic restraint. The alternating bands of flint which the clothier John Topp employed for the construction of Stockton House, Wiltshire, no doubt helped to reduce the amount of stone that he had to purchase, but they also created a striking and attractive appearance. The gentry houses of mid-Wales, the west Midlands and Lancashire and Cheshire are invariably built of timber, while their equivalents in the limestone and sandstone regions are of stone. Brick could be a status material, particularly in the earlier part of the sixteenth century, as at Plaish Hall, Shropshire, but it quickly became a

Stockton House, Wiltshire. Typical square, compact, late Elizabethan gentry house with emphasised porch and gables, built of local stone and flint

common choice for the gentry in those areas where more traditional materials were not easily secured.

To a certain extent, the material available in a particular locality dictated the architectural form of the regional house, even at the gentry level. Poor or intractable stone generally meant buildings with thick walls, a minimum of carved decoration and a comparatively low roof line. It also stimulated regional practices which effectively disguised its true nature, such as the fashion for harling in Scotland or lime-washing in the south-west of England. Timber as a principal building material, on the other hand, encouraged a tendency to promote to the full the potential for surface decoration; the inherent contrast in colour between the framework and its infill is best seen in the western counties of England and the eastern counties of Wales, but it was not eschewed as close to London as Southall Manor House in the historic county of Middlesex.

Apart from the potent but essentially geographical differences between a gentry house built of timber and one constructed of stone or brick, the way that timber was used as a building material had important implications for the form of the house. Framed houses were erected in modules governed by the maximum usable length of timber that contemporary sylvicultural practice provided. Although it was possible to pile one module on top of another to achieve an impression of considerable height, as in the gate-house at Little Moreton Hall, it was very rarely that timber-framed buildings were constructed of more than a single module in depth. Con-

Plaish Hall, Shropshire, c.1540. The arched lights to the windows are typical of that date, but the H-plan and the use of brick are both advanced features for the region

Little Moreton Hall, Cheshire, 1559 and 1570s. The flamboyant qualities of decorated timber-framing, characteristic of the western counties, displayed to the full

sequently, timber-framed country houses invariably exhibit an extended rather than a compact plan and their degrees of status are marked by additional ranges often erected by successive generations. Pitchford Hall, Shropshire, illustrates the rising fortunes of the Otley family of wool merchants during the sixteenth and early seventeenth centuries: it developed from a single late medieval range into an L-plan which was then further extended before the present E-plan was evolved. On a smaller scale, many late medieval houses like the Manor House at Chalgrove, Oxfordshire, were given a balanced appearance in the sixteenth century by the addition of a further wing. Both flanking wings at Penarth, near Newtown, in Powys, are additions of about 1600.

Nowhere in the British Isles are the regional characteristics of the gentry house more clearly illustrated than in the tower-houses of Scotland. They are essentially classless buildings erected by small lairds and great nobles alike, and it is virtually impossible to associate different types of towers with different social categories. In a society which was economically straitened and politically unstable, those who could afford to build in permanent materials required the same sort of accommodation. The tower-house struck just the right balance between the claims of domestic comfort and those of defence, giving the maximum security in return for a fairly modest financial outlay.

The medieval tower-house in both Scotland and northern England had been a simple rectangular block. When the Scottish domestic building boom began in the second half of the sixteenth century this traditional form was modified to

Penarth,
Newtown, Powys.
A medieval house
remodelled c.1600
by the addition of
the decorated
flanking wings and
the insertion of a
chimneystack in
the hall

provide more flexible accommodation and to respond to developments in firearm defence. Extra rooms linking with the main apartments of hall and chambers in the body of the tower were provided by short attached wings, and advantage could be taken of this more convenient arrangement to capitalise on the growing availability of handguns. The defence of the tower moved from the exposed wall-head to the lower storeys where gun-loops afforded greater protection to the defenders and where the wings could be utilised to provide covering fire along the exposed faces of the tower, particularly in the vicinity of the vulnerable entrance. The extra accommodation could be arranged in a single wing attached to the main tower and sheltering the entrance in the re-entrant angle, as in a truncated form at Crathes Castle begun shortly after 1553 or more generously in the Burnetts' other castle at Muchalls of the early seventeenth century. Alternatively and more commonly, two wings could be positioned at diagonally opposite corners of the main block providing an unobstructed field of fire around all four sides of the tower.

The Z-plan, as this arrangement is generally called, emerged in its fully developed form immediately after the Scottish Reformation, with Terpersie Castle of 1561 and Claypotts Castle of 1569 being among the earliest dated examples. It continued in vogue throughout the whole period of renewed building activity in Scotland which lasted into the 1630s. Its defensive features gradually became less pronounced, although the defended entrance cautiously persisted and the principal rooms, entered from a narrow staircase,

Above: Muchalls Castle, Grampian Region, c.1607–27. L-plan house with enclosed forecourt and gun-loops flanking the gateway

Left: Crathes, Grampian Region, c.1553–95. Tower-house on truncated L-plan with plain harled walls and decorated cap-houses. The protected entrance is in the re-entrant angle. The large window is a later insertion

Above right: Claypotts Castle, Tayside Region, 1569–88. Classic example of the Z-plan tower-house. Uncompromisingly defensive

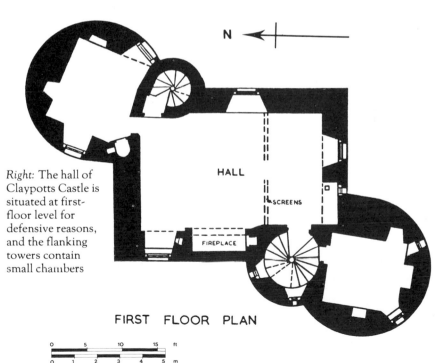

N ←

HALL

SCREENS

Right: The hall of Claypotts Castle is situated at first-floor level for defensive reasons, and the flanking towers contain small chambers

FIREPLACE

FIRST FLOOR PLAN

0   5   10   15   ft
0   1   2   3   4   5   m

remained on the upper floors; but the upper works grew increasingly more decorative than functional, with rainwater spouts playfully modelled as cannon and a profusion of corbelled-out conical turrets and gabled cap-houses making a high display above the plain battered walls below. The public show which crowned the exterior of the house was echoed by the rich decoration of the principal rooms, and the late-flowering of the tower-house coincided with a fashion for opulent plasterwork and painted ceilings.

Deliberate irregularity is an essential characteristic of Z-plan and L-plan towers, but the conflicting attractions of symmetrical planning were beginning to appear in Scottish domestic architecture in the early seventeenth century. Tower-houses could be created in a symmetrical form by placing both flanking wings on the same elevation, as at Craigston, Pitreavie and Castle Stewart. At the same time, a less bellicose house type of low profile with projecting wings was pointing Scottish architecture in the direction of long-established trends south of the border. The house of this form that George Bruce, a wealthy merchant, built at Culross at the turn of the century still had its principal rooms on the upper floor, but by 1626 when John Hamilton built his house at

Craigevar Castle, Grampian Region, c. 1610–26. *Above:* Interior of the hall showing the exuberant plasterwork typical of early seventeenth-century decoration throughout the British Isles

Right: Craigevar is a tower-house perfected as a conscious architectural device with its inherent qualities of height and crowning decoration fully exploited

Preston, Lothian, the main rooms had descended to the ground floor and there was no provision for defence against intruders.

The marked similarity of form exhibited by the greater mass of Scottish building in the later sixteenth and early seventeenth centuries is not so easily discernible in England and Wales during the same period, although a general preference for compactness of plan provides a common link with the courtier house. Greater political stability and economic prosperity provided more freedom for diverse experiments in creating the ideal gentry home, or so it must have seemed to those men who were not constrained by conservative attitudes. Such contrasting philosophies as guided the individual builders militate against easy generalisations. Sir Richard Clough, for example, returned to Wales in 1567 from Antwerp, where he had been resident agent to Sir Thomas Gresham, and built himself an extraordinary Flemish villa in the shape of a square with a steep pyramid roof crowned by a chamber with a towering cupola. Bach-y-Craig at Tremeirchion, Clwyd, the first recorded use of brick in Wales, was linked by an arcaded range with a gate-house of equally fantastic form. Both the gate-house and the linking range survive in a much

Haddon Hall, Derbyshire. Long gallery, c. 1600. Such decorative motifs as the bay windows, the delicately patterned ceiling and the richly modelled panelling are characteristic of the most refined interiors of the period

Right: Flemingston Court, South Glamorgan. Early sixteenth-century house with a pointed arch to the through-passage. The importance of the hall is still emphasised by its dominant window

Below: The Palace, Culross, Fife Region, begun 1597. Scottish asymmetrical H-plan house with the principal rooms still on the first floor and with characteristic crow-stepped gables

mutilated form incorporated into the farmhouse which now stands on the site, and a hint of the demolished house itself can be seen from the dormered roof of Clough's town house in Ruthin. Such architectural bravado had no imitators, unless the more sober Cemmaes Bychan in Montgomeryshire of 1632 is considered to be a belated response. Elsewhere in Wales the gentry were more restrained. Houses such as

Flemingston Court in Glamorgan, with its accentuated through passage and tall hall window, would have looked distinctly old-fashioned to English eyes, while even the more self-consciously designed Old Gwernyfed, Velindre, with its symmetrical E-plan and circular forecourt pavilions, is cautiously under-fenestrated. The timber-framed lobby-entry houses with decorated porches, which abound in Montgomeryshire, are undoubtedly the most distinctively attractive of all the smaller gentry houses in the Principality; but the same plan was probably more appropriate to the housing needs of the yeomanry in the more prosperous social hierarchy to the east of the Marches.

Not that the richest yeoman would readily concede that he had not already penetrated the lower ranks of the gentry. Limited social mobility between classes was an important aspect of Elizabethan society, and architectural aspirations could be a significant indication of a man's ambitions. Many of the developments already described in relation to the courtier house were rapidly adopted lower down the social scale. Decorative plasterwork and fashionable Flemish and even Classical motifs were easily copied. The more sophisticated Court taste for romantic chivalry can be discerned in buildings such as Kinnersley Castle, with its dominant central tower and

Kinnersley Castle, Hereford and Worcester, c.1585–1601. The embattled tower suggests the adoption of the courtier sham castle theme at a gentry level

The Vicarage, Berriew, Powys, 1616. Characteristic Montgomeryshire lobby-entry house (the gable-end chimneys are a later alteration) with a decorated jettied porch

castellated entrance porch, or the even more uncompromisingly tower-like Claverdon Leys in Warwickshire. The crenellated chimneys at Toseland Hall probably represent a timid expression of the same theme. A similar fascination for the curious device resulted in such houses as Gayton Manor, Northamptonshire, which is planned in the form of a Greek cross. The Trinitarian inspiration which must lie behind the inconvenient Y-plan that the Reverend Thomas Smith chose for his parsonage house at Goodrich in 1636 is an excellent example of the lengths to which some builders were prepared to go.

These are oddities, but they show that their builders wished to emulate the intellectual games of their social superiors, albeit on a limited budget. The same was true of the more conventional trappings of the great house. The gentry in both England and Wales continued to build gate-houses long after they had gone out of general fashion among the Court circle, and even those who seem to have realised what an expensive nonsense such public posturing could be often sought to achieve a similar symbolic effect by the erection of an entrance gate inscribed with their arms or a fashionable piece of decoration. If the gate was flanked by garden walls it could effectively reproduce the courtyard appearance of a grander house. Many gentry houses took on the ostentatious glazing and opulently decorated porches, the great chambers and the long galleries that characterised the mansions of the period. With certain notable exceptions, however, these novelties were not adopted in the mistaken pursuit of a way of life that most of their owners neither wanted nor needed. They were grafted on to their own vigorous architectural traditions in the forms that were best suited to their individual requirements and pockets. In 1642 Bishop Fuller wrote that

a house had better be too little for a day than too great for a year. And it's easier borrowing of thy neighbours a brace of chambers for a night than a bag of money for a twelve-month. It is vain therefore to proportion the receipt to an extraordinary occasion.

Such advice was no doubt salutory for the builders of the prodigy houses, but it had rarely been necessary for the builders of the manor houses.

Left: Blackmoor Farm, Cannington, Somerset, c.1500. Hall house on the medieval pattern with irregular projecting wings and porch

Below: Marske Hall, Cleveland, 1625. A sophisticated rectangular design which uses simple projections to achieve a disciplined elevation and an interesting sky-line in an economic fashion

Stibbington Hall, Cambridgeshire, 1625. A gentry E-plan house with a fashionable shaped gable to the porch and detached gateway economically creating a courtyard in front

For all the regional variety and diversity in size of the gentry house, it was a direct descendant in England and Wales of the medieval hall house. The economy of space and propensity towards symmetry of form, if not of detail, that were characteristic of the prototype were retained and transformed by its sixteenth-century successor. Compactness of plan was an enduring feature of the gentry house long before its economic advantages recommended it to the ambitious courtier. The lineage of the simple rectangular plan can be traced through the century from early houses such as Abbey House, Witchampton, Dorset, through more architecturally ambitious examples such as Bassingthorpe Manor, Lincolnshire, of 1568, to the disciplined compositions of Felbrigg Hall, Norfolk, Woolbridge Manor, Dorset, and Marske Hall, Yorkshire, all built in the early seventeenth century. If it is arguable that the courtier E-plan developed from a courtyard house like Sutton Place, the gentry E-plan and H-plan which evolved at about the same time in houses such as Eastbury House, Essex, can be traced in a separate line from the grander hall houses with flanking wings as illustrated by houses such as Chalgrove Manor or Blackmoor Farm, Cannington, Somerset.

While the dilettante courtiers were playing with the compact square plan as a lighthearted holiday home, the more practical merchant and the country gentleman whom he saw as his equal were exploiting its possibilities to the full to

Left: Whitehall, Shrewsbury, Shropshire, 1578–82. Square double-pile house with central cupola and ordered symmetry about the principal elevations

Below: Barnham Court, West Sussex, c.1640. The decorative brickwork, regular fenestration, bold cornice and Dutch gables are hallmarks of the Artisan Mannerist style

Right: Chastleton
House,
Oxfordshire,
begun 1602.
Square plan
around a small
central court. The
staircase towers
and projecting
porch balanced by
the hall bay
window are both
functionally useful
and dramatically
effective

Below: The
rhythmic
symmetry of
Chastleton House
gives added
emphasis to its
height

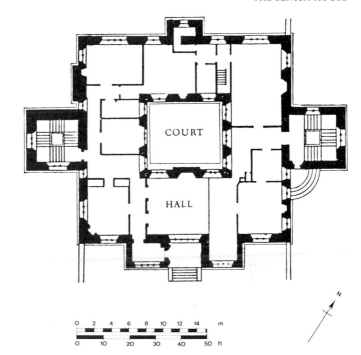

provide a striking principal residence with the minimum of expense. Together they created the double-pile plan, as exemplified by Whitehall, Shrewsbury, of 1578–82 for the lawyer Richard Prince, and its near-relation, the square-block plan arranged around a central light-well, as at Barlborough Hall, Derbyshire, built at about the same time for another lawyer, or Chastleton, Oxfordshire, of 1603 for Walter Jones, a Witney wool merchant. Similar developments were taking place in eastern Wales where John Games, the High Sheriff of Breconshire, was building himself a double-pile house at Llanfaes in 1582.

Wraxall Manor House, Dorset, c.1630. The architectural qualities of discipline, order and symmetry brought to perfection by the anonymous designer of this small manor house

At Chastleton, Jones was able to provide himself with all the amenities of gracious living in a remarkably compact fashion. The house has an imposing hall, a first-floor great chamber, a top-floor gallery, and two very spacious staircases. All this was achieved at a reasonable cost by making the building both deep and tall, and placing the staircases in flanking projecting towers. This latter feature shows that the gentry were just as responsive as the nobility to the architectural potential of projecting and receding planes in wall surfaces and the dramatic effect of an emphatic roof line. The careful way that all these elements are disposed at Chastleton indicates a considerably accomplished controlling hand in the design, and a similar quality is displayed in most of the gentry houses of the later sixteenth and early seventeenth centuries throughout the country. Their anonymous designers had brought to such perfection the discipline of handling the elements of architectural mass and relating them to the details of fenestration, gables and chimneystacks that their creations can bear comparison with anything else in Europe of the same period. Whether it be the quiet confidence of a building like Wraxall Manor House in Dorset, the exuberant flamboyance of the Artisan Mannerist merchant houses around London and the Home Counties characterised by their decorative brickwork, Dutch gables and rectangular windows, or the dramatic culmination of the Scottish tower-house tradition, the smaller British country house is a proud contribution to our cultural heritage.

5

THE FARMHOUSE

I n certain parts of the kingdom, particularly Scotland, the far
north of England and much of western Wales, no houses
from a social level lower than the gentry house survive from
the sixteenth century. In the remainder of the country, the
smallest standing buildings were the houses of relatively
prosperous farmers and craftsmen. The buildings of the vast
majority of the population, of the peasantry and the urban
poor have not survived, and are known only from historical
documents and archaeological excavations.

Like the gentry house, the study of the English and Welsh
farmhouse is primarily a regional inquiry. At an economic
level the boundaries of agricultural prosperity and the
differences in land tenure go far to explain the uneven
distribution of the sixteenth- and early seventeenth-century
farmhouse. The wealth of examples that can still be seen in the
south-east is not simply the result of accidental survival. It was
readily apparent to the composer of the popular Elizabethan
rhyme that

> A knight of Cales,
> And a gentleman of Wales,
> And a laird of the North Country;
> A yeoman of Kent,
> With his yearly rent,
> Will buy them out, all three.

Despite the disparities of wealth and numbers and the
altered state in which so many farmhouses have come down to
us, it is still possible to offer some general observations to
enable recognition and understanding.

At this level the builder had no choice in the materials that he was able to use. If he lived in the timbered regions of southern and eastern England, the west Midlands, north-east Wales, or Lancashire and Cheshire, he built himself a timber-framed house. If he lived on the limestone belt extending from Dorset in the south to parts of Lincolnshire in the north, he was able to use that excellent building stone. If he lived elsewhere, he made do with whatever was available in the locality ranging from earth mixed with straw, through flint and poor-quality stone rubble, to the hard dressed stone of the Pennines. Brick, although increasingly used for chimneys, was still generally beyond his means.

The lack of choice dictated by surface geology did not preclude further regional differences in the way that similar materials were used. The simple, understated framing of the Kentish house contrasts subtly with the square-panelled framework of its equivalent in the west Midlands, and far more emphatically with the exuberantly decorated surface of a Lancashire or Cheshire timber building. In East Anglia the framework might be covered up altogether, disguised under a pargeted coating of plaster. Similarly, it is not just the tones of its stonework that differentiate a farmhouse in Northampton-shire from one in Dorset.

The buildings that survive at this level represent a housing revolution which was to be far more lasting in its effects than the more fashionable experiments of Court and gentry. In a very real sense, the changes which took place in the houses of the yeomen and prosperous husbandmen during the course of the sixteenth and early seventeenth centuries were to influence the housing of the middle classes right up to the beginning of World War II. Whether the Great Rebuilding of 1570 to 1640, first identified and christened by W. G. Hoskins in a seminal article published in 1953, was as widespread or as restricted in time as was once thought, does not really matter. Even though later detailed research has modified the concept and revealed other periods of great building activity in different parts of the country, the important point is that approximately between those dates significant numbers of farmers in a large area of England and part of Wales either built themselves new houses in a way that broke completely with their medieval predecessors or built in permanent materials for the very first time. The new house types were gradually adopted in those other parts of the country whose Great Rebuilding came at a later period.

Manor Farm, Chalgrove, Oxfordshire. Late-medieval timber-framed hall house remodelled in the sixteenth century by the insertion of a chimneystack and the subdivision of the hall. Fashionably rendered and refenestrated in the nineteenth century

At the beginning of the sixteenth century almost everybody who was not of gentry status lived in a house dominated by a single room open to the roof and heated by an open fire placed in the middle of the floor. By the outbreak of the Civil War in 1642 this was no longer true. A complex subdivision of the space available within the house had taken place and a substantial part of the population had begun to go to bed upstairs for the first time. The Middle Ages had ended and the modern period had begun.

In the early years of the sixteenth century, even in the prosperous south-east, open-hall houses continued to be built on the plan that had been established several hundred years before. At its most developed it comprised a hall extending for the full height of the building, entered by a screens-passage and flanked at either end by storeyed bays with specialised service and storage functions. The hall was the only heated room and there was no intercommunicating access between the upper storey chambers at either end. In the grandest examples, which were possibly built for the lesser gentry, the storeyed ends were contained in separate wings aligned at right angles to the hall range. It is probable that the upper storey chambers in these buildings had a regular domestic use, but in the smaller hall houses, where all the accommodation was contained under a single roof, the upper rooms often seem to have been of an inadequate size and too difficult of access to have been used for other than seasonal storage. The smallest hall houses which have survived were simple structures of only two bays with a loft over one bay, the other bay left open to the roof.

The same factors that have been described as stimulating new building among the higher ranks of society made themselves felt in a modified way lower down the social scale. But perhaps the most potent force for change was the staggering rise in food prices which took place through the sixteenth century. This enabled the primary producers, whether freeholders or copy holders on fixed rents, to accumulate reserves of capital which, after a generation or so, they were able to invest in building. The same notions of privacy and greater comfort which they saw being practised in the manor houses were now available to them. The agent by which they were able to achieve this desirable state was the enclosed fireplace with its own flue to take the smoke away.

William Harrison wrote in 1577 of how men marvelled at 'the multitude of chimneys lately erected' in his own village, 'whereas in their young days there were not above two or three, if so many . . .'. The chimneystack, which was frequently constructed of easily portable brick, brought the medieval house a new lease of life and has ensured that many of them have survived to our own day. Once the open hearth was replaced by a proper fireplace, it was no longer necessary to leave the larger part of the house open to the roof simply so that the smoke could find its own way out. The hall could be horizontally subdivided with an upper floor which not only provided an extra room, but also allowed access between the flanking upper storey chambers. Other rooms, by being provided with their own chimneystacks, could be brought into regular domestic use for a greater part of the year. The growing availability of glass enabled draught-free lighting and the addition of a porch diminished one of the important functions of the screens-passage. With more light and no smoke from an open hearth, it was possible to enjoy to the full the somewhat gaudy effects of decoratively painted beams and walls and even ceilings. Within the space of less than a hundred years, the housing conditions of an important segment of society had been thoroughly transformed.

The flexibility of the hall house enabled it to adapt to these momentous changes, but, equally, the opportunity was present to rethink the whole concept of the small house to take advantage of all the new possibilities of smaller rooms, better heating and a more extensively used upper storey. Not unexpectedly there was a variety of shortlived solutions, but by the early seventeenth century three distinct new house types had evolved, each of which was preferred in different parts of the country. By far the most popular, and the one with the widest distribution, was the lobby-entry house. In its smallest form, the chimneystack was placed in the centre of the house with an entrance lobby to the front and a staircase to the rear. The stack could heat the rooms to either side on both floors and provided the opportunity for a dominant decorative central feature where it broke through the ridge of the roof. It was a beautifully economical plan, with all the essential services of chimneystack, draught-free lobby and staircase confined to a narrow bay, leaving the remainder of the building free for unobstructed domestic life. It was easily extended by the addition of further bays in either direction, although these would require additional chimneystacks if they were to be heated, and it exhibited the minimum of radiant heat loss.

The earliest known example of a lobby-entry house is the brick hunting lodge built in about 1525 for Baron Hussey and now known as Old Hall Farm at Kneesall in Nottinghamshire. But this isolated Court example does not preclude a separate and slightly later genesis of the type at the farmhouse level. Whatever its origins, by the seventeenth century it had become the most common house in southern England and East Anglia to the south and east of the limestone belt and in a further area, including part of Wales, to the north and west. Its

Greystone Stores, Little Milton, Oxfordshire; early seventeenth century. A lobby-entry house which retains its original mullioned windows at first-floor level

Lobby-entry plan. The typical post-medieval farmhouse plan in those areas of England and Wales with a persistent timber-framed tradition

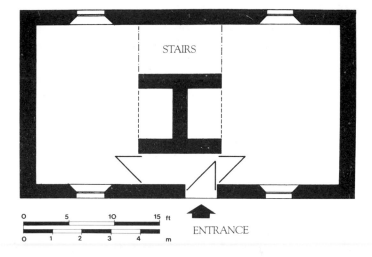

STAIRS

0   5   10   15 ft
0   1   2   3   4 m

ENTRANCE

solution to the domestic changes posed in the sixteenth century was so complete that it continued to be chosen until the popularity of central heating rendered the chimneystack redundant.

The post-medieval house in the limestone uplands took a somewhat different course, suggestive of a more conservative approach to the traditional tripartite division of the farmhouse. Here, the continued emphasis on the retention of the screens-passage leading through from front to rear of the house produced a different relationship between the chimneystack and the entry. The fireplace was generally placed at one end of the largest ground-floor room, backing on to the through passage. There was usually a further unheated room beyond, and the other side of the passage retained the service rooms in their traditional position. The central room, although reduced to a single storey, was initially the only heated room and accordingly retained a dominant position in the domestic arrangements of the house, akin to the medieval hall. The staircase to the upper storey was usually placed on the rear wall of the modified hall. The principal advantage of the through passage was that it provided direct access to the service rooms from both the street and the yard at the rear without interfering with the other rooms of the house. It also continued to emphasise the importance of the hall which had to be entered before access could be gained to the remainder of the house. The tenacious adherence to the symbolic form of an earlier way of life despite radically altered circumstances presupposes different cultural preferences that are not easily understood. In certain areas, such as the Cotswolds, this house type was displaced in the late seventeenth and early eighteenth centuries by the lobby-entry form.

In the west of England and the western parts of Wales a further plan was evolved, with the through passage retained and the newly acquired chimneystack proudly displayed on an outside wall.

Whatever plan was adopted, all these houses with their new fireplaces and stairs, their smaller rooms arranged on two floors, and their glazed windows, were fully equipped to provide comfortable living conditions for the next 250 years. It is a mark of the enduring strength of the Elizabethan housing revolution that even today, if you ask a child to draw a house, you will inevitably be presented with the elevation of a lobby-entry house, often with its most important element smoking furiously.

Below: Through-passage plan. The common farmhouse plan in the upland areas

Bottom: Manor House, Upper Swell, Gloucestershire, early seventeenth century. Through-passage house in the Cotswolds with an added porch

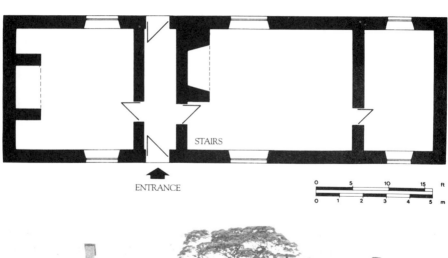

STAIRS

ENTRANCE

6

THE TOWN HOUSE

Four centuries of urban decay and redevelopment have made it a far more difficult task to describe the appearance of an Elizabethan town house than to analyse an Elizabethan country house. Particular buildings in Canterbury, York, Shrewsbury or Chester in England, Llanidloes in Wales and Culross in Scotland, to pick at random the examples that immediately come to mind, might hint at the sixteenth- or seventeenth-century prosperity of the town, but they give a very blurred and incomplete picture of what it was really like.

In London, for example, none of the great courtier mansions that formerly lay between the Thames and the Strand has survived. The York Watergate, forlornly land-locked in the Embankment Gardens, is the sole reminder of Old Somerset House, Salisbury House, York House and Hungerford House, themselves the sixteenth- and early seventeenth-century products of the despoliation of the earlier episcopal mansions of the Bishops of Carlisle, Durham and Norwich. Now that they have gone it is impossible to recapture what must have been one of the most dominant architectural features of the principal city in the kingdom.

Mansions of such grandeur were purely a Court phenomenon, of course, and there was nothing strictly comparable in the provincial cities and towns. In architectural terms they were hardly distinguishable from large country houses set down in the town, and they were equipped with the full complement of courtyards, rooms and lodgings that the magnates would have provided in their rural seats. An impression of their nature, if not of their enormous scale, can be gleaned from Plas Mawr in Conwy with its gate-house and double courtyard. In Scotland, the towering mass of Provost

Skene's House in Aberdeen provides the most notable surviving example now that the 'great ludging' built for the Dowager Countess of Home at Moray House, Edinburgh, has been reduced to a mere fragment of its former size. The remodelled Argyll lodging, close to the Scottish Court at Stirling Castle, is also worthy of note.

However, the largest houses that survive in most British towns were generally the residences of the successful merchants and entrepreneurs who were invariably the wealthiest citizens and who seem frequently to have moved on after two or three generations to become country gentlemen. In the timber-framed regions it is the scale of the houses and the extravagance of decoration that draw the eye: qualities of self advertisement which were no doubt good for trade. There is a particularly splendid sequence in Shrewsbury beginning with the house built in about 1575 for Robert Ireland, a successful wool merchant, and including Owen's Mansion placed almost opposite in 1592 by one of his business rivals. Rowley's House, built at the same period for Roger Rowley, a draper and brewer, is not quite so flamboyant but is similarly timber-framed and jettied. It is typical of the self-assurance that

Below: Provost Skene's House, Aberdeen, Grampian Region, sixteenth century. A grand town mansion with projecting wings and corbelled-out turrets in the Scottish fashion

Right: Ireland's Mansion, Shrewsbury, Shropshire, c.1575. Richly modelled town house proclaiming the prosperity of Ireland's wool business. The decorative framing is typical of the western counties

second-generation wealth brings that the mansion erected by his son next door relies more on the novelty of its brickwork and the sophistication of its architectural detailing to announce its presence. A similar refinement of taste is characteristic of the town houses of successful lawyers and officials, as illustrated by Richard Prince's Shrewsbury mansion at Whitehall, or Moncreif House in Falkland.

These men were at the very point of the pyramid of civic society. Beneath them was a seething mass of shopkeepers, craftsmen, artisans and all the other shadowy and often unsavoury characters who populated the towns of Shakespeare and Jonson. As far as one can tell from the much altered surviving physical evidence, they were generally housed in narrow buildings, often of only one room's width, with a side entry that led both into the house and to the yard at the rear. Each narrow unit might have a shop or workshop facing on to the street, entered from the side passage, with a further living room behind. Various other living rooms, often sublet or in multiple tenancies, would be on the floors above. Depending on the depth of the plot or the commercial pressures on the site, there might be a separate detached kitchen at the rear or further rows of workshops and meaner dwellings extending at right angles to the street frontage. Alternatively, in conformity with the practice of those who took their money from the town making their principal residence there, the shops and tenements on the street front might screen an imposing town house from the hubbub of the world outside. An excellently preserved example of this type of layout can still be seen in Oxford where the jettied and gabled Kemp Hall was built for Alderman William Boswell in 1637 at the rear of a late medieval tenement fronting the High Street. Boswell's house faces a narrow passage which used to communicate with a further house at the rear of the plot. Other examples are known in York, Tewkesbury and elsewhere in England.

At the commercial heart of the town, where space was at an expensive premium, the shops and tenements on the street front could be extended only in an upward direction and the most picturesque examples are often four or five storeys high, with each successive storey being progressively further jettied out to secure the maximum usable space. Jettied buildings could only be successfully constructed in timber and this was presumably one of the most important reasons why so many towns in the sixteenth century were predominantly timber-framed even in areas where good building stone was easily available. Away from the prime sites, town buildings were often only two storeys high and spread more generously across wider plots. Contemporary maps of provincial towns show how quickly the suburbs were reached from the crowded marketplaces and here farm buildings and orchards were likely to be encountered as well as rows of artisan housing interspersed with the occasional larger house.

The variety of their architecture, and their often tortuous relationship with their neighbours, suggests that many town buildings were the results of individual speculations, with one man leasing one or two burgage plots and erecting a single structure which would provide him with the accommodation that he required and possibly give him a small investment income from letting the remainder of the building or parts of the site. However, there is also a great deal of evidence of more controlled development still visible in many English towns. Buildings such as Abbot's House, Butcher Row, Shrewsbury, with its ground-floor row of separate shops and the uniform architecture above, speak of a more extensive speculation. Indeed, as more and more apparently disparate groups of urban buildings are examined by the trained eye of the building archaeologist, it is becoming clear that certain parts of the sixteenth-century town were just as likely to present a picture of terraced uniformity as they were the irregular jumble of

Abbot's House, Butcher Row, Shrewsbury, Shropshire. Early sixteenth-century urban speculation with original shop-fronts on the ground floor

picturesque buildings so beloved of nineteenth-century topo-
graphical artists.

Only the wealthy or influential investor was likely to be
able to assemble sufficient land on a site close to a town centre to
create a terrace of any length, and it is significant that many of the
early sixteenth-century examples are closely linked with the
church. The most comprehensible development in its newly
restored form is in Church Street, Tewkesbury, where the
Abbey seems to have been responsible for building a terrace of
at least twenty-three units, each with its own shop and hall on
the ground floor, and a chamber above. The deliberate
architectural emphasis provided by a larger central unit is also
present in the similar row recently discovered adjoining Battle
Abbey in Sussex, and in the row which hides behind an
eighteenth-century brick front in Friday Street, Henley-on-
Thames. No ecclesiastical connection can be discovered for
the latter, but, as it is situated in a street away from the market
centre of the town, there would not have been too much
difficulty in securing a site of sufficient dimensions to make a
comprehensive development worthwhile. The economic
advantages of building a series of units to let is manifest from
the 'shopping precinct' incorporated on the ground floor of
the Moot Hall at Elstow in Bedfordshire.

The terraces at both Tewkesbury and Battle still retained
the hall heated by an open hearth of medieval tradition. By the

Friday Street,
Henley-on-
Thames,
Oxfordshire.
Sixteenth-century
row of timber-
framed tenements
built as a single
speculation and re-
fronted in the
eighteenth
century

middle of the sixteenth century the same sorts of processes that have already been noted in the countryside were at work in the towns: medieval houses were modernised and altered, and new house types were evolved. The characteristic features were the same. Enclosed fireplaces with proper chimney-stacks, a proliferation in the number of rooms with more specialised and more private functions, and a greater use of the upper parts of buildings with a corresponding emphasis on the staircase, were the most noticeable changes. Given the limitations on site width and the need for convenient access to the rear, the side-passage house continued as the most viable urban plan although now it was invariably graced with an imposing chimneystack and an adequate staircase, and it often extended upwards for three storeys. Indeed, this type continued through the eighteenth and nineteenth centuries and supplied most of the characteristics of the typical terraced house of those centuries.

In the suburban areas, where the pressures on space were less and the plots tended to be considerably broader, the new farmhouse plan types soon emerged. One example, a two-storey, lobby-entry house with large dormer windows lighting the roof at 35 Holywell, Oxford, is dated 1626. Holywell, just outside the line of the city wall, still preserves a decidedly seventeenth-century air for much of its length.

Although the fact might be difficult to appreciate now,

34–50 Church Street, Tewkesbury, Gloucestershire. Early sixteenth-century timber-framed row of ground-floor shops with living accommodation above. Probably built as an investment by the Abbey

constant efforts were made by the city fathers to control the siting, materials and even the numbers of new buildings that were erected in the sixteenth-century town. Their ordinances might not always have met with success, but they display awareness of a need for fairly strict planning in the interests of safety, good government, and the proper functioning of the town. The marked increase in population in the sixteenth century led to greatly increased social and physical pressures on the thriving towns. The growth of London had so alarmed the Government by 1580 that a royal proclamation forbade the building of any new houses within three miles of the gates of the city. Further proclamations under James I and Charles I grew ever more restrictive. Despite their original intention to halt a potentially dangerous growth of the capital, the proclamations evolved in practice into a system of licensing building in such a way that responsible control was exercised over its proper planning, not least its 'Uniformities and Decency' specifically mentioned in the proclamations of 1625 and 1630. Inigo Jones, as Surveyor of the King's Works,

Holywell Street, Oxford. Situated just outside the city wall, many of the seventeenth-century houses are spread over more generous plots headed the commission entrusted with the administration of the system. He also designed the new residential quarter at Covent Garden for which the Earl of Bedford had been granted a licence in 1631. The concept of a square surrounded by gentlemen's residences overlooking a communal garden and served by its own church, was to have a profound influence on the subsequent planning of fashionable British towns.

Its immediate effect was restricted to London where a new Classical formality appeared in the large terraced houses built in Great Queen Street in 1636 and Lincoln's Inn Fields from 1638. Lindsey House, the sole survivor of this speculation, seems light-years away from the vernacular traditions of Tewkesbury. It symbolises the architectural transformation that was to affect the larger cities in the land after the Restoration.

Lindsey House, Lincoln's Inn Fields, London, 1640. The beginnings of Classical formality in the streets of the metropolis

7

PUBLIC BUILDINGS

Towns and villages were composed of many other build-ings besides their houses, inns and shops. Their places of worship are considered in the final chapter, and it remains to discuss what can be described loosely as their public buildings – the buildings which provided for the government, education and welfare of the population.

The most imposing building of this nature to be found in most towns was appropriately enough the market house, predecessor of the modern town hall. In England and Wales this invariably had an open arcaded ground floor which provided shelter for some of the stalls on market day. Above this was a large chamber which acted as a meeting room for the regulation of the market and the government of the affairs of the town. The Scottish tolbooth or Town House differed from this pattern only by virtue of having an enclosed ground floor, sometimes used as the town gaol.

The civic authorities went to some expense to ensure that the physical symbol of their power was a dominant feature of the town. It was usually sited at the head of the wide marketplace, initially at least, isolated from the ordinary buildings of the town. Its form of a solid mass, seemingly hovering above the ground, effectively drew attention to its dual function. Its decoration was often striking. For those few market halls for which we have documentary information, it is clear that their construction was entrusted to only the very best craftsmen in the locality: Walter Hancock at Shrewsbury, John Abel at Brecon, Leominster and Kington, and William Grumbold at Rothwell.

The expense of building Rothwell Market House was shared by the inhabitants of the town and two local magnates,

The Town House, Culross, Fife Region, 1626 (with added tower of 1783). The imposing centre for the administration of the town

Sir Christopher Hatton and Sir Thomas Tresham. The latter was the prime instigator of the project, commissioning the design and paying for the workmanship. Although planned before his conversion to Catholicism, it unashamedly reflects the burning desire for architectural self-advertisement which was to characterise the rest of Tresham's building career. It is embellished with ninety shields which were to bear the arms of his friends and neighbours, a public demonstration of his local importance and the range of his connections. The only hint of embarrassment at such a brazen display comes at the end of the Latin inscription which runs round the building above the pilasters decorated with his trefoils:

This was the work of Thomas Tresham, Knight. He erected it as a tribute to his sweet fatherland and county of Northampton, but chiefly to this town, his near neighbour. Nothing but the common weal did he seek; nothing but the perpetual honour of his friends. He who puts an ill construction on this act is scarcely worthy so great a benefit . . .

A desire for immortality in stone, for some permanent way of ensuring that a man's name lived on after his physical remains had turned to dust, was an enduring characteristic of an age which had seen its traditional religious certainties swept away. One way of achieving this was by a self-important

Market House, Rothwell, Northamptonshire, 1578. Architecturally impressive testament to the generosity and social standing of Sir Thomas Tresham

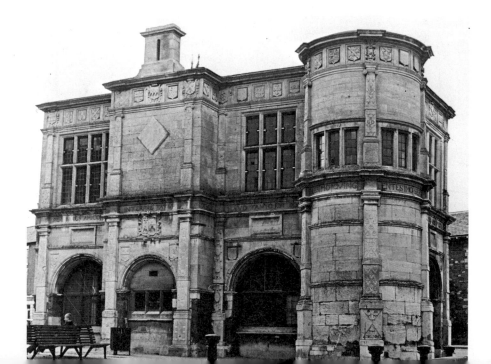

monument in the parish church. Another was by an act of public benefaction which contributed to 'the common weal' yet at the same time left your name on the lips of everyone who benefited and in the gaze of all who passed by. Such was Tresham's Market House and so, too, on a much more widespread scale, were all the almshouses for the relief of the aged and the needy which were built throughout the land in the sixteenth and seventeenth centuries.

They ranged in size from the full-blown courtyard plans complete with hall, chapel and gate-house of such ambitious foundations as Heriot's Hospital in Edinburgh or Abbot's Hospital, Guildford, to the humble row of three or four cottages, such as Sir John Strode built by the church at Beaminster. They were founded by kings and noble lords, archbishops and humble clerics, merchants, lawyers, and successful tradesmen. No matter what form they took, or whether they catered for a hundred people or four, they invariably had one characteristic in common: the name of the benefactor was usually attached to the foundation and prominently displayed on the fabric. Such foundations met a real social need.

One of the reasons that public charity markedly increased during the sixteenth century was the dissolution of the traditional providers of alms and succour, the monasteries.

Market House, Ledbury, Hereford and Worcester, begun 1617. Typical timber-framed market hall with an open ground floor and a large chamber above

Abbot's Hospital, Guildford, Surrey, 1619–22. Quadrangular group of almshouses built at the expense of George Abbot, Archbishop of Canterbury, with a dominating gate-house

Their demise, and the legislation associated with it, also destroyed many of the haphazard provisions for formal education made by medieval society. This was another area where private individuals could step into the breach and create a personal memorial in return for an act of public good. Individuals, such as Wolsey and Colet, had founded schools before the dissolution, but the practice expanded considerably after the middle of the century. Many of our still flourishing institutions, in both the public and the private sectors, can trace their origins back to that period. Some, such as Shrewsbury, Thame and Guildford, were quite elaborate creations, but the majority were simple rectangular buildings with a single schoolroom and possibly lodgings for the master. No coherent architectural type emerged, but such school buildings were a familiar part of the fabric of many late sixteenth- and early seventeenth-century towns.

The need for literate administrators to service the machinery of the Tudor state was a powerful stimulus to education which touched not only the ambitious gentry but also the hereditary nobility who wished to maintain their position in an increasingly competitive society. Times were changing and the most important public positions were going to those men with trained minds who were capable of clear analysis and who could write official papers and memoranda. Their skill in diplomacy was far more important than their military expertise. 'Learning to a gentleman', Sir John Strode informed his son in 1632, 'is like a diamond set in a gold ring: one doth beautify the other.' The new schools were the foundation of the system, the universities and the Inns of Court were where the process was brought to fruition.

This sequence is present in the school that Wolsey founded at Ipswich in 1527 to complement the new college that he had begun to build in Oxford two years previously. The great expansion in the universities, however, was to come later in the century. In Oxford, St John's College was founded by the London merchant Sir Thomas White in 1555, and Trinity College was refounded in the same year by Sir Thomas Pope, the Treasurer of the Court of Augmentation. Jesus College was founded as a Protestant institution in 1571 by Dr Hugh Price, Treasurer of St David's Cathedral in Wales. In the early years of the seventeenth century Wadham was founded

Almshouses, Mapledurham, Oxfordshire. Founded in 1613 by John Lister for six poor inhabitants of the parish

by the Somerset landowners Nicholas and Dorothy Wadham, and Pembroke followed in 1624. At the same time some of the older foundations were expanding, with new quadrangles being added at Merton between 1608 and 1610, Lincoln (1608–31), Oriel (1620–42), and University (begun in 1634). Duke Humfrey's Library was reconstructed by Sir Thomas Bodley between 1598 and 1602 and further extended between 1613 and 1620 when the Schools Quadrangle was built. A Botanic Garden was established for the University in 1621 by the Earl of Danby. The building activity at Cambridge, details of which are in the gazetteer, was just as impressive. With a few notable exceptions, such as the allegorical gateways of Dr Caius in Cambridge, the Classical frontispieces at Merton, Wadham and the Bodleian, Nicholas Stone's gateways to the Botanic Garden, and the proto-Baroque parts of Canterbury Quadrangle, St John's, all at Oxford, the chosen style at the universities right up to the Civil War was late-Perpendicular Gothic. As late as 1640 the staircase leading up to the hall at Christ Church was given a magnificently convincing fan-vault.

St John's College, Cambridge. Library, 1623–4. Deliberately designed with 'the old fashion of church window' as the most appropriate style

This was not in any spirit of revival of the sort that appeared in domestic architecture of the latter part of the sixteenth century. It was more that the functional requirements of the colleges had not changed since William of Wykeham had devised their most practical architectural expression at New College in the late fourteenth century. The inward-looking courtyard plan with its porter's lodge, hall, chapel and sets of lodgings was perfectly designed to meet the needs of the expanded universities of the sixteenth century. It was a static form which must have seemed to those who used it to have acquired its own immutable style of dress. In comparison with the architectural adventures that were taking place in the world outside, it was recognised that this dress might appear outdated, but it was nevertheless deemed to be the most appropriate one for the dignity of the institution. As the College explained to Bishop Williams who had donated the money to build a new library at St John's, Cambridge, in 1624: 'men of judgement liked the best the old fashion of church windows, holding it the most meet for such a building'.

A similar attitude can be discerned at the Inns of Court in London, which acted as a kind of finishing school in the education of many of the nobility as well as providing a professional training for the gentry. The need for some knowledge of the law in that litigious age, together with the

St John's College, Cambridge. Second Court, 1598–1602. A Cambridge example of collegiate architectural conservatism

Overleaf: The Feathers Hotel, Ludlow, Shropshire. Highly decorated timber-framing used to draw attention to the commercial function of the building

attractions of the proximity of the Court, led to a parallel expansion in those institutions. The new halls that the societies of Gray's Inn, Staple Inn and the Middle Temple built in the period all perpetuated the Gothic traditions of the hammerbeam roof.

One other class of urban building requires brief mention. Inns and taverns were an important feature of daily life in every town and city throughout the land. The smaller drinking-houses were probably little different from the houses and shops already discussed. The larger establishments, which provided accommodation as well as food and drink, had their own distinctive forms, with impressive street frontages advertising their presence and often galleried courtyards behind giving independent access to the individual rooms. Examples of this type of building are often to be seen today, either substantially in their original form, such as the George, Dorchester, or the Feathers, Ludlow, or more often disguised by later alterations.

8

ECCLESIASTICAL BUILDINGS

It is a reflection of its relative importance that church building should form the final chapter of this account of British architecture in the sixteenth and early seventeenth centuries. This is not to say that people did not continue to build new churches or to extend and repair those that already existed. Indeed, contrary to popular belief, so much ecclesiastical building went on during the period that if the gazetteer were to include it all, there would scarcely be room for other buildings. But much of it was of a minor nature and there is little evidence of the dynamic invention which illuminated domestic architecture. Religious uncertainty not unnaturally bred architectural uncertainty and most builders played safe with a watered-down Gothic that could offend no one but which hardly uplifted the spirit.

Nothing of this could have been predicted at the start of the century. In England and Wales the late flowering of the Perpendicular style was still in full flow. These were the years when Henry VII's chapel was built at Westminster Abbey and the crowning octagon was placed on top of the Boston Stump. In Aberdeen the twin spires were added to the west front of St Machars Cathedral and the chapel to King's College was constructed. At a parish level, many of the splendid West Country and East Anglian churches were completed or further embellished during the early decades of the sixteenth century, and new churches of compelling self-confidence and architectural unity, such as St James, Barton-under-Needwood, were built. A single patron, such as the Duke of Buckingham, did not hesitate to lavish money on the various churches of his scattered manors, adding towers at Brecon and St Bride's Wentlooge, an aisle of impressive dimensions at Eastington,

Left: Cleeve Abbey, Somerset. The lavishly decorated Refectory built by Abbot William Dovell just before the dissolution of the Abbey

and thoroughly remodelling his principal church at Thornbury, while simultaneously building himself the grandest mansion in the land.

Such works of piety by the laity were designed to demonstrate their standing and to increase their chances in the life hereafter. Among the monastic orders there seems to have been a late flurry of building, apparently oblivious of the gathering storms, which suggests a similar concern with public

Below: St James, Barton-under-Needwood, Staffordshire, begun 1517. An outstanding and rare example of total architectural unity at a parochial level

Right: St Leonard, Sunningwell, Oxfordshire. West porch, c.1551. Only the Gothic window tracery betrays the uncompromisingly Classical spirit of this charming polygonal addition

Below: St Mary, Thornbury, Avon. Richly modelled tower added in the early sixteenth century. It forms a striking feature as seen from Buckingham's Privy Garden at Thornbury Castle

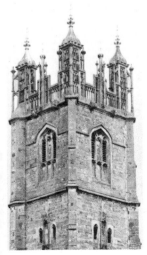

recognition, and a weakness for worldly comfort. Faced with the magnificent lodging that the Prioress built for herself at Carrow Abbey, Norwich, in the early sixteenth century, Sir Nikolaus Pevsner cannot refrain from commenting that 'in its sumptuousness and worldliness [it] almost seems to justify the Dissolution'. Contemporary lodgings and monastic buildings of similar splendour can be instanced from the abbeys of Cleeve, Forde, Muchelney, St Osyth and Much Wenlock in England and Lincluden and Arbroath in Scotland, while the free-standing campanile erected at Evesham Abbey by Abbot Lichfield is a remarkable testimony of architectural lavishness and clerical arrogance.

Such open displays of wealth no doubt contributed to the ultimate fate of the monasteries, but the English Reformation when it came was as much an expression of growing nationalism and statehood as an attack on the declining standards of the church. As far as its architectural development is concerned, there is evidence that had Henry VIII not felt it essential to assert his supremacy in matters both spiritual and temporal within his kingdom, advanced ecclesiastical taste could still have exercised an important influence on design. There is a greater corpus of Early Renaissance work dating from the 1520s, '30s and '40s in the fittings of English churches than can be assembled from all the known domestic examples and it is tempting to see them as an indication of a growing movement of potential significance. In the event, the break with Rome, the militant Protestantism under Edward VI, the subsequent Marian reaction and the eventual Elizabethan compromise, stifled the development of any consistent style. The screens at King's College, Cambridge, and Carlisle Cathedral, the windows at Barham, Barking and Henley in Suffolk and Kirtling in Cambridgeshire, the porches at Sunningwell, Oxfordshire, Totnes in Devon and Sherborne St John in Hampshire, the Cathedral gateway at Canterbury, Bishop Gardener's Chantry at Winchester, the Draper Chantry at Christchurch, and the pulpit at Wells remain isolated works which have never been assessed in toto.

The bewildering turns in ecclesiastical doctrine seem to have inhibited ecclesiastical invention and possibly to have reduced the funds available for lavish building. New churches continued to be built, whether financed by individuals, such as Richard Chernocke who, according to his monument, 're-edified his parish church' of St Nicholas, Holcot, Bedfordshire, or by nationwide contributions as with St Michael, Arthuret. They have the beauty of architectural uniformity but little excitement.

The belief, which permeated the universities as well, in an immutable style considered appropriate to the lasting traditions of the institution must have provided a necessary sense of security in coping with radical doctrinal changes. The porches, towers and even the memorial chapels which were added in this period often seem to be characterised by the quiet self-effacement which must have been an important ingredient in the unmolested survival of many parishioners as they wrestled with their consciences.

Church interiors were a different matter and the large amount of Elizabethan and Jacobean woodwork, particularly pulpits, which still survives in many parish churches, is testimony not only to changing liturgical requirements but also to the infiltration of domestic architectural fashions. As

Chapel of St Michael, Rycote Park, Oxfordshire. Interior refitted in the early seventeenth century with woodwork reminiscent of domestic decoration of the period

long as the fabric remained recognisably Gothic, there was greater scope for freedom in the design of fittings and in some churches, such as Standish in Lancashire and Metheringham in Lincolnshire, even the piers of the arcades took on a Classical form. It is significant that the decreasing emphasis on a separate chancel, which led to the simple rectangular form of such early seventeenth-century churches as Langley, Shropshire, and Groombridge, Kent, was not accompanied by any similar trend.

In Scotland the Reformation did not occur until 1560. The requirement for a single chamber within which the congregation could freely hear the preaching of the Word led to the 'cleansing' of extant churches and the creation of simple oblong spaces in the few new churches that were built. The

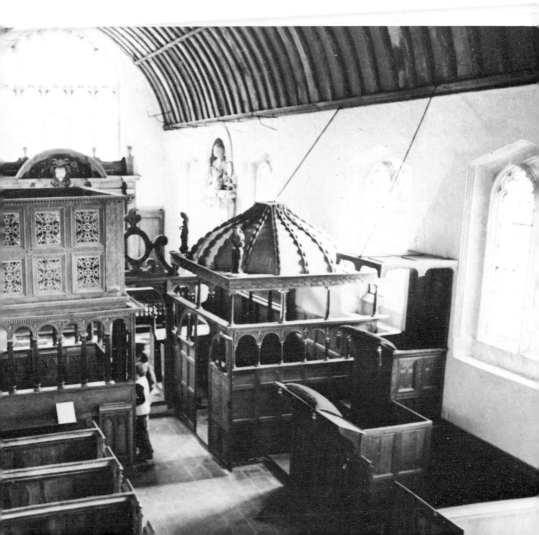

Langley Chapel
Shropshire, 1601.
A simple building
with no distinction
between nave and
chancel but
retaining vestigial
Gothic detail

St Mary, Oxford.
South porch, 1637,
by N. Stone.
The twisted
columns, bold
scrolls and
interrupted
pediment are rare
Mannerist motifs
for an English
ecclesiastical
building

striking square plan subdivided by internal piers supporting the central tower, which was adopted by the parishioners of Burntisland in 1592, was not repeated anywhere else, and the typical Scottish Reformed church is a simple single-cell with Gothic detailing. By the seventeenth-century, a projecting aisle containing the laird's loft had produced a distinctive T-plan which remained popular into the eighteenth century.

In England in the years leading up to the Civil War there is evidence of a revived confidence in church building, much of it associated with the high church vision of Bishop Laud or of his known supporters. In some parts of the country, such as Somerset and Shropshire, it seems to have taken the form of a

St Mary, Leighton Bromswold, Cambridgeshire. West tower, c.1630. An admirable provincial attempt to integrate reticent Classical details with the essentially Gothic form of the tower

revival of full-blooded Gothic detail. Elsewhere there is the exuberant Mannerism of the porch to St Mary the Virgin, Oxford, and the Classical competence of the tower at Leighton Bromswold. This activity was not to last, but it makes a welcome antidote to the reticence of much that had preceded it.

The final words must be on Inigo Jones. In this sphere, as with all his other achievements, it is difficult to integrate his buildings into the general story of British architecture in the early seventeenth century. His two royal chapels, both for clandestine Catholic worship, his Classicising of old St Paul's and his Protestant church for the Earl of Bedford's Covent Garden speculation, show him to have been totally removed from the architectural aspirations and the insular vision of his compatriots. Isolated like the Court that sustained him, his influence was to be realised only by generations yet unborn.

St Paul, Covent Garden, 1631–8, by Inigo Jones. The only remaining element of the Duke of Bedford's influential experiment in town planning. A Tuscan temple fit for Protestant worship

GAZETTEER

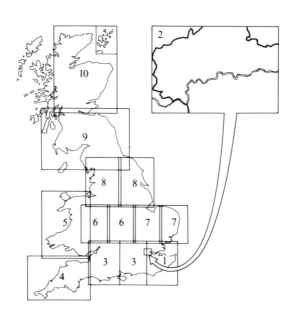

MAPS

Key to Symbols

⊙ town or village with various good buildings of the period

○ large modern town

⌂ house

♟ palace or very large house

✚ church or chapel

⊕ monastery

‡ cathedral

♜ castle or fort

🏛 town hall or government institution

📖 college, school or library

▣ hospital or almshouse, etc.

◩ theatre or place of entertainment

▲ industrial or commercial building

⌒ bridge

■ other building or monument

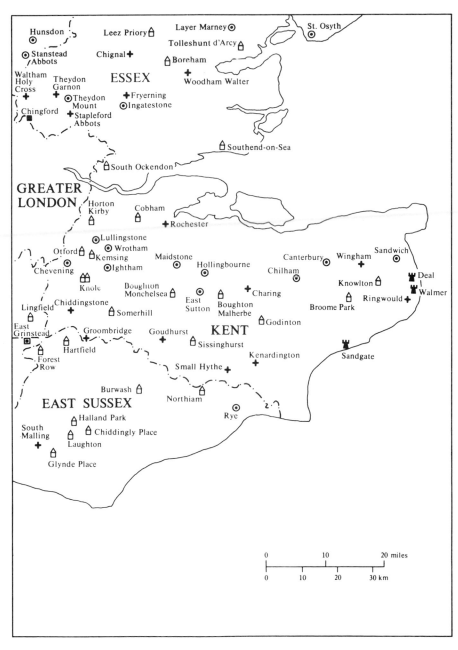

1 South-East England

2 London

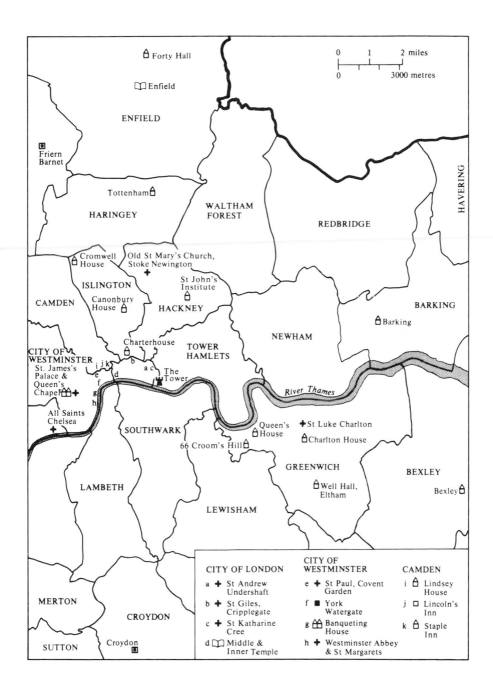

Forty Hall

Enfield

ENFIELD

Friern
Barnet

Tottenham

HARINGEY

WALTHAM
FOREST

REDBRIDGE

HAVERING

Cromwell
House

Old St Mary's Church,
Stoke Newington

ISLINGTON

St John's
Institute

CAMDEN

Canonbury
House

HACKNEY

BARKING

Barking

Charterhouse

TOWER
HAMLETS

NEWHAM

CITY OF
WESTMINSTER
St. James's
Palace &
Queen's
Chapel

i j k
e
f
g
h

b
d

a c
The
Tower

River Thames

All Saints
Chelsea

SOUTHWARK

Queen's
House

St Luke Charlton

66 Croom's Hill

Charlton House

GREENWICH

BEXLEY

LAMBETH

Well Hall,
Eltham

Bexley

LEWISHAM

MERTON

CROYDON

SUTTON

Croydon

CITY OF LONDON	CITY OF WESTMINSTER	CAMDEN
a ✚ St Andrew Undershaft	e ✚ St Paul, Covent Garden	i Lindsey House
b ✚ St Giles, Cripplegate	f ■ York Watergate	j □ Lincoln's Inn
c ✚ St Katharine Cree	g Banqueting House	k Staple Inn
d Middle & Inner Temple	h ✚ Westminster Abbey & St Margarets	

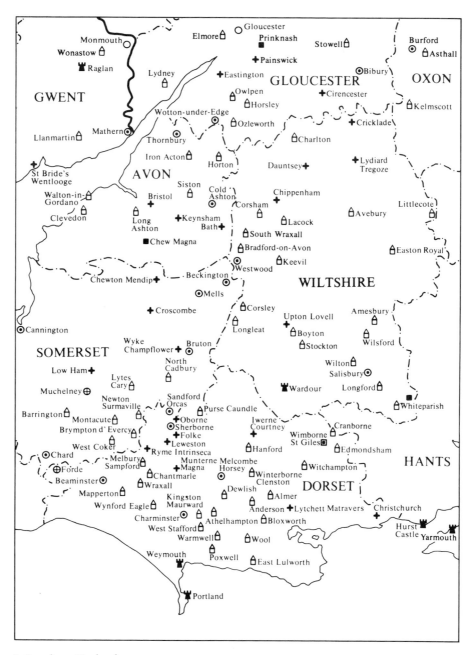

3 Southern England

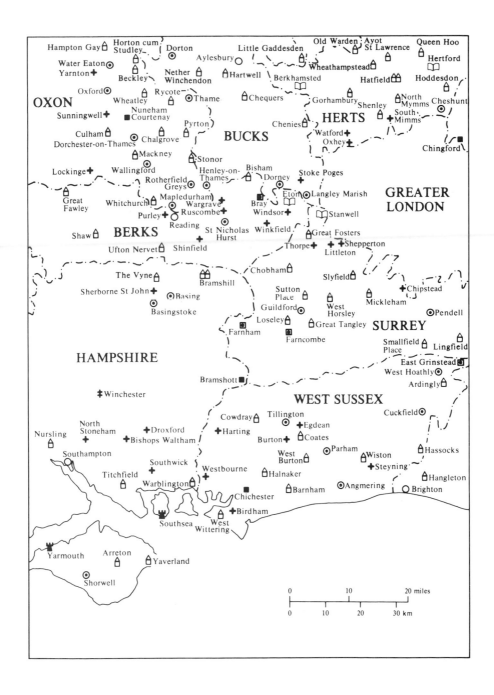

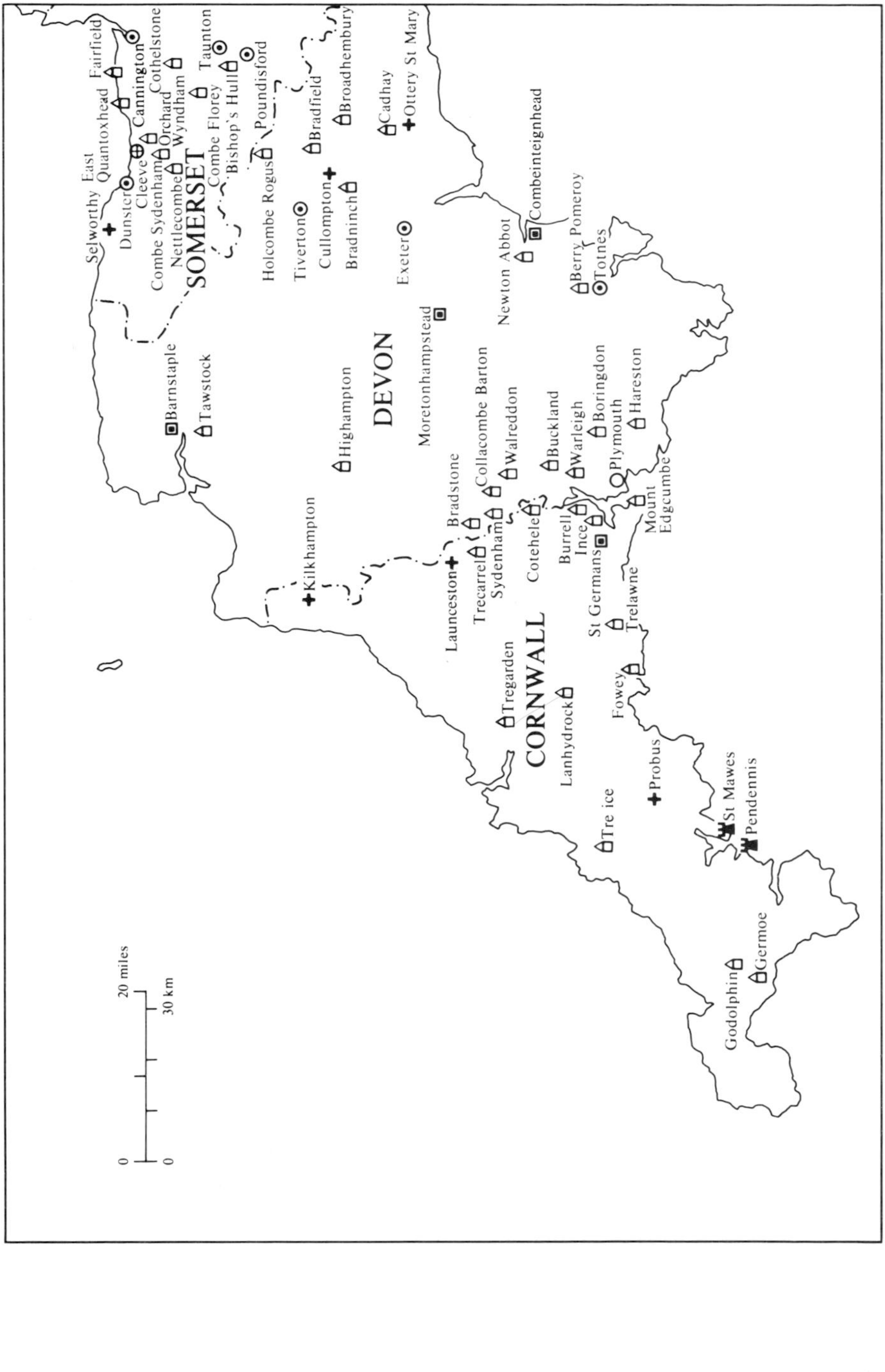

Selworthy East
Quantoxhead Fairfield
Dunster Cannington Cothelstone
Cleeve Taunton
Combe Sydenham Orchard Wyndham
Nettlecombe Combe Florey
Bishop's Hull Poundisford
Bradfield
Broadhembury
Holcombe Rogus Cadhay
Tiverton Otery St Mary
Cullompton Combeinteignhead
Bradninch
SOMERSET
Exeter
Newton Abbot Berry Pomeroy
Totnes

Barnstaple
Tawstock

DEVON

Highampton
Moretonhampstead
Collacombe Barton
Kilkhampton Walreddon Buckland
Bradstone Warleigh
Trecarrel Sydenham Boringdon
Cotehele Hareston
Burrell Plymouth
Ince Mount
Launceston St Germans Edgcumbe
Trelawne

Tregarden
Lanhydrock Fowey

CORNWALL

Tre ice Probus
St Mawes
Pendennis

Godolphin Germoe

20 miles
30 km
0
0

4 South-West England

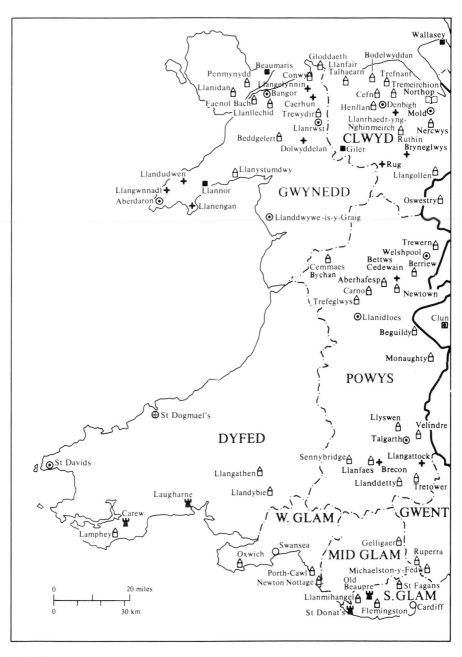

5 Wales

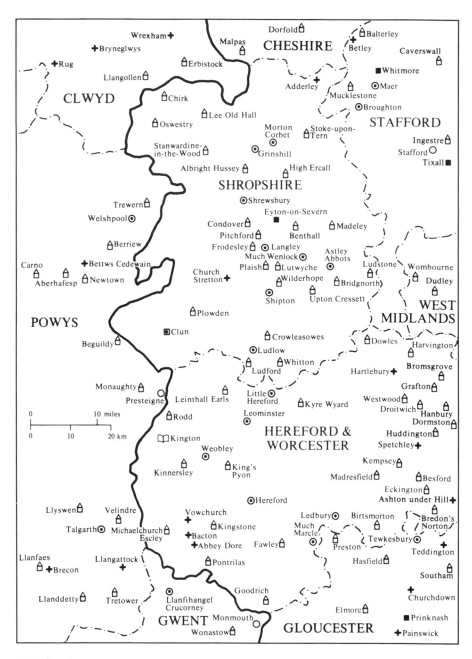

6 Midlands

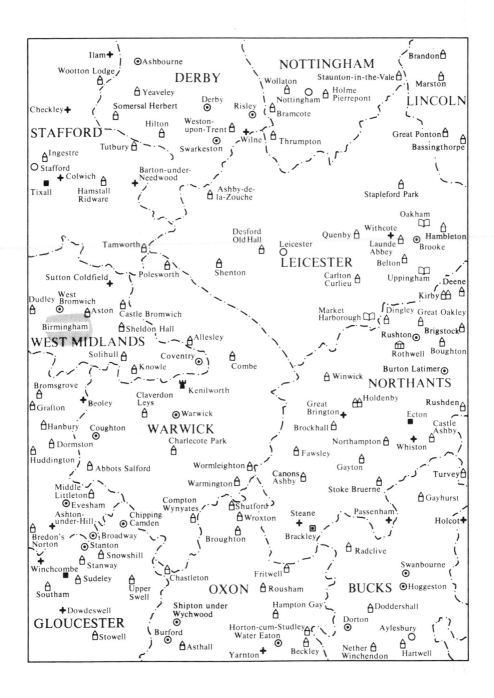

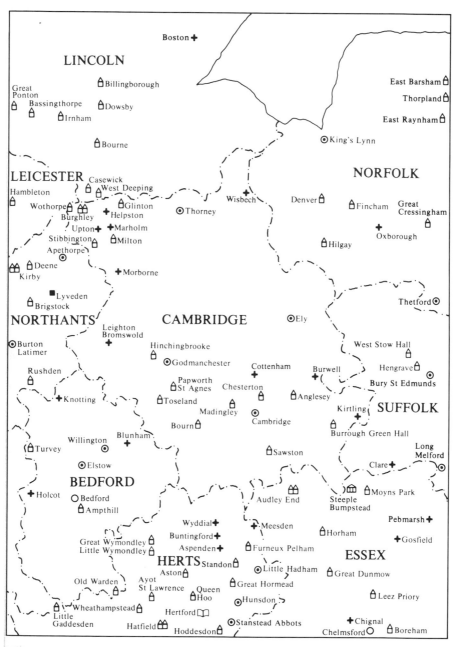

7 East Anglia

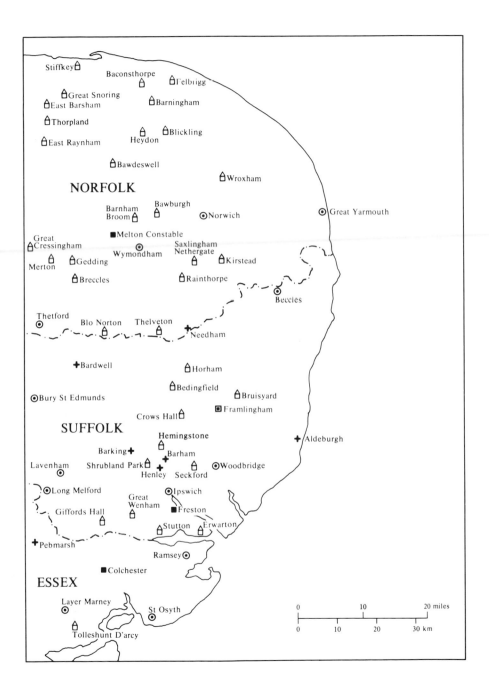

Stiffkey

Baconsthorpe

Felbrigg

Great Snoring

East Barsham

Barningham

Thorpland

East Raynham

Heydon

Blickling

Bawdeswell

Wroxham

NORFOLK

Barnham Broom

Bawburgh

Norwich

Great Yarmouth

Great Cressingham

Melton Constable

Wymondham

Saxlingham Nethergate

Merton

Gedding

Kirstead

Breccles

Rainthorpe

Beccles

Thetford

Blo Norton

Thelveton

Needham

Bardwell

Horham

Bedingfield

Bruisyard

Bury St Edmunds

Framlingham

Crows Hall

SUFFOLK

Hemingstone

Aldeburgh

Barking

Barham

Lavenham

Shrubland Park

Henley

Seckford

Woodbridge

Long Melford

Great Wenham

Ipswich

Giffords Hall

Freston

Stutton

Erwarton

Pebmarsh

Ramsey

Colchester

ESSEX

Layer Marney

St Osyth

Tolleshunt D'arcy

0   10   20 miles

0   10   20   30 km

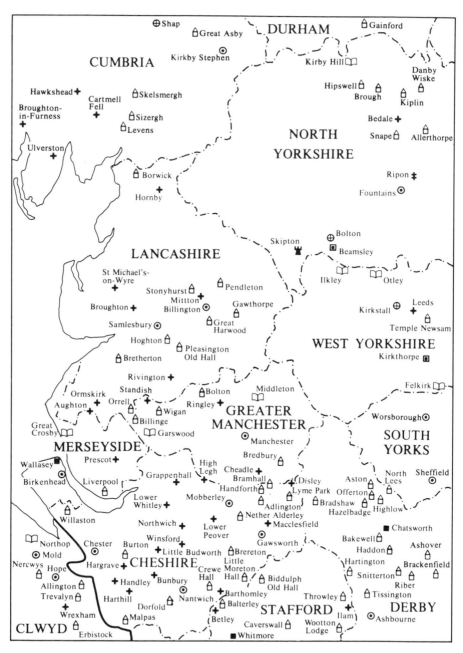

8 Northern England

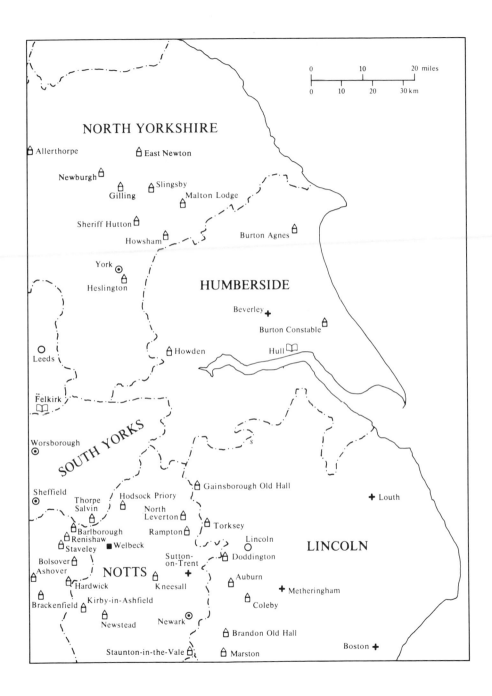

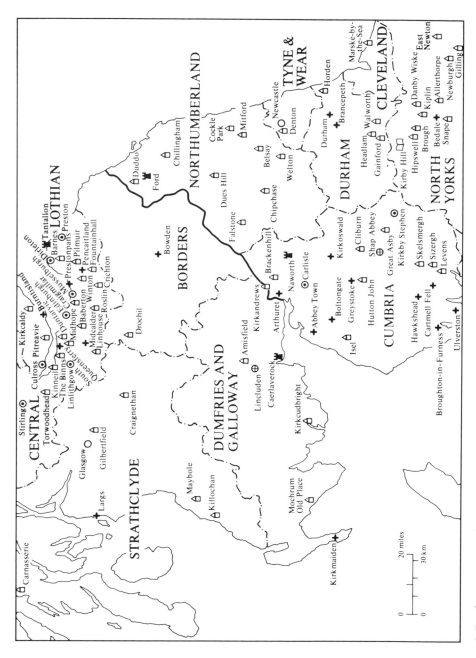

9 Border Country and Southern Scotland

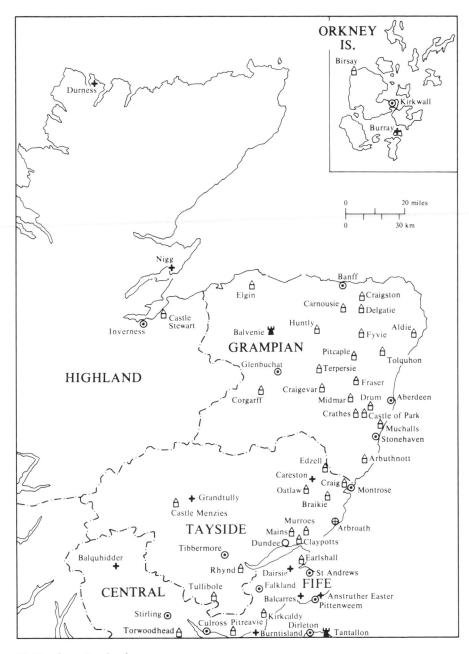

ORKNEY
IS.

Birsay

Kirkwall

Burray

0   20 miles

0   30 km

Durness

Nigg

HIGHLAND

Inverness

Castle
Stewart

Elgin

Balvenie

GRAMPIAN

Glenbuchat

Corgarff

Craigevar

Banff

Carnousie

Huntly

Craigston

Delgatie

Fyvie   Aldie

Pitcaple   Tolquhon

Terpersie

Fraser

Midmar   Drum   Aberdeen

Crathes   Castle of Park

Muchalls

Stonehaven

Arbuthnott

Edzell

Careston

Oatlaw   Craig   Montrose

Braikie

Grandtully

Castle Menzies

TAYSIDE

Murroes

Mains   Arbroath

Tibbermore

Dundee   Claypotts

Balquhidder

Rhynd   Earlshall

Dairsie   St Andrews

CENTRAL   Tullibole   Falkland   FIFE

Balcarres   Anstruther Easter

Pittenweem

Stirling

Kirkcaldy

Torwoodhead   Culross Pitreavie   Dirleton

Burntisland   Tantallon

10 Northern Scotland

135

GAZETTEER

A National Grid Reference number is cited immediately after location and county name beginning each entry. Pages of the main text bearing direct reference to the subject of each entry are indicated in brackets (italicised page numbers refer to illustrations).

Abbey Dore, Hereford and Worcester. SO3830. *St Mary* (formerly Dore Abbey), restored c. 1633–4 for Lord Scudamore, woodwork by John Abel.

Abbey Town, Cumbria. NY1750. *St Mary* (formerly Holme Cultram Abbey), W porch 1507 for Abbot Chamber, with dog-tooth ornament, E window c. 1605.

Abbots Salford, Warwickshire. SP0751. *Salford Hall*, shaped gables, porch dated 1602.

Aberdaron, Gwynedd. SH1827. *St Hywyn*, S aisle early C16. *Bodwrdda*, late medieval gentry house refronted in brick in 1621, projecting wings and mullioned windows.

Aberdeen, Grampian Region. NJ9305. *St Machars Cathedral* (111), central tower completed and choir rebuilt in early C16 for Bishop Elphinstone. S transept and W spires for Bishop Dunbar, 1522. Nave ceiling 1518–31 (largely renewed in 1867). *King's College Chapel* (111), 1500–5 with remarkable W tower surmounted by arched diadem (replacement of 1634, designed by Dr William Gordon, Professor of Medicine). Together with the Round Tower (c. 1525), the only surviving original buildings of the University.

Provost Skene's House (94, *94*), tall rectangular block, projecting wings and corbelled turrets with conical caps, C16, remodelled in late C17. See also *The Tolbooth*, Castlegate, 1615; *Provost Ross's House*, 1599; and *Wallace's Tower*, c. 1600 (recently re-erected from its original site in Nether Kirkgate).

Aberhafesp, Powys. SO0692. *Plas-yn-pentre*, medieval timber-framed hall house remodelled c. 1600 with added porch of 1706.

Adderley, Salop. SJ6639. *St Peter*, N chapel, 1635–7 with Gothic detail.

Adlington Hall, Cheshire. SJ8880. Large timber-framed house with hammerbeam roof (1505) and dais canopy in hall. Alterations (including porch) of c. 1581.

Albright Hussey, Salop. SJ5017. Timber-framed house, 1524, with brick additions of 1601.

Aldeburgh, Suffolk. TM4656. *St Peter and St Paul*, nave, N aisle and N chapel, 1525–9. S aisle and S chapel, 1534–5. S porch, 1539. Chancel, 1545.

Aldie Castle, Grampian Region. NK0639. Early C16 tower house with later extensions.

Allerthorpe Hall, North Yorkshire. SE3386. Dated 1608. Brick, with two low round towers giving Gothic flavour.

Allesley, Warwickshire. SP2981. *Stone House*, dated 1608 with nearly symmetrical gabled front and central porch.

Allington, Clwyd. SJ3656. *Trefalun*, gabled gatehouse, 1576, with Classical detail and short single-storey wings.

Almer Manor, Dorset. SY9098. Stone and flint late C16 symmetrical house with 5-sided projecting porch and matching bay window.

Amesbury, Wiltshire. SU1541. *Diana's House* and *Kent House*, Pewsey Road. Ogee-capped gatehouse 'conceits' dated 1600 and 1607, built for Earl of Hertford on site of dissolved priory.

Amisfield, Dumfries and Galloway Region. NX9983. Richly modelled tower house of the Charteris family, dated 1600.

Ampthill, Bedfordshire. TL0337. *Houghton House*, impressive ruins of the brick H-plan house commenced c. 1615 for Mary, Countess of Pembroke. Main range 2 rooms deep and hall entered in the centre. Classical frontispieces to N and W, possibly additions of c. 1640.

Anderson Manor, Dorset. SY8797. Tall, compact, brick, double-pile house, 1622, for John Tregonwell. Disciplined design with central canted porch and two banks of axially placed chimneystacks.

Anglesey Abbey, Cambridgeshire. TL5362. Parts of an Augustinian priory incorporated in the house of c. 1600. Much altered in 1861 and 1926.

Angmering, West Sussex. TQ0704. *St Margaret*, tower of 1507. *Ecclesden Manor*, 1634, gabled house of flint with brick dressings and a 2-storeyed porch.

Anstruther Easter, Fife Region. NO5603. Rectangular *church*, 1634, with projecting 'Laird's aisle'. Upper stages of small W tower added in 1644.

Apethorpe, Northamptonshire. TL0295. *Apethorpe Hall*, large double-courtyard house with hall range and part of N (gatehouse) range dating from c. 1500, W court from 1530–50, and magnificent E elevation with projecting porch, arcaded loggia and stepped and shaped gables added c. 1620–5 for Sir Francis Fane. Some excellent interior decoration survives. *St Leonard*, S chapel added in 1621, late Perp in style but with Classical plasterwork. Tower, 1633, with Y tracery.

Arbroath, Tayside Region. NO6441. (113.) *Abbot's House*, first floor hall and associated chambers built c. 1500 over vaulted undercroft of c. 1200.

Arbuthnott House, Grampian Region. NO8074. Medieval tower house extended by Robert Arbuthnott (1522–79) and further altered in C18 and C19.

Ardingly, West Sussex. TQ3331. *Wakehurst Place*, built in 1590 for Sir Edward Culpeper as courtyard house but subsequently reduced to present E-plan. Central porch with Tuscan columns, windows with old-fashioned arched lights.

Arreton Manor, Isle of Wight. SZ5386. H-plan house, 1639, for Sir Humphrey Bennet.

Arthuret, Cumbria. NY3767. (114.) *St Michael*, rebuilt 1609 in convincingly Perp style.

Ashbourne, Derbyshire. SK1846. *Grammar School*, Church Street, ambitious stone building of 1585–1603 with symmetrical gabled front and 2 entrance doors. *Owfield's Almshouses*, Church Street, 1614–30, stone, gabled, altered in 1848. See also various timber-framed town houses in Church Street and Victoria Square (formerly the Shambles).

Ashby-de-la-Zouche, Leicestershire. SK3516. *Castle*, C16 garden buildings to S include ruins of octagonal and quatrefoil brick towers and triangular summer-house of stone. Various windows, porches and fireplaces in the castle date from late C16.

Ashover, Derbyshire. SK3563. *Eastwood Hall*, ruins of large Elizabethan fortified manor house destroyed in the Civil War.

Ashton-under-Hill, Hereford and Worcester. SO9938. *St Barbara*, chancel dated 1624 with curious tracery to E window.

Aspenden, Hertfordshire. TL3528. *St Mary*, S porch c. 1525, S chancel chapel 1622.

Asthall, Oxfordshire. SP2811. *Manor House*, H-plan with symmetrical gabled front of c. 1620 for Sir William Jones. Remodelled and greatly extended in 1916.

Astley Abbots, Salop. SO7096. *St Calixtus*, chancel rebuilt in 1633 in strong Gothic style with hammerbeam roof. See also *Dunvall*, late Elizabethan decorated timber-framed house with projecting wings and handsome brick chimneystacks.

Aston, Hertfordshire. TL2722. *Astonbury House*, tall Jacobean brick house with symmetrical S front and shaped gables to N front.

Aston Hall, Birmingham, West Midlands. SP0789. Important brick house on half H-plan of 1618–35 for Sir Thomas Holte. Double-pile main range with hall entered in its centre. Set on a hill with fanciful skyline of shaped gables, ogee-capped turrets, disciplined ranks of chimneystacks, and dominant central tower. Ground floor loggia on S front and good contemporary interior fittings.

Aston Hall, Derbyshire. SK1883. Dated 1578 in elaborate strapwork cartouche. Central doorway on S front with Roman Doric columns and broken pediment.

Athelhampton Hall, Dorset. SY7794. Enchanting manor house of c. 1500 for Sir William Martyn, Lord Mayor of London, with magnificent bay window. Considerably extended in mid-C16 including parlour range with Renaissance detail.

Auburn Hall, Lincolnshire. SK9262.

1587–1628 remodelling of earlier house for Sir John Meres. Very tall and flat S front in brick.

Audley End, Essex.TL5238. (15, *15*.) The most magnificent of all the courtier mansions of the Jacobean age. Begun in 1603 on the site of Walden Abbey for Thomas Howard, Earl of Suffolk. The present hall range with twin porches for the King and Queen flanking a central bay window, and two projecting wings, formed only the central core of an enormous double-courtyard house. The hall alone retains its original interior decoration, principal rooms having been remodelled by Robert Adam in the 1760s. See also the double-courtyard late C16 brick almshouses of the *College of St Mark* in the village.

Aughton, Lancashire. SD3804. *St Michael*, N aisle and chancel chapel c. 1540.

Avebury Manor, Wiltshire. SU0969. c. 1557 on site of small Benedictine cell. Much enlarged c. 1600.

Ayot St Lawrence, Hertfordshire. TL1915. *Bride Hall*, early C17 brick, E-plan house with 2-storeyed porch. Wings originally gabled but one now hipped.

Baberton, Lothian Region. NT1968. House of 1622 for Sir James Murray, Master of King's Works. 3 storeys high on half H-plan with circular stair turrets in re-entrant angles. Alterations, 1765.

Baconsthorpe Castle, Norfolk. TG1238. Gatehouse, 1560, is the most substantial surviving part of moated C15 mansion built for the Heydons.

Bacton, Hereford and Worcester. SO3732. *St Faith*, W tower of c. 1574.

Bakewell, Derbyshire. SK2169. *Holme Hall*, 1626 for Bernard Wells. 3 bays with projecting central porch and flanking canted bay windows.

Balcarres, Fife Region. NO4704. *Church* with ruined mortuary chapel, 1635.

Balquhidder, Tayside Region. NN5320. Ruined *church*, 1631.

Balterley, Staffordshire. SJ7650. *Hall O'Wood*, large timber-framed house of late C16 with decorative framing and projecting wings.

Balvenie Castle, Grampian Region. NJ3240. Ruined medieval castle remodelled, 1547–57, for John Stewart, Earl of Atholl.

Banff, Grampian Region. NJ6863. Some late C16 and early C17 town houses survive around old Market Place.

Bangor, Gwynedd. SH5872. *Cathedral*, W Tower, 1532, for Bishop Skeffington. See also C16 *Town Hall*, formerly Bishop's Palace.

Bardwell, Suffolk. TL9473. *St Peter and St Paul*, chancel, 1553.

Barham, Suffolk. TM1451. (114.) *St Mary*, vestry has large terracotta early Renaissance window, c. 1525. The nave clerestory is also of the early C16.

Barking, Suffolk. TM0753. (114.) *St Mary*, One N window with terracotta Early Renaissance detail of c. 1525.

Barlborough Hall, Derbyshire. SK4778. (56, 84.) Most attractive tall, compact square house with crowning staircase lantern built in 1580s for Francis Rodes, lawyer and seneschal to the Earl of Shrewsbury. Heath Old Hall, West Yorkshire, an almost identical twin demolished in 1961, but it also has similarities to Wootton Lodge, Staffordshire (*q.v.*). A garden building was altered in 1582 by addition of large semicircular bay window and was probably a banqueting house.

Barnes, Lothian Region. NT5376. House built for Sir John Seton in early 1590s on a very unScottish plan with flanking wings, central entrance, extruded staircase towers, and pavilioned forecourt.

Barnham Court, West Sussex. SU9604. (82.) Brick Artisan Mannerist house of c. 1640 with Dutch gables and pilasters.

Barnham Broom Hall, Norfolk. TG0807. Brick house, c. 1530, with stepped gables and polygonal buttresses. Addition of c. 1614 with fashionably pedimented windows.

Barningham Hall, Norfolk. TG1435. Brick with stone dressings for Sir Edward Paston, 1612. Compact plan with polygonal angle buttresses, pedimented windows, and extraordinary 2-storeyed dormers on main elevation.

Barnstaple, Devon. SS5533. *Penrose's Almshouses*, Lichdon Street, founded in 1627. Striking collonaded symmetrical street elevation with courtyard behind.

Barrington Court, Somerset. ST3918. (6o.) Famous example of E-plan house, 1552–64, for William Clifton of Norwich and London. 2 storeys high with further dormered attic storey and a 3-storeyed porch. Twisted finials to the gables and decorated chimneystacks.

Barthomley, Cheshire. SJ7652. *St*

Bertoline, S chapel of c.1528 for Crewe Family.

Barton-Under-Needwood, Staffordshire. SK1818. (111, *112*.) *St James*, begun 1517 for Dr John Taylor, Chaplain to Henry VIII, and possessed of architectural quality of complete visual unity, rare for an English parish church. The octagonal apsidal end to chancel is prominently adorned with coats of arms.

Basing, Hampshire. SU6652. *St Mary*, built in brick, 1519, for John Paulet of *Basing House*. The ruins of the latter, rebuilt after 1531 for Sir William Paulet, Marquess of Winchester, survive. Famous as the house from which Inigo Jones was ignominiously carried naked by Parliamentary troops during the Civil War.

Basingstoke, Hampshire. SU6351. *St Michael*, nave and aisles, c. 1500, 2-storeyed S porch, 1539. *Holy Trinity*, Chapel Hill; ruins of brick guild chapel built for Lord Sandys of The Vyne, 1524.

Bassingthorpe Manor House, Lincolnshire. SK9628. (81.) Compact rectangular plan with stepped gables and finely decorated chimneystacks. Unusual high oriel window on the churchyard side with semicircular gable. Dated 1568, it was built for Thomas Coney and is adorned with his punning 'device' of a rabbit.

Bath, Avon. ST7566. *Abbey*, begun in 1499 for Bishop King and completed after the Dissolution between 1572 and the early C17.

Bawburgh Hall, Norfolk. TG1508. Brick, 1634, with stepped gables and 2 square stone summer-houses in front.

Bawdeswell Hall, Norfolk. TG0420. Brick, 1633, with large shaped gables.

Beaminster, Dorset. ST4801. *St Mary*, one of the most spectacular towers in the county, 1503, with N chapel built for John Hillary, 1505. *Almshouses* (105), small, single storey building in churchyard erected for Sir John Strode in 1630. *Parnham House*, large picturesque unsymmetrical E-plan house, essentially

Bassingthorpe Manor House, Lincolnshire, 1568. A simple rectangular plan given deliberate architectural interest by its decorated gables and chimneystacks and projecting oriel

of mid-C16, for Robert Strode. Early Renaissance frieze in the present tea-room.

Beamsley, West Yorkshire. SE0752. Hospital. *Almshouse*, 1593, extended in mid-C17 for Lady Anne Clifford, Countess of Pembroke. The conventional street range hides the extraordinary circular building containing a central chapel in the garden behind.

Beaumaris, Anglesey, Gwynedd. SH6076. *Court House* of 1614 with hammerbeam roof.

Beccles, Suffolk. TM4290. *St Michael*, magnificent detached tower of 1515–47. *Roos Hall*, Bungay Road. Tall, compact brick house, 1593, with stepped gables, pedimented windows, and polygonal corner buttresses with decorated pinnacles.

Beckington, Somerset. ST7951. *The Abbey*, hospital of the Augustinian canons built in 1502, remodelled early C17. *Beckington Castle*, large, compact, stone house of late C16 with 3 steep gables to street and 3-storeyed castellated porch.

Beckley Park, Oxfordshire. SP5711. Rare survival of hunting lodge, c. 1540, for Lord Williams of Rycote. Tall, compact, brick building with 3 projecting gabled turrets to rear.

Bedale, North Yorkshire. SE2688. *St Gregory*, S chapel, 1556.

Beddgelert, Gwynedd. SH6552. *Hafodlwyfog*, stone, gentry house, 1638, with gable-end chimneystacks and central entrance.

Bedingfield, Suffolk. TM1768. *Fleming's Hall*, elongated house, c. 1550, with brick ground floor and timber-framing above. Shaped end gables, polygonal chimneystacks and a 2-storeyed off-set brick porch.

Beguildy, Powys. SO2078. *Bryndraenog*, fine medieval hall house with additions dated 1636.

Belsay Castle, Northumberland. NZ1078. House, 1614, adjoining tower of medieval castle. Porch with coupled Tuscan columns.

Belton, Leicestershire. SK8101. *Old Hall*, early C17 with projecting gabled wings and massive hall fireplace.

Benthall Hall, Salop. SJ6502. Gabled house, c. 1583, for the Catholic Benthalls with decoration said to represent the Stigmata. Excellent contemporary interiors.

Beoley, Hereford and Worcester. SP0669. *St Leonard*, late C16 N chapel in Perp style.

Berkhamsted, Hertfordshire. SP9907. *Grammar School*, long, brick schoolroom, c. 1544, with traceried windows.

Berriew, Powys. SJ1800. (*79*.) *The Vicarage*, lobby-entrance, timber-framed house with projecting, jettied porch, 1616. Converted to gable-end chimneystacks in C19.

Berry Pomeroy Castle, Devon. SX8261. Medieval castle extended by symmetrical residential ranges in the late C16 and early C17 for the Seymours.

Besford Court, Hereford and Worcester. SO9144. Close-studded timber-framed range, c. 1500, altered c. 1600. Greatly extended in C20.

Betley, Staffordshire. SJ7548. *St Margaret*, chancel rebuilt, 1610.

Bettws Cedewain, Powys. SO1296. *St Beuno*, sturdy, plain, typical Welsh border tower, c. 1520.

Beverley, Humberside. TA0339. *St Mary*, crossing tower of this supremely beautiful church was rebuilt c. 1520–30 after collapse in 1520.

Bibury, Gloucestershire. SP1106. *Arlington Row*, famous picturesque row of early C17 weavers' cottages. *Bibury Court*, roughcast, gabled manor house, 1633, for Sir Thomas Sackville. *Ablington Manor*, roughcast, gabled house with off-set buttressed porch and side-wall chimneystack, 1590 for John Coxwell.

Biddulph Old Hall, Staffordshire. SJ8857. Considerable ruins remain of courtyard mansion built in 1580s and sacked in the Civil War.

Billingborough Hall, Lincolnshire. TF1134. Stone, gabled house, c. 1520 for William Toller.

Billinge, Lancashire. SD5300. *Birchley Hall*, gabled with projecting wings and porch and hall bay in re-entrant angles, 1594.

Billington, Lancashire. SD7235. *Old St Leonard Church*, c. 1557. Low building with bellcote, nave and chancel in one. *Hacking Hall*, gabled, symmetrical façade with projecting wings and porch, and hall bay in re-entrant angles, 1607.

The Binns, Lothian Region. NT0478. 3-storeyed symmetrical house with twin stair turrets and contemporary plasterwork. Built 1621–30 for Thomas

Dalyell, Edinburgh merchant, and greatly enlarged c. 1810.

Birdham, West Sussex. SU8200. *St James*, tower, c. 1545.

Birkenhead, Merseyside. SJ2890. *St Oswald*, Hoylake Road, Bidston. Tower, c. 1504–21. *Bidston Hall*, c. 1620 for Earl of Derby. Central semicircular bow with entrance into middle of hall, loggia to garden front and forecourt with arched gateway.

Birsay, Orkney. HY2327. Ruins of the large courtyard mansion with square angle pavilions begun in 1574 for Robert, Earl of Orkney.

Birtsmorton Court, Hereford and Worcester. SO8035. Large timber-framed house, c. 1580.

Bisham Abbey, Berkshire. SU8585. Adapted and remodelled as a house for Sir Philip Hoby after 1553. Stepped brick gables. Hall chimneypiece has similar ornament to conduit house in Bristol.

Bishop's Hull Manor, Somerset. ST2024. E-plan dated 1586 on porch.

Bishops Waltham, Hampshire. SU5517. *St Peter*, SW tower, 1584–9. N aisle, 1637. Both Gothic.

Blickling Hall, Norfolk. TG1728. (51, 53.) 1619–27 for Sir Henry Hobart, Lord Chief Justice; supervised and partly executed by Robert Lyminge who had occupied similar position at Hatfield. 2 irregular sized courtyards with 4 prominent, ogee-capped, corner towers. Narrow symmetrical entrance front with shaped gables and an elaborate frontispiece. Long E front with alternating canted and rectangular projecting bays. N and W fronts sympathetically created by the Ivorys of Norwich, 1765–79. The 2 low service ranges flanking the entrance have Dutch gables. Of the magnificent interiors, the plasterwork of the long gallery and great chamber by Edward Stanyon and the (altered) staircase by Lyminge himself are the most memorable.

Blo Norton Hall, Norfolk. TM0179. Early C16 timber-framed house with brick end walls, altered and enlarged c. 1585.

Bloxworth House, Dorset. SY8794. Brick E-plan, 1608, with 3-storeyed gabled porch and stair projection in one of the re-entrant angles.

Blunham, Bedfordshire. TL1551. *St James and St Edward*, W tower 1583.

Bodelwyddan, Clwyd. SJ0076. *Faenol-faur*, half H-plan house with stepped gables built in 1597 for John Lloyd, registrar of diocese of St Asaph.

Bolsover Castle, Derbyshire. SK4770. (58, 59.) Little keep built as lodge, 1612–21, for Sir Charles Cavendish to designs by John Smythson. On the site of genuine medieval castle, it is the most exhilarating and perfect of all the Jacobean fantasy castles. The recently restored interiors are a remarkable survival. The N part of the separate terrace range was built as accommodation, 1629–30, for guests and retainers for Sir William Cavendish. The gallery was erected to receive the King on his return from Scotland, 1633–4, and the hall block was built shortly after, possibly to the designs of Huntingdon Smythson. The state-rooms and the great riding school are probably post-Restoration.

Bolton, Greater Manchester. SD7211. *Hall i 'l' Wood*, one of the most exuberantly decorated timber-framed houses in the north-west. c. 1500, remodelled in late C16, and restored in 1899 for Lord Leverhulme.

Bolton Abbey, North Yorkshire. SE0753. Priory Church of Augustinian canons. W tower begun 1520.

Boltongate, Cumbria. NY2340. *All Saints*, possibly early C16 with a sensational, steeply-pointed, stone tunnel-vault carrying the roof with no timber superstructure.

Boreham, Essex. TL7509. *New Hall*, the S range, with 7 symmetrical bay windows and central entrance framed by Roman Doric columns, is surviving part of the house that Earl of Sussex built in 1573 on the site of Henry VIII's mansion of Beaulieu. See also the chapel built to contain his monument in the church.

Boringdon, Devon. SX5457. Remains of the mansion built by the Parkers after 1582 include the entrance tower.

Borwick Hall, Lancashire. SD5273. C14 pele tower incorporated in house of c. 1590–5 for Robert Bindloss, Kendal clothier.

Boston, Lincolnshire. TF3244. (111.) *St Botolph*, crowning octagon at the top of incomparable stump dates from c. 1510–20.

Boughton House, Northamptonshire. SP9081. Substantial remains of house, c. 1550 for Sir Edward Montagu, survive within present late C17 house.

Boughton Malherbe, Kent. TQ8849.
Boughton Place, one wing, from 2 periods
in C16, survives from home of the
Wottons and birthplace of Sir Henry
Wotton, author of *The Elements of
Architecture*.

Boughton Monchelsea Place, Kent.
TQ7749. One range of square courtyard
house, c. 1567–75 for Robert Rudston,
remains. Stone with a 2-storeyed porch
and gabled dormers.

Bourn Hall, Cambridgeshire. TL3256.
Asymmetrical, gabled brick house, 1607,

Bolsover Castle, Derbyshire, 1612–21. The remarkably preserved interiors offer a
tantalising glimpse of the private decorative taste of a Jacobean magnate

with projecting bays.

Bourne, Lincolnshire. TF0920. *Red Hall*, double-pile brick house built in early C17 for Gilbert Fisher. Gabled with 2-storeyed porch.

Bowden, Borders Region. NT5530. Early C17 *church* with added aisles, 1644 and 1661. Altered in 1909.

Boyton Manor, Wiltshire. ST9539. Square, gabled, roughcast house of compact plan with central 2-storeyed porch. 1618 for Thomas Lambert.

Brackenfield, Derbyshire. SK3759. *Ogston Hall*, W range of c. 1500, the remainder C17 and Victorian.

Brackenhill Tower, Cumbria. NY4469. Medieval type of pele tower built by Richard Graham, 1586.

Brackley, Northamptonshire. SP5837. *Almshouses* founded in 1633 by Sir Thomas Crewe of Steane. Handsome stone range in local vernacular.

Bradfield House, Devon. ST0509. One of the largest Elizabethan houses in the county. Symmetrical with projecting wings and porch, and hall bay in the re-entrant angles. Hammerbeam roof and Early Renaissance frieze in hall. Inscribed dates of 1592 and 1604, but part dates from mid-C16.

Bradford-On-Avon, Wiltshire. ST8260. *The Hall*, tall, compact, double-pile plan, ostentatiously glazed on entrance front with projecting bays and porch. c. 1610 for John Hall, wealthy clothier.

Bradninch Manor, Devon. SS9903. 1547 for Peter Sainthill. Altered c. 1600 and again in C18.

Bradshaw Hall, Derbyshire. SK0380. L-plan, gabled with multi-mullioned windows. Dated 1620 on handsome gateway.

Bradstone Manor House, Devon. SX3880. Early C17 for Cloberry family with attractive gabled and pinnacled gatehouse.

Braikie, Tayside Region. NO6250. L-plan tower-house of 1581 with stair corbelled-out in the re-entrant angle above 1st floor.

Bramcote Manor House, Nottinghamshire. SK5037. Jacobean remodelling of earlier brick house with diaper-work and steep gables.

Bramhall Hall, Cheshire. SJ8984. Considered to be one of the best timber-framed mansions in England. C15 core greatly extended in late C16 and early C17 in an elaborately decorated fashion. Further alterations in the late C19.

Bramshill House, Hampshire. SU7559. 1605–c. 15 for Lord Zouche and one of the largest houses of the time. Decoration concentrated on grand and rather grotesque 3-storeyed frontispiece flanked by open loggia. Remainder comparatively plain, apart from crowning openwork parapet. Unusual plan with long range running back at right angles from entrance front.

Bramshott Place, Hampshire. SU8432. Miniature brick gatehouse of c. 1575 with tiny oriel and shaped gables.

Brancepeth, Durham. NZ2238. *St Brandon*, refitting of chancel in 1638 for John Cosin in consciously Gothic fashion. Porch of same date, however, has semicircular gable and is decorated with pilasters.

Brandon Old Hall, Lincolnshire. SK9048. L-plan, 1637.

Bray, Berkshire. SU9079. *Jesus Hospital*, large brick almshouse of 28 units set around a courtyard. Founded by the London Fishmongers' Company, 1627.

Breccles Hall, Norfolk. TL9594. E-plan brick house, 1583, for Woodhouse family, greatly extended by Lutyens after 1908.

Brecon, Powys. SO0428. (111.) *St Mary*, W tower built c. 1510–20 for Edward Stafford, Duke of Buckingham, at cost of £2,000.

Bredbury, Greater Manchester. SJ9391. *Ardern Hall*, tall tower with stepped gables and unusual tripartite window with trefoiled lights. Ruined; said to have been dated 1597.

Bredon's Norton Manor House, Hereford and Worcester. SO9339. Much altered house with detached stone garden gateway dated 1585 and decorated with similar motifs to those at Woollas Hall, Eckington (*q.v.*).

Brereton Hall, Cheshire. SJ7764. Symmetrical brick building, 1586, with extraordinary frontispiece comprising two octagonal towers linked by arch at top and orginally with ogee roofs. Gabled end pavilions with 2-storeyed canted pedimented bays. Possibly a courtyard house originally.

Bretherton, Lancashire. SD4720. *Carr House*, 1613 for 'Thomas Stones of London haberdasher, and Andrew Stones of Amsterdam, merchant', according to the inscription over the entrance. Brick, symmetrical, with slightly projecting wings and a 3-storeyed porch.

Bridgnorth, Salop. SO7193. *Bishop Percy's House*, Cartway, elaborately decorated timber-framed town house, 1580.

Brigstock Manor House, Northamptonshire. SP9485. Early C16.

Bristol, Avon. ST5872. *St Mark*, College Green, E end of chancel, early C16. Poyntz chantry chapel, 1520–36.

Broadhembury, Devon. ST1004. *The Grange*, late-Elizabethan H-plan house with good plaster ceilings and fireplaces.

Broadway, Hereford and Worcester. SP0937. *The Lygon Arms*, stone house of C16 and early C17 with recessed centre flanked by gabled wings. Now a hotel. See also many other good minor houses of the period in the village.

Brockhall Hall, Northamptonshire. SP6362. 3-storeyed Elizabethan half H-plan house with projecting bays in the re-entrant angles.

Bromsgrove, Hereford and Worcester. SO9570. Former *Hop Pole* Inn, New Road, 1572, with decorated timber framework.

Brooke, Leicestershire. SK8405. *St Peter*, N aisle, chancel and porch, c. 1579. Round-arched arcade has no medieval precedent. *Brooke Priory*, gate lodge and archway of c. 1600.

Broome Park, Kent. TR2148. 1635–8 for Sir Basil Dixwell on a symmetrical H-plan of brick with shaped and pedimented gables. One of the most accomplished of the Artisan Mannerist houses.

Brough Hall, North Yorkshire. SE2197. Tall Elizabethan house remodelled c. 1730.

Broughton, Lancashire. SD5234. *St John Baptist*, W tower dated 1533.

Broughton, Staffordshire. SJ7633. *St Peter*, 1630–4 in Gothic style. *Broughton Hall*, large flamboyantly timber-framed 3-storeyed house, 1637.

Broughton Castle, Oxfordshire. SP4138. Large medieval moated house thoroughly remodelled and extended in an up-to-date 'Sharington' Classical fashion in 1551–4 for Richard Fiennes, with further work carried out by his son.

Broughton-In-Furness, Cumbria. SD2087. *St Mary Magdalene*, consecrated in 1547 with additions, 1874 and 1900.

Bruisyard Hall, Suffolk. TM3266. 3-storeyed brick house of 1610 with central porch with stepped gable.

Bruton, Somerset. ST6834. *St Mary*, clerestory of 1506–23. *Sexey's Hospital* High Street, founded 1638. The original W court contains the hall and chapel and a wooden gallery giving access to upper tenements. *King's School*, founded in 1619 by Bishop Fitzjames of London, Abbot Gilbert and Dr Edmunds. Original building survives in Old School.

Brympton D'Evercy House, Somerset. ST5414. Remodelling c. 1520 of earlier house with additions, late C17.

Bryneglwys, Clwyd. SJ1447. *Yale Chapel* attached to S E of church and separated internally by oak piers. Late C16.

Buckland Abbey, Devon. SX4866. Sanguine remodelling of Cistercian church to form house for Sir Richard Grenville in the 1570s. Original form of the building is still clearly visible both within and without.

Bunbury, Cheshire. SJ5658. *St Boniface*, S chancel chapel of c. 1527 for Sir Ralph Egerton. The screen is painted with Early Renaissance decoration.

Buntingford, Hertfordshire. TL3629. *St Peter*, 1614–26 of brick on Greek Cross plan. Apse and porch added, 1899.

Burford, Oxfordshire. SP2512. Various C16 and early C17 stone and timber-framed houses. Fragments of Sir Lawrence Tanfield's house, c. 1580, in much-altered *Burford Priory*.

Burghley House, Cambridgeshire. TF0406. (9, 24, 48–9, 56.) One of the most important of all Elizabethan courtier houses. Built on courtyard plan between c. 1550 and 1587 for William Cecil, Lord Burghley, it epitomises the changing sophisticated taste of those years from comparatively disciplined Classic to exuberantly lively Gothic. Internal elevations of courtyard reflect the former, hammerbeamed hall and turreted form of completed house the latter.

Burntisland, Fife Region. NT2385. (117.) *St Columba's*, built 1592 on square plan with central tower carried on semicircular arches. Good interior fittings of early C17. Upper part of the tower added in C18.

Burray, Orkney. ND4796. Roofless *church* of 1621.

Burrell House, Cornwall. SX4259. 1621 with added wing of 1636.

Burrough Green Hall, Cambridgeshire. TL6355. Brick house of c. 1575. Porch and bay window have Ionic pilasters on ground floor and taller pilasters above.

Burton Hall, Cheshire. SJ5063. Square, tall house with large gable to each side (one now missing) and irregularly placed windows. Said to date from 1569.

Burton, West Sussex. SU9617. *Church* extensively restored, 1636, on instructions of Archbishop Juxon.

Burton Agnes, Humberside. TA1063. Mansion built for Sir Henry Griffith, 1601–10. Long main front with semicircular bows to projecting end bays and entrance formed in similar fashion to Chastleton (*q.v.*). Frontispieces dated 1601, tunnel-vaulted long gallery on top floor, and excellent staircase. Much allegorical decoration. Gatehouse with 4 octagonal corner turrets and ogee roofs.

Burton Constable, Humberside. TA1836. c. 1600 for Sir Henry Constable. 2-storeyed brick house with projecting wings and broad embattled towers which were originally capped by staircase turrets with ogee roofs. Remodelled in Jacobean style, 1760.

Burton Latimer Hall,

Northamptonshire. SP9074. Jacobean house originally on half H-plan. *School,* W of the church. Small single-storeyed building of 1622 with gabled central entrance.

Burwash, East Sussex. TQ6724. *Batemans,* 1634, probably for an ironmaster, originally on symmetrical plan with projecting gabled porch. Subsequently famous as home of Rudyard Kipling.

Burwell, Cambridgeshire. TL5866. *St Mary,* chancel of c. 1515–30 paid for by abbot of Ramsey. Perfect late Perp church.

Bury St Edmunds, Suffolk. TL8564. *St James* (now cathedral), c. 1510–30 and completed under Edward VI. Extended after 1960. Also various *town houses* of the period.

Cadhay, Devon. SY0896. Large house built c. 1540 for John Haydon, wealthy lawyer, extended after 1587.

Caerhun, Gwynedd. SH7770. *Church,* S chapel, 1591, for Edward Williams and his wife.

Caerlaverock Castle, Dumfries and Galloway Region. NY0265. (66.) Medieval castle on triangular plan

St Columba's, Burntisland, Fife Region, 1592. This striking plain square box with a central tower presented difficulties of internal planning and had no imitators elsewhere in Scotland

remodelled in early C16 with further alterations in 1630s in Classical style on E side of courtyard.

Cambridge, Cambridgeshire. TL4458. Most significant collegiate work of the period includes: *Christ's*, refounded 1505 by Lady Margaret Beaufort, mother of Henry VIII. First Court is principally of this date and gateway to St Andrew's Street is the showpiece. *Emmanuel*, founded in 1584 by Sir Walter Mildmay, Chancellor of Exchequer. Second Court incorporates parts of dissolved house of Black Friars. Brick buildings, 1633–4, with curved gable and shallow projecting bays. *Gonville and Caius* (48, 49, 108), refounded 1557 by Dr Caius. Caius Court has S side closed with only wall and gate pavilion. W range is of 1565 and E of 1567. Both are traditional in style, but the 3 gateways symbolising passage of student through college, designed by founder, are important examples of intellectual Classicism. *Jesus*, founded 1497 by Bishop Alcock of Ely. Gatehouse c. 1500. *King's* (27, 114), fabric of the chapel not completed until 1515. *Magdalene*, refounded 1542 by Lord Audley of Audley End. In First Court, hall range is of 1519 and the W range was completed in 1574. *Peterhouse*, contains work of the late C16 and early C17. *Queen's*, picturesque timber-framed President's Lodge and Gallery, c. 1540, and brick range in Walnut Tree Court, 1617–18. *St Catharine's*, brick Gostlin Court completed in 1637. *St John's* (108, 109), founded 1511 by Lady Margaret Beaufort. First Court, 1511–20, of brick with a 3-storeyed gatehouse. Second Court, 1598–1602, by Ralph Symons. Library with Gothic windows of 1623–4. *Sidney Sussex*, founded 1594 by Lady Frances Sidney. Hall Court of 1594 by Ralph Symons and Sir Francis Clarke's range of 1628, but both much altered by Wyatville. *Trinity*, refounded by Henry VIII. Great Gate 1519–35. Great Court principally for Dr Thomas Nevile, 1597–1605 (Fountain 1602). Larger than any other quadrangle in Oxford or Cambridge. Nevile's Court completed in 1614. *Trinity Hall*, brick library with stepped gables, c. 1560–70. In the town, the rebuilding of *St Mary-the-Great* started 1478. Nave roof finished 1508; Lady Chapel 1522; W window 1536; W tower completed 1593–1608. Octagonal *Hobson's Conduit* with its ogee cupola was erected in 1614 to conduct water to the city from Trumpington.

Cannington Priory, Somerset. ST2539. Late C16 house on site of nunnery built for Rogers family. *Blackmoor Farm* (80, 81), remarkably well-preserved medium-sized house of c. 1500 for Sir Thomas Tremail. Irregular E-plan with chapel in N wing.

Canons Ashby, Northamptonshire. SP5750. Begun 1551 for John Dryden on site of Augustinian priory. Stone and brick around small courtyard. Further additions for Sir John Dryden, 1630s.

Canterbury, Kent. TR1557. *Cathedral*, central tower (Bell Harry) completed 1503. *Christ Church Gate* (114), entrance to Cathedral precinct. 1517–21 with Early Renaissance stone pilasters. *Manwood's Hospital*, St Stephen's Green, brick almshouse with stepped gables of 1570 for Sir Roger Manwood. Similar to his school at Sandwich. Various timber-framed houses of the period in the town and the brick gateway surviving from *Place House*, St Dunstan's Street, the suburban mansion of the Ropers.

Careston, Tayside. NO5260. *Church*, 1636, restored 1808.

Carew Castle, Dyfed. SN0403. Medieval castle thoroughly remodelled c. 1500 for Sir Rhys ap Thomas and extended late C16 for Sir John Perrot.

Carlisle, Cumbria. NY3955. *Abbey* gatehouse 1527 for Prior Slee and the defensive Prior's lodging of c. 1510–20. *Castle*, remodelled c. 1540 for Henry VIII and further altered c. 1580.

Carlton Curlieu Hall, Leicestershire. SP6997. Stone, c. 1630, with large shaped gables.

Carnasserie Castle, Strathclyde Region. NR8398. Ruined elongated tower-house.

Carno, Powys. SO0095. *Plasauduon*, early C17 timber-framed lobby entrance house with storeyed porch and service wing at rear.

Carnousie, Grampian Region. NJ6749. Ruined Z-plan house, 1577, for the Ogilvy family.

Cartmel Fell, Cumbria. SD4188. *St Anthony*, c. 1505, unfinished W tower with saddle-back roof. Nave and chancel in one.

Casewick Hall, Lincolnshire. TF0709. S range, 1621, for William Trollop of Thurlby.

Castle Ashby, Northamptonshire. SP8659. (60, 62.) Large mansion, begun

1574 for Lord Compton. 3 sides of courtyard with polygonal staircase turrets near ends of wings and open loggia to hall range. Extra storey with lettered balustrade added c. 1620 and Classical screen across S end of court c. 1634.

Castle Bromwich Hall, West Midlands. SP1489. Early C17 brick E-plan house remodelled 1657.

Castle Menzies, Tayside Region. NN8349. Elongated Z-plan with pedimented dormers dated 1577.

Castle of Park, Grampian Region. NO7797. L-plan tower-house, 1590.

Castle Stewart, Highland Region. NH7449. (74.) Symmetrically planned tower-house with projecting wings containing semicircular staircase towers in rear re-entrant angles. Offset corbelled cap-houses at corners of main block.

Caverswall Castle, Staffordshire. SJ9542. Tall symmetrical house c. 1615 for Matthew Cradock with high staircase tower at rear. Roofline originally balustraded, but building possibly in sham castle fashion.

Cefn, Clwyd. SJ0370. *Dolbelydir*, stone house, late C16, with gable-end chimneystacks.

Cemmaes Bychan, Powys. SH8306.(77.) Square house with steeply pitched roof and central cluster of 4 chimneystacks. Timber-framed with two tiers of dormers when built in 1632 for Lewis Anwyl. Refaced in stone c. 1850.

Chalgrove, Oxfordshire. SU6396. (70, 81, 88.) *Manor Farm*, late medieval timber-framed hall house extended in early C16 and remodelled in late C16.

Chantmarle, Dorset. ST5802. (20.) Truncated survivor of E-plan house, for Sir John Strode 1612–23. Very plain with finely-jointed ashlar and old-fashioned arch-headed windows.

Chard, Somerset. ST3208. *The Grammar School*, originally private house dated 1583 with central porch. *Court House*, Fore Street. Group of late Elizabethan houses.

Charing, Kent. TQ9549. *St Peter and St Paul*, tower completed 1537, S chapel early C16, nave roof rebuilt 1592 after fire, chancel roof rebuilt 1620.

Charlecote Park, Warwickshire. SP2656. Much altered brick mansion begun by Sir Thomas Lucy in 1558. See especially gatehouse, porch, stables and brewhouse.

Charlton Park, Wiltshire. ST9589. c. 1610 for Countess of Suffolk, whose husband had built Audley End (q.v.). 4 ranges around courtyard with corner turrets carrying ogee caps. Projecting wings on the entrance front.

Charminster, Dorset. SY6792. *St Mary*, early C16 W tower for Sir Thomas Trenchard emblazoned with stylised Ts outside and in. C17 E window to chancel. *Wolfeton House*, early C16 courtyard house of the Trenchards remodelled in late C16 in a way which owes much to Longleat. Early C17 *Riding School* is earliest surviving example in country.

Chastleton House, Oxfordshire. SP2429. (83, 84, 85.) Begun 1602 for Walter Jones, Witney wool merchant. Tall, compact house of stone with massive square battlemented staircase towers at either end. Square plan around small courtyard with side entrance through projecting porch matched by hall bay. Excellent unspoilt interiors include great chamber and top-floor tunnel-vaulted long gallery.

Chatsworth, Derbyshire. SK2570. Hunting tower with 4 circular angle turrets with domed caps of c. 1580.

Cheadle, Greater Manchester. SJ8788. *St Mary*, S chapel completed 1530, tower and nave 1541. Chancel rebuilt 1556–8 for Lady Catherine Buckley, former Abbess of Godstow.

Checkley, Staffordshire. SK0237. *St Mary*, extensively remodelled in early C17 in Perp style.

Chenies Manor House, Buckinghamshire. TQ0198. Brick S range, c. 1530, for the Earl of Bedford with 6 massive chimney projections incorporating closets.

Chequers, Buckinghamshire. SP8405. 2-storeyed gabled brick N range, 1565. Much altered by Sir Reginald Blomfield, 1909–12.

Cheshunt, Hertfordshire. TL3502. *Dewhurst Charity School*, modest gabled brick building, 1640. Nothing remains of Lord Burghley's *Theobalds* (37), perhaps most influential prodigy house of late C16.

Chester, Cheshire. SJ4066. *Cathedral*, pre-dissolution abbey cloister walks, c. 1524–30. Many timber-framed buildings throughout town from C16 and early C17, although present appearance is largely Victorian.

Chesterton Hall, Cambridgeshire. TL4560. Jacobean brick symmetrical façade with 3 dormers capped by semicircular gables.

Chevening Park, Kent. TQ4857. Externally all C18, but encasing a double-pile brick house known from drawings which is exceptionally advanced if the tradition that it was built for the 13th Lord Dacre who died in 1630 is correct. *St Botolph*, W tower begun after 1518.

Chew Magna, Somerset. ST5763. *Church House* c. 1510 and 11 bays long.

Chewton Mendip, Somerset. ST5952. *St Mary Magdalen*, early C16 tower of great height.

Chichester, West Sussex. SU8605. Perp *Market Cross*, 1501, for Bishop Story.

Chiddingly Place, East Sussex. TQ5414. Fragments of the early Elizabethan mansion of the Jefferays.

Chiddingstone, Kent. TQ5045. *St Mary*, rebuilt 1625–9 after fire. Nave and chancel in one. Windows with cinque-foiled lights but semicircular arch to S porch.

Chignal, Essex. TL6611. *St Nicholas*, early C16 and all brick.

Chilham, Kent. TR0753. *St Mary*, early C16 W tower. *Castle*, strange brick mansion, 1616, for Sir Dudley Digges by medieval octagonal keep. Polygonal building around an open court. Battlemented with 3-storeyed gabled porch and 4-storeyed corner turrets with ogee caps.

Chillingham Castle, Northumberland. NU0625. 3-storeyed frontispiece of c. 1625 to great hall.

Chingford, Essex. TQ3893. *Queen Elizabeth's Hunting Lodge*, timber-framed, 3 storeys with upper floor originally open and an attached staircase wing. Rare survival.

Chipchase Castle, Northumberland. NY8875. E-plan addition to medieval castle, 1621, with 3-storeyed frontispiece.

Chippenham, Wiltshire. ST9173. *St Andrew*, W tower and spire of 1633.

Chastleton House, Oxfordshire; begun 1602. A scaled down long gallery in a successful merchant's house is given a deceptive appearance of length by its curved ceiling – a device used to similar effect at Burton Agnes, Humberside.

Gothic.

Chipping Camden, Gloucestershire.
SP1539. Lodges, gateway, and summer-houses survive of former mansion of Sir Baptist Hicks of c. 1613. *Almshouses*, 1612 for Hicks on an I-plan, symbolic of King James. *Market Hall*, 1627, also for Hicks.

Chipstead, Surrey. TQ2756. *St Margaret*, brick crossing tower, 1631.

Chirk, Clwyd. SJ3037. *Bryncunallt*, brick E-plan house, 1612, with shaped gables to wings and porch. Castellated chimneystacks.

Chobham, Surrey. SU9761. *Lucas Green Manor House*, late C16 gabled brick house with hood-moulds to windows.

Christchurch Priory, Dorset. SZ1693. Early C16 chancel and Lady chapel. Harys Chantry chapel, 1525, Gothic. Draper Chantry (114), 1529, and Countess of Salisbury Chantry, c. 1541, have Early Renaissance details.

Churchdown, Gloucestershire. SO8819. *St Bartholomew*, W tower, 1601.

Church Stretton, Salop. SO4593. *St Lawrence*, E window in revived Decorated style, 1630s.

Cirencester, Gloucestershire. SP0201. *St John the Baptist*, nave 1516–30.

Clare, Suffolk. TL7645. *St Peter and St Paul*, chancel rebuilt 1617–19.

Claverdon Leys, Warwickshire. SP1964. (79.) Early C17 tower-house of stone with few windows, an almost pointed arch to the entrance, and a corbelled-out chimneystack with two brick shafts. Given its geographical location, it is almost certainly a fantasy castle.

Claypotts Castle, Tayside Region. NO4531. (71, *73*.) One of the most completely preserved small Z-plan tower-houses, 1569–88 for John Strachan.

Cleeve Abbey, Somerset. ST0541. (*112*, 113.) Refectory lavishly remodelled by William Dovell, the last abbot (1507–37), and one of the finest rooms of its period in the county.

Clevedon Court, Avon. ST4271. Medieval house remodelled c. 1570.

Cliburn Hall, Cumbria. NY5824. Dated 1567 but windows still with cusped arched lights.

Clun, Salop. SO3081. *Trinity Hospital*, single-storeyed almshouses, 1618, around courtyard, with stepped dormers.

Coates Manor House, West Sussex. SU9917. Small early C17 house of 3 bays with central gable.

Cobham Hall, Kent. TQ6768. Earlier house extensively remodelled and enlarged in brick c. 1580–1603 for Lord Cobham. 2 long wings with octagonal turrets in the outer angles and various projecting bays. Sumptuous Classical porch on S side of N wing.

Cockle Park Tower, Northumberland. NZ2091. Oblong tower-house of c. 1520, with bartizans on two N corners and machicolation between. Essentially medieval.

Colchester, Essex. TM0025. *Bourne Mill*, Bourne Road. Fishing lodge of 1591 with large, elaborately shaped and decorated gables. A pretty conceit.

Cold Ashton, Avon. ST7472. *Holy Trinity*. Rebuilt 1508–40 for rector, Thomas Key. *Manor House*, c. 1629 for John Gunning, mayor of Bristol. Symmetrical S front with 2 projecting gabled wings. Central entrance with Roman Doric order and pediment flanked by oval windows.

Coleby Hall, Lincolnshire. SK9760. c. 1628 for William Lister. Brick E front with 6 steep gables.

Collacombe Barton, Devon. SX4376. Medieval manor house of Tremayne family, extended in 1574 by tall central hall block with projecting porch and entrance forecourt.

Colwich, Staffordshire. SK0121. *St Michael*, gothic W tower, 1640.

Combe Abbey, Warwickshire. SP4079. Cistercian house altered and extended c. 1600 for Lord Harington.

Combe Florey, Somerset. ST1531. Gabled gatehouse, 1593.

Combe Sydenham, Somerset. ST0736. Medieval house remodelled c. 1580.

Combeinteignhead, Devon. SX9071. *Bouchier Almshouses*, 1620.

Compton Wynyates, Warwickshire. SP3341. (*10, 42, 43,* 43.) Justly renowned brick courtyard house of the early C16 for Sir William Compton.

Condover Hall, Salop. SJ4906. (*25, 26, 63.*) A beautifully disciplined H-plan house of 1586–98 for Thomas Owen, a merchant's son who became a prominent lawyer and member of the Council of Wales. Carefully symmetrical with 2 soaring staircase towers and open loggia to the garden front, it is a larger gentry house at its most sophisticated. Associated with the masons Walter Hancock and Lawrence Shipway.

Conwy, Gwynedd. SH7877. (60, 61, 93.) *Plas Mawr*, begun 1576 for Robert Wynn as H-plan with central passage entrance. 2 polygonal staircase turrets of differing heights in the re-entrant angles (see Barking, Eastbury House). Wealth of rather crude but flamboyant plasterwork in principal rooms. Gatehouse and forecourt c. 1595. Described by Peter Smith as 'the most perfect and most complete memorial to Elizabethan Wales'.

Corgarff Castle, Grampian Region. NJ2508. Late C16 plain tower-house interestingly remodelled as a Hanoverian garrison after the final Jacobite rising.

Corsham Court, Wiltshire. ST8770. 1582 for Thomas Smythe, haberdasher and Collector of the Customs of London. Subsequently much altered and extended.

Corsley, Wiltshire. ST8246. *Manor Farmhouse*, built c. 1563 for Sir John Thynne who lived there after 1567 fire at Longleat. Attractive detached gateway announces its status.

Cotehele, Cornwall. SX4268. The most important Tudor house in the county. Rambling courtyard mansion rebuilt in late C15 and early C16 for the Edgcumbe family with NW tower dated 1627.

Cothelstone Manor, Somerset. ST1831. Mid-C16 house with projecting wings and gatehouse decorated with wealth of baluster and candelabra shapes.

Cottenham, Cambridgeshire. TL4567. *All Saints*, upper parts of tower of 1617–19 in yellow and pink brick with stepped battlements, bulbous ogee pinnacles and Y-tracery.

Coughton Court, Warwickshire. SP0860. Early C16 courtyard house with stone gatehouse and projecting timber-framed wings for the Throckmorton family. Hall block demolished. *St Peter*, E end c. 1518, completing work started in late C15.

Coventry, West Midlands. SP3379. *Ford's Hospital*, Greyfriars Lane, large timber-framed almshouse founded in 1529. Various restored *timber-framed houses* in Spon Street.

Cowdray House, West Sussex. SU8821. (42.) Substantial ruins remain of courtyard mansion begun in 1490s for Sir David Owen and continued after 1535 for Sir William Fitzwilliam. Completed after 1542 for Sir Anthony Browne. Described by Ian Nairn as 'an absolutely consistent epitome of Tudor architecture at its plainest and most sober'.

Craig Castle, Tayside Region. NO7056. (14.) Courtyard house with gateway and low towers built in the early C16 for Wood family and altered in early C17 for Earl of Southesk.

Craigevar Castle, Grampian Region. NJ5609. (14, *74*, *75*.) Supreme example of a stepped L-plan tower-house, built c. 1610–1626 for William Forbes, a wealthy merchant. 6 storeys with plain, battered walls and small windows, capped by exuberant sky-line. Profusion of internal plasterwork.

Craigmillar, Lothian Region. NT2871. (65.) Ruined medieval tower-house with a 3-storeyed E range of c. 1550.

Craignethan Castle, Strathclyde Region. NS8146. (65.) Greatly ruined tower-house within rectangular courtyard of 1532–40 for Sir James Hamilton.

Craigston Castle, Grampian Region. NJ7655. (74.) Tower-house of 1604–7 on half H-plan for John Urquhart. Defensive elements of upper works treated as playful decoration.

Cranborne Manor House, Dorset. SU0513. (56, *57*.) Medieval hunting lodge remodelled by William Arnold for Robert Cecil, 1608–11, as fairy-tale castle. Symmetrical and compact with projecting angle towers and arcaded loggias in the centre of each front. Gothic decoration mixed with various Classical motifs. S forecourt and tiny brick lodges added, 1620.

Crathes, Grampian Region. NO7396. (71, *72*.) Tower-house built by Bell family for Alexander Burnett, c. 1553–c. 1595. Plain harled exterior, deliberately unsymmetrical, with rainwater spouts disguised as cannon. Three complete painted ceilings inside.

Crewe Hall, Cheshire. SJ7353. Brick house, 1615–36, for Sir Randolph Crewe carefully reconstructed in the late 1860s by E. M. Barry following a fire. Original stables with shaped gables.

Crichton Castle, Lothian Region. NT3862. (*65*, 65.) Medieval tower-house with extraordinary courtyard façade added in 1580s for Earl of Bothwell. Open ground floor loggia with a diamond-faceted elevation above punctuated by large rectangular windows. Spacious stone staircase of a sophisticated design. Bothwell had been in Italy in 1581 and the whole composition is without precedent in the British Isles.

Cricklade, Wiltshire. SU0993. *St Sampson*. Crossing tower begun 1512–13 and completed in early 1550s at the expense of Duke of Northumberland and Hungerfords.

Croscombe, Somerset. ST5844. *St Mary*, chapel 1507–12; complete interior refurnishing 1616.

Crowleasowes, Salop. SO5478. Remarkable late Elizabethan house with profusion of ornamental brick decoration and large chimney with diagonal stacks.

Crows Hall, Suffolk. TM1962. Fragment of moated brick house, 1508, with polygonal buttresses and a 4-arched bridge over moat.

Cuckfield, West Sussex. TQ3024. Jacobean *Grammar School* of 6 bays and 2 storeys N of the church. *Cuckfield Park*, brick gatehouse with 4 angle turrets, 1580s, altered C19.

Culham Manor House, Oxfordshire. SU5095. Medieval grange of abbots of Abingdon, thoroughly remodelled and enlarged in stone c. 1610 for Thomas Bury. Further altered in C20.

Cullompton, Devon. ST0207. *St Andrew*, W tower 1545–9 with the arms of Bishop Vesey of Exeter. Outer S aisle c. 1525–6 for John Lane, wool merchant, his generosity commemorated by a prominent inscription.

Culross, Fife Region. NS9885. *The Palace* (17, 74, 77), begun 1597 for wealthy merchant, George Bruce. Roughly half H-plan with further ranges to the N. Only 1½ storeys high with crow-stepped gables crowned by chimneystacks. Separate taller range built in 1611 to the N, apparently in anticipation of a Royal visit, although the ground floor stabling and byres make the story unlikely. Recently restored contemporary paintings on boards in the rooms above include selection from Geoffrey Whitney's *Choice of Emblemes*. Culross is the best-preserved of all the wealthy coastal burghs and contains an impressive array of early C17 stone harled houses, especially around *The Study*. *The Town House* (*102*), 1626, was altered in 1783.

Dairsie, Fife Region. NO4117. *Parish church* built 1621 for Archbishop Spottiswoode. Rectangular block with polygonal tower corbelled-out at SW corner. Regular pointed fenestration with thick, cinque-foiled tracery. Hipped roof replaces original flat roof with balustrading.

Danby Wiske, North Yorkshire. SE3398. *Lazenby Hall*, c. 1640, with windows similar to those at Slingsby Castle.

Dauntsey, Wiltshire. ST9882. *St James*, Gothic W tower, 1630, for Earl Danby.

Deal Castle, Kent. TR3752. One of the best preserved castles built for Henry VIII, c. 1539–40. 6-lobed plan.

Deene Park, Northamptonshire. SP9492. Medieval house remodelled in courtyard form by the Brudenells after 1514. Important Renaissance work of c. 1570, including hall, porch and, possibly *ex situ*, bay window with an ogee gable. Further alterations in early C17.

Delgatie Castle, Grampian Region. NJ7550. Much altered tower-house with painted ceiling dated 1597.

Denbigh, Clwyd. SJ0567. Parts still remain of cathedral-sized *church* commenced c. 1578 for Robert Dudley, Earl of Leicester, and never completed. *Plas Clough*, a more conventional brick house with stepped gables for Sir Richard Clough. Begun 1567, the year that he was building Bach-y-Craig, Tremeirchion (q.v.).

Denton Hall, Northumberland. NZ1965. 3-storeyed house, 1622, with gabled ends and entrance porch off-set in the medieval way.

Denver Hall, Norfolk. TF6106. Brick house, c. 1520, with stepped gables, terracotta decoration, and small detached gatehouse of 1570.

Derby, Derbyshire. SK3536. *All Saints* (cathedral since 1927), extremely ornate early C16 W tower of great architectural quality. The remainder rebuilt 1723–5 by James Gibbs. *St Werburgh*, Friar Gate, 1601–8, new tower following collapse of earlier tower.

Desford Old Hall, Leicestershire. SK4703. Medium-sized brick manor house of c. 1640 with triple-gabled front and projecting porch. Variant on lobby-entrance plan.

Dewlish, Dorset. SY7798. *Manor Farm House*, square, gabled, double-pile house of c. 1630.

Dingley Hall, Northamptonshire.

SP7687. Built in late 1550s (porch dated 1558; gatehouse range 1560) on site of preceptory of the Knights Hospitallers of St John for Edward Griffin, ironically a fanatical Catholic. Earliest example of Renaissance architectural decoration in the county. E and S wings rebuilt in late C17.

Dirleton, Lothian Region. NT5183. *Parish church*, 1612, long and wide with round-headed windows. S aisle added 1664. *Castle* (65), 3-storeyed W range of domestic apartments added c. 1520 for Lord Ruthven.

Disley, Cheshire. SJ9784. *St Mary*, commenced early C16 and consecrated 1558. Tower and roof survive, remainder rebuilt 1824–35.

Doddershall House, Buckinghamshire. SP7220. Moated half H-planned house with hall range of c. 1525 containing Early Renaissance decoration to the E. S wing remodelled in late C17 and W wing in early C19.

Doddington Hall, Lincolnshire. SK89 70. (63.) 1593–1600 for Thomas Taylor, the Bishop of Lincoln's Recorder. Tall, elongated H-plan of brick with stone dressings. Entrance front with projecting 3-storeyed porch and square turrets in re-entrant angles, all capped with octagonal prospect rooms. Plain garden front with straight projecting chimney-breasts. Very careful and disciplined design.

Dolwyddelan, Gwynedd. SH7352. *Old Church*, primitive structure of early C16 with later C16 S chapel added for Robert Wynne, the builder of Plas Mawr, Conwy (q.v.). Separated from the body of the church by a Classical arcade.

Dorchester-On-Thames, Oxfordshire. SU5794. *Abbey church of St Peter and St Paul*, W tower reconstructed 1602. Several timber-framed buildings of the period in the High Street, especially *No. 55*, an impressive double-jettied house with prominent axial brick chimneystack and ostentatious array of original fenestration; *No. 39*, lobby entrance remodelling of 2 late medieval tenements; *George Inn* (109), galleried courtyard inn of early C16.

Dorfold Hall, Cheshire. SJ6352. Double-pile brick house, 1616, for Ralph Wilbraham, with projecting wings and balustraded porch and hall bays in the re-entrant angles. Great chamber with tunnel-vaulted plaster ceiling above hall.

Forecourt with angle pavilions.

Dormston Manor, Hereford and Worcester. SO9857. Picturesque timber-framed house of c. 1600.

Dorney, Buckinghamshire. SU9379. *St James*, brick W tower of early C16 and Gerrard Chapel of early C17. *Dorney Court*, probably originally L-plan when built c. 1500, with hall in longer wing, but later alterations have obscured the original arrangements.

Dorton House, Buckinghamshire. SP6714. Large brick Jacobean house with 2 long wings and projecting bays in re-entrant angles. Built for Sir John Dormer and contemporary plan of the house is incorporated in his portrait of c. 1625 in hall at Rousham, Oxfordshire. See also the weather-boarded bell turret of c. 1630 on church of *St John Baptist*.

Dowdeswell, Gloucestershire. SP0019. *St Michael*, central spire rebuilt 1577. S transept 1630.

Dowles Manor House, Hereford and Worcester. SO7878. Excellent example of Elizabethan manor house with central hall range and flanking cross wings. Stone ground floor with close-studded timber-framing above. Well-preserved wall paintings inside.

Dowsby Hall, Lincolnshire. TF11 29. Square, tall, double-pile house of c. 1610 for Sir William Rigdon. 2 contemporary plans of the building are contained in Thorpe collection.

Drochil Castle, Borders Region. NT1544. Fragment of Z-plan tower-house built c. 1578. for Regent Morton.

Droitwich, Hereford and Worcester. SO9063. *St Peter's Manor*, St Peter's Lane, 3-storeyed, gabled, timber-framed house, early C17.

Droxford, Hampshire. SU6018. *St Mary and All Saints*, W tower 1599.

Drum Castle, Grampian Region. NJ7900. Addition of c. 1619 to medieval tower-house shows awareness of the architectural qualities of symmetry.

Duddo Tower, Northumberland. NT9342. Ruins of early C17 fortified house.

Dudley Castle, West Midlands. SO9490. Medieval castle remodelled in mid-C16 by Duke of Northumberland and important example of mid-century Classical movement. First floor hall with open loggia and long gallery. Some work was possibly carried out by John Chapman who had worked at Lacock and

Longleat.

Dues Hill Grange, Northumberland. NT9700. Gabled bastle-house, 1602, with vaulted ground floor. Indicative of need for defence in the area at this date.

Dunster, Somerset. SS9943. *Castle* remodelled c. 1589–c. 1620 for George Luttrell by William Arnold. Heavily altered in C19 by Salvin. *Yarn Market*, picturesque, octagonal, market hall erected c. 1589 at Luttrell's expense. *Luttrell Arms*, the town residence of the abbots of Cleeve greatly altered for Luttrell, 1622–9.

Duntarvie Castle, Lothian Region. NT1276. Ruins of late C16 symmetrical house built for Durham family.

Durham Castle, Durham. NZ2742. Chapel of 1542 for Bishop Tunstall.

Durness, Highland Region. NC4067. Ruined *church*, 1619, with N aisle of 1692.

Earlshall Castle, Fife Region. NO4621. (14.) Mid–C16 Z-plan tower-house with elongated main block.

East Barsham Manor House, Norfolk. TF9133. Perfect early Tudor house, c. 1520–30, of brick for Sir Henry Fermor. Rambling house with battlements, finials and projecting porch. 2-storeyed gatehouse with polygonal angle buttresses and elaborately carved brickwork.

East Grinstead, West Sussex. TQ3938. *Sackville College*, High Street, almshouse founded 1617 by Earl of Dorset and dated 1619. Long 2-storeyed street range with triple gables over centre and further gables over end bays. Courtyard behind.

Eastington, Gloucestershire. SO7705. (111.) *St Michael*, long S aisle added in early C16 for Duke of Buckingham and adorned with his initials.

East Lulworth, Dorset. SY8582. (56.) *Lulworth Castle*, sham castle built c. 1608 as lodge for Viscount Bindon. Square central block with 4 round corner towers and mixture of Gothic and Classical motifs. Similar dimensions but far more exciting design than Ruperra (q.v.).

East Newton Hall, North Yorkshire. SE6479. c. 1620–30. Surviving wings of house with similar windows to Slingsby Castle.

Easton Royal, Wiltshire. SU2060. *Holy Trinity*, 1591 for Earl of Hertford to replace friary church demolished previous year. Plain simple box with no division between nave and chancel,

windows with arched heads.

East Quantoxhead, Somerset. ST1343. *Court House*, early C17 stone house incorporating earlier building for Luttrell family.

East Raynham, Norfolk. TF8825. *Raynham Hall*, 1619–c. 1630 for Sir Roger Townshend. An important and enigmatic double-pile brick house with Classical portico flanked by Dutch gables on garden elevation. Despite existence of early building accounts and brave analysis by John Harris, it remains architectural puzzle, difficult to reconcile with anything else of the period.

East Sutton, Kent. TQ8349. *Charlton Court*, one range dated 1612 of projected larger house for Sir Edward Filmer, with shaped gables and projecting bays. Possibly abandoned for *East Sutton Park*, in more commanding position, bought by Sir Edward in 1610 and subsequently extended.

Eckington, Hereford and Worcester. SO9241. *Woollas Hall*, tall, gabled, stone manor house dated 1611. 3-storeyed porch with similar decoration to Bredon's Norton Manor House (q.v.).

Ecton Hall, Northamptonshire. SP8263. Oval, Classical summer-house of remarkable purity, said to date from 1630s.

Edinburgh, Lothian Region. NT27. *Tron Kirk*, begun 1637 to designs of John Mylne, the King's Master Mason. Altered and truncated in late C18, but much original detail survives. *Castle* (35, 36), great hall alongside Crown Square, c. 1500; Half-Moon Battery, Portcullis Gate and Chamber above, 1574; double-pile King's lodgings with Jacobean decoration, 1617. *Holyrood House* (33), N W tower 1529–32, remainder after 1671. *Heriot's Hospital* (105), begun 1628, completed end of C17. Symmetrical courtyard plan on grand scale with square corner towers and polygonal towers in centre of each side. Open loggia on 2 internal elevations of courtyard. *Moray House*, Canongate (94), grand town house for Dowager Countess of Home by William Wallace. Originally quadrangular with orchards and gardens, but only N and W sides together with garden gateway survive. For other town houses of the period, see *John Knox's House* and *Huntly House*.

Edmondsham House, Dorset. SU0611. Probably early C17. Tall, compact, symmetrical entrance front with shaped gables. Original effect weakened by later flanking wings.

Edzell Castle, Tayside Region. NO5968. (65, 66.) Early C16 tower-house extended around large courtyard c. 1580 and completed by delightful pleasance, 1604, for Lord Edzell. Elaborate conceit symbolising the qualities and destiny of the builder with carved figures copied directly from C16 German engravings.

Egdean, West Sussex. SU9920. Brick *church*, 1622.

Elgin, Grampian Region. NJ2162. *103 High Street*, dated 1634 and built for Andrew Leslie of Glen Rothes.

Elmore Court, Gloucestershire. SO7715. Hall and solar wing with excellent internal decorations survive of house built 1564–88 for John Guise.

Elstow, Bedfordshire. TL0547. *St Mary and St Helen*, W window c. 1580. *Hillersdon Hall*, ruins of E-plan house built by Thomas Hillersdon after 1616 with stone from abbey and incorporating church as N wing. *Moot Hall* (98), early C16 timber-framed building with ground floor divided into 6 shops.

Ely, Cambridgeshire. TL5380. *Bishop's Palace*, brick E tower built for Bishop Alcock (1486–1501), W tower and W wing for Bishop Goodrich in 1550. Remodelled in late C17. Also various disguised *town houses* of the period.

Erbistock, Clwyd. SJ3544. *Eyton Manor Farm*, compact, gabled plan with jettied porch and rear kitchen wing, 1633.

Erwarton Hall, Suffolk. TM2234. Brick house of c. 1570 has been much altered but charming gatehouse with 4 semicircular gables, round angle buttresses, and forest of pinnacles, of c. 1549, survive intact.

Eton College, Berkshire. SU9678. Principal buildings of C16 include Lupton's chapel of c. 1510–15, his towering gatehouse and flanking wings, the W range of Cloisters, and completion of hall.

Evesham, Hereford and Worcester. SO6848. *Abbey* (113), Abbot Lichfield's Tower built after 1513 as free-standing campanile is ostentatious demonstration of monastic wealth. His chapel begun shortly before 1513 at *All Saints* for his own burial, and the chapel that he added to *St Laurence* c. 1520, are indications of Lichfield's personal desire for immortality.

Exeter, Devon. SX9292. *Guildhall*, High Street. Altered and extended 1592–4 in grotesque fashion. Some other timber-

Falkland Palace, Fife Region. South range, 1537–41. Strongly influenced by French taste and justly described as 'a display of early Renaissance architecture without parallel in the British Isles'

framed buildings in the city escaped the devastation of both German bombers and grandiose schemes for postwar redevelopment.

Eyton-On-Severn, Salop. SJ5706. (26.) Only one octagonal brick banqueting house remains of mansion built in 1607 for Sir Francis Newport.

Faenol Bach, Gwynedd. SH5369. House with stepped gables and tall chimneys built 1571 and enlarged 1626.

Fairfield House, Somerset. ST1843. Large symmetrical E-plan with canted bays to projecting wings and 3-storeyed porch dated 1589.

Falkland, Fife Region. NO2507. *Palace* (34–5, 36), courtyard façades built 1537–41, with strong French Classical influence, are of great national importance. By contrast, the fortified gatehouse, usually dated 1541, is in conventional Scottish tradition. Other parts include King's Stables, rebuilt 1531 with attached tennis court of 1539, and Chapel Royal of c. 1500–12 with interior decorations of 1633. *Moncreif House* (96), tall, thatched stone town house for a court official, 1610. A few other houses of similar period in the town.

Falstone, Northumberland. NY7287. - Fortified farm pele S of the church, dated

1604 on lintel. Usual vaulted ground floor.

Farncombe, Surrey. SU9745. *Wyatt Almshouses*, 1622 for Richard Wyatt of London. 10 units of brick with a central gabled chapel and coupled chimneys at rear.

Farnham, Surrey. SU8446. *Windsor Almshouses*, 1619 with central stepped gable.

Fawley Court, Hereford and Worcester. SO5730. Nearly symmetrical remodelling in stone c. 1630 of earlier timber-framed house. Conservative arched lights to windows.

Fawsley Hall, Northamptonshire. SP5556. Large early C16 house for Sir Edmund Knightley with magnificent bay window to hall. Ruins of Dower House, possibly earliest use of brick in the county.

Felbrigg Hall, Norfolk. TG1939. (81.) 1615–24 for Thomas Windham. Tall, compact rectangular block of flint and brick with a central porch and flanking canted bays capped with lettered parapets (for other examples of this conceit see Castle Ashby and Temple Newsam). Shaped gables at either end and an impressive group of chimneystacks.

Felkirk, West Yorkshire. SE3812. Small

Felbrigg Hall, Norfolk, 1615–24. A rectangular block is effectively transformed by emphatically projecting bays and towering chimneystacks. (Later range to the left)

C16 *school* in churchyard.

Fincham Hall, Norfolk. TF6806. Early C16 brick polygonal tower with late C16 additions.

Flemingston Court, South Glamorgan. ST0170. (*77*, 78.) Unspoilt C16 stone house with through-passage and side-wall chimneystack.

Folke, Dorset. ST6513. *St Lawrence*, rebuilt and refurnished 1628. Characteristic local window with triple stepped lights.

Ford Castle, Northumberland. NT9437. S front added before 1589 to N range of medieval castle. Much altered in C19.

Forde Abbey, Dorset. ST3505. (113.) Much ostentatious work carried out for Thomas Chard, Abbot 1521–39, including E window in Chapter House, great hall with magnificent entrance porch and private rooms to the W, and remodelling of N range of cloisters.

Forest Row, East Sussex. TQ4235. *Brambletye*, ruins of impressive symmetrical house built 1631 for Sir Henry Compton. Tall central porch, canted bays, and 4-storeyed angle towers with ogee caps. Parts of gatehouse also survive.

Fountainhall, Lothian Region. NT4467. Late C16 medium-sized house with crow-stepped gables extended in early C17.

Fountains, North Yorkshire. SE2768. *Abbey*, large N tower was built for Abbot Huby shortly before the Dissolution. *Hall*, very tall compact house with lively projections partly built of stone from Abbey c. 1611 for Sir Stephen Proctor.

Fowey, Cornwall. SX1251. *Place*, the medieval house of Treffry family with lavishly decorated bay windows added in early C16.

Framlingham, Suffolk. TM2863. *Poor House*, founded in ruins of Castle by Sir Robert Hitcham. Brick S wing of 1636.

Fraser Castle, Grampian Region. NJ7314. Large, beautiful, tower-house with a decidedly French air. Main block with flanking rectangular tower built 1575. Round tower completing Z-plan added c. 1618 when fanciful upper-works with mock battlements and false gun gargoyles were created. 2 lower courtyard wings added, 1630s.

Freston Tower, Suffolk. TM1739. Brick tower, c. 1550, and 6 storeys high overlooking estuary. Some windows are pedimented.

Fritwell Manor House, Oxfordshire. SP5229. 2-storeyed gabled E-plan of c. 1600.

Frodesley Lodge, Salop. SJ5199. Plain, gabled, Elizabethan stone house with semicircular stair tower.

Fryerning, Essex. TL6400. *St Mary*, early C16 brick tower with stepped battlements and pinnacles.

Furneux Pelham Hall, Hertfordshire. TL4327. Early C16 brick with stepped gables.

Fyvie Castle, Grampian Region. NJ7637. Upper parts of towers added in 1599 for Earl of Dunfermline, producing symmetrical composition. Magnificent stair dated 1603.

Gainford Hall, Durham. NZ1716. Tall, compact, almost square house built in 1603 with gabled projections in centre of each side – those to front and rear with lavishly glazed top chambers. Triple roof with row of 11 chimneys rising from centre. Very accomplished design.

Gainsborough Old Hall, Lincolnshire. SK8189. Remodelling in 1597–1600 of late C15 mansion for William Hickman, London merchant.

Garswood, Greater Manchester. SJ5599. *School*, founded 1588. Rectangular range of 3 bays with central doorway.

Gawsworth, Cheshire. SJ8869. *St James*, chancel and W tower c. 1500–36. *Old Hall*, large timber-framed courtyard house, dated 1570 on N front, with Elizabethan gatehouse.

Gawthorpe Hall, Lancashire. SD8033. Tall, square house of 1600–5 for Rev. Lawrence Shuttleworth, possibly incorporating earlier pele tower. Similar in conception to houses like Barlborough Hall (q.v.).

Gayhurst, Buckinghamshire. SP8446. Stone 3-storeyed E-plan with bay windows in re-entrant angles and porch with 2 orders of attached columns. Small shaped gables to central range. Begun 1597 for William Mulso. Altered in C18 and C19.

Gayton Manor House, Northampton-shire. SP7054. (*13*, 79.) Compact Greek Cross plan with projections at end of each wing. Built c. 1570 for the Tanfield family.

Gedding Hall, Suffolk. TL9497. Brick, c. 1530, with polygonal turrets. Extended 1897.

Gelligaer, Mid Glamorgan. ST1196. *Llancaeach Fawr*, tall L-plan house for Pritchard family with 1st floor hall, projecting 2-storeyed porch at one end and latrine tower in re-entrant angle with rear wing. Small windows indicate continuing need for defence both when it was built in early C16 and when remodelled in early C17.

Germoe, Cornwall. SW5829. *Pengersick Castle*, embattled early C16 tower, originally with attached hall.

Giffords Hall, Suffolk. TM0137. Delightful early C16 courtyard house behind 2-storeyed brick gatehouse.

Gilbertfield Castle, Strathclyde Region. NS6460. Ruined L-plan tower-house, c. 1610.

Giler, Clwyd. SH8849. Gabled gatehouse, 1623, with plaster overmantel in upper room.

Gilling Castle, North Yorkshire. SE6176. Medieval tower-house remodelled in late C16 for Fairfax family. Magnificent great chamber.

Glenbuchat Castle, Grampian Region. NJ3318. Ruined Z-plan tower-house, 1590, with elongated main block. *Church*, 1629, greatly altered in C18.

Glinton Manor House, Cambridgeshire. TF1506. Compact house, c. 1630, with ogee gables.

Gloddaeth, Gwynedd. SH8080. C16 hall and solar wing for the Mostyns with large addition of 1870s by W. E. Nesfield.

Glynde Place, East Sussex. TQ4509. Flint courtyard house, 1569, for William Morley. Symmetrical W front with central entrance and 3 gabled projections divided by 2 prominent chimney breasts. E range much altered.

Godinton, Kent. TQ9843. Symmetrical façade with projecting wings and shaped gables added c. 1628 to earlier timber-framed building. Greatly extended C19, C20.

Godmanchester, Cambridgeshire. TL2470. *St Mary*, Perp W tower, 1623. *Grammar School*, founded 1559. Small brick building with projecting 2-storeyed porch.

Godolphin Hall, Cornwall. SW6031. Early C16 hall with Jacobean range opposite.

Goodrich, Hereford and Worcester. SO5719. (20, *20*, 79.) *Newhouse Farm*, strange, 3-storeyed Y-shaped house with projecting porch built as a conceit in 1636 for Rev. Thomas Smith.

Gorhambury, Hertfordshire. TL1107. (50.) Only ruined porch survives from Sir Nicholas Bacon's mansion begun 1563 and extended in 1570s.

Gosfield, Essex. TL7829. *St Katharine*, N chancel chapel built c. 1560 for Sir John Wentworth to house his monument.

Goudhurst, Kent. TQ7337. *St Mary*, Gothic W tower of 1638–40 but with a Classical doorway.

Grafton Manor, Hereford and Worcester. SO9469. Brick house with stepped gables remodelled 1567–9 for John Talbot. Porch and S window of upper parlour are in unusually pure Classical idiom.

Grandtully, Tayside Region. NN9152. *St Mary*, long, simple building of early C16 with painted wooden ceiling of 1636.

Grappenhall, Cheshire. SJ6385. *St Wilfred*, rebuilt 1525–39.

Great Asby, Cumbria. NY6813. *Gaythorne Hall*, early C17, square plan with staircase and porch projections in centre of each side. Central chimneystacks.

Great Brington, Northamptonshire. SP6665. *St Mary*, Spencer Chapel possibly designed c. 1520 by Thomas Heritage, rector of parish and Surveyor of Royal Works.

Great Cressingham Priory, Norfolk. TF8501. Fragment of sumptuous brick house of c. 1545 with Gothic terracotta panels.

Great Crosby, Merseyside. SJ3199. *Merchant Taylors' School for Girls*, Liverpool Road, incorporates original boys' school founded 1620 by John Harrison. Stone with 2-storeyed porch.

Great Dunmow, Essex. TL6221. *Clock House*, tall symmetrical brick building with shaped gables of c. 1600. Timber-framed building behind.

Great Fawley, Berkshire. SU3981. *South Fawley Manor House*, gabled front with 2 orders of pilasters and embattled staircase tower. 1614 for Sir Francis More.

Great Fosters, Surrey. TQ0169. Large gabled, brick house, 1598, asymmetrically composed. Stables of 1630s are in fashionable Artisan Mannerist style.

Great Harwood, Lancashire. SD7332. *Marholme*, medieval house remodelled

1561, further altered 1607.

Great Hormead, Hertfordshire. TL4020. *Brick House*, tall brick manor house with stepped gables, early C16.

Great Oakley Hall, Northamptonshire. SP8686. L-shaped plan of c. 1555 with elaborate porch.

Great Ponton, Lincolnshire. SK9230. Early C16 *Rectory*, with stepped gables and important scheme of wall-paintings on upper floor.

Great Snoring, Norfolk. TF9434. *Rectory*, substantial part of brick manor house, built c. 1525 for Sir Ralph Shelton, with Early Renaissance terracotta friezes.

Great Tangley, Surrey. TQ0246. 1584 and one of few decoratively timber-framed houses in south-east.

Great Wenham, Suffolk. TM0738. *Wenham Place*, one brick wing surviving of mansion built c. 1540.

Great Wymondley, Hertfordshire. TL2128. *Delamere House*, tall brick house, c. 1600, with plain gables on N front.

Great Yarmouth, Norfolk. TG5207. Remains of merchants' houses in The Rows which survived devastation of World War II still give good impression of late C16 prosperity – particularly *Nos 7 and 8, Row 111*; *The Merchant's House, Row 117*; and *No. 4 South Quay*.

Greystoke, Cumbria. NY4330. *St Andrew*, early C17.

Grinshill, Salop. SJ5223. *The Manor House*, 1624. Carefully composed 3-bay front with plain gables. *Stone Grange*, 1617 for Shrewsbury School as retreat in times of plague. Simple plain rectangle with 2 entrances.

Groombridge, Kent. TQ5337. (115.) *St John the Evangelist*, simple brick box, 1625 for John Packer, to celebrate failure of marriage negotiations between Prince Charles and Infanta of Spain. Semicircular arch to porch is the only concession to Classical spirit.

Guildford, Surrey. TQ0049. *Grammar School* (106), impressive gabled stone courtyard complex of 1557–86 with schoolroom on 1st floor of S range. *Abbot's Hospital* (105, 106), 1619–22 brick almshouses for George Abbot, Archbishop of Canterbury. Dominant gatehouse flanked by wings with shaped gables on street elevation. 3-storeyed quadrangle behind. Remarkably complete original furnishings.

Haddon Hall, Derbyshire. SK2366. (76.) Highly attractive medieval house extensively altered in C16, including NW gate tower and apartments to E built c. 1530 for Sir George Vernon and the long gallery range c. 1600 for John Manners. Interior decorations of same period.

Halland Park Farm, East Sussex. TQ5016. Fragments of brick courtyard house, 1595 for the Pelhams.

Halnaker, West Sussex. SU9008. Ruins of medieval house remodelled c. 1540 for Lord de la Warr.

Hambleton Old Hall, Leicestershire. SK9007. Gabled early C17 H-plan with loggias on both garden and entrance fronts.

Hampton Gay, Oxfordshire. SP4816. *Manor House*, ruins of late C16 stone, gabled, E-plan house.

Hamstall Ridware, Staffordshire. SK1019. *Hamstall Hall*, only ruined brick gatehouse, tower and loggia remain of courtyard mansion built for the Fitzherberts, late C16.

Hanbury, Hereford and Worcester. SO9663. *Mere Hall*, decorated timber-framed house with flanking wings of c. 1560.

Handley, Cheshire. SJ4657. *All Saints*, W tower, 1512.

Handforth Hall, Cheshire. SJ8883. Truncated remains of large timber-framed house dated 1562 over doorway.

Hanford House, Dorset. ST8411. Large stone house, 1623 for Sir Robert Seymer. Symmetrical gabled entrance front with Classical frontispiece. Small central courtyard.

Hangleton Manor, East Sussex. TQ2907. Simple flint house, c. 1540, with off-set gabled porch.

Hardwick Hall, Derbyshire. SK4663. (16, 20, 26, 54, 55, 56.) Masterpiece of architectural massing built with 'more glass than wall' for Bess of Hardwick, 1590–7. Almost certainly designed by Robert Smythson, it is essentially a long 3-storeyed double-pile block with flat balustraded roof, enlivened by 3 symmetrically placed 4-storeyed towers at each end carrying initials of builder. The staterooms, including magnificent long gallery, are on top floor, and this is reflected architecturally by ascending height of the windows. Perhaps the least altered of all the Elizabethan great houses, it is also one of the most magically satisfying. Ruins of *Old Hall*, remodelled by Bess from 1581 and abandoned in favour of her new scheme in 1590, stand a short distance to W.

Hareston, Devon. SX5653. Small early C16 manor house with open hall, 2-storeyed porch, and chapel wing for John Wood, died 1537.

Hargrave, Cheshire. SJ4862. *St Peter*, 1627 for Sir Thomas Moulson, later Lord Mayor of London. Hammerbeam roof.

Hartfield, East Sussex. TQ4737. *Bolebrooke*, substantial fragment of Elizabethan brick mansion. Gatehouse with polygonal turrets and ogee caps.

Harthill, Cheshire. SJ4955. *All Saints*, c. 1609. Nave and chancel in one and hammerbeam roof.

Harting, West Sussex. SU7819. *St Mary and St Gabriel*, extensively renovated in 1576 after fire.

Hartington Hall, Derbyshire. SK1360. Gabled symmetrical front, 1611.

Hartlebury, Hereford and Worcester. SO8470. *St James*, W tower 1587 for Bishop Sandys.

Hartwell House, Buckinghamshire. SP7912. Jacobean mansion with corbelled bow windows to symmetrical N front. Extended C18.

Harvington Hall, Hereford and Worcester. SO8875. Picturesque remodelling of medieval house in brick for Pakington family, c. 1560-75.

Hasfield, Gloucestershire. SO8227. *The Great House*, late C16 timber-framed house.

Hassocks, West Sussex. TQ3015. *Danny Park*, E front c. 1582-93 on E-plan for George Goring, later Earl of Norwich. Tall, with deliberate prominence given to hall window.

Hatfield House, Hertfordshire. TL2309. (37, *50-1*, 51, 53, 58.) 1607-12 for Robert Cecil, Earl of Salisbury, with work supervised by Robert Lyminge. Unusually large E-plan presages move towards compactness among courtier houses. Sequence of apartments for King and Queen in separate wings. Original entrance front with open loggia crowned by clock tower possibly designed by Inigo Jones. Present entrance on plain N front. *St Etheldreda*, N chapel added, 1618, to contain Salisbury's tomb. Generally Perp but with 3-bay Tuscan arcade (cf. Watford).

Hawkshead, Cumbria. SD3597. *St Michael*, long and low with low W tower. Dated 1578 on S aisle and 1633 on clerestory.

Hazelbadge Hall, Derbyshire. SK1780. Rectangular stone lodge, 1549, with arms of Vernons and Swynnertons.

Headlam Hall, Durham. NZ1818. Early C17 symmetrical manor house.

Helpston, Cambridgeshire. TF1205. *St Botolph*, chancel windows of 1609 with pointed quatrefoil at top of each light.

Hemingstone Hall, Suffolk. TM1453. Brick house, 1625, with shaped gables.

Hengrave Hall, Suffolk. TL8268. (42, 43-4, 45.) 1525-40 for Sir Thomas Kytson, London merchant. Courtyard house of brick and stone with several innovatory features, especially Classical detail to entrance oriel of 1538, corridor access around 3 sides of courtyard, and double-pile range including hall. See also N chapel of church built in 1540.

Henley, Suffolk. TM1551. (114.) *St Peter*, W tower c. 1500. Large S window with terracotta Renaissance decoration c. 1525.

Henley-On-Thames, Oxfordshire. SU7682. *St Mary*, tower, 1521-47, for John Longland, Bishop of Lincoln. Also various timber-framed houses in town, including disguised row of tenements in *Friday Street* (98, 98).

Henllan, Clwyd. SJ0267. *Foxhall-newydd*. Ruined tall gentry house, 1608.

Hereford, Hereford and Worcester. SO5040. *Cathedral*, Audley Chapel, c. 1500. N porch 1519. *Aubrey's Almshouses*, Berrington Street, low timber-framed range founded 1630. *Coningsby Hospital*, Widemarsh Street, almshouses founded 1614 for Sir Thomas Coningsby. 4 stone ranges around courtyard, incorporating dissolved house of Order of St John of Jerusalem. Ruins of Coningsby's town house created out of Blackfriars survive in park behind. *The Old House*, High Town, elaborately timber-framed building of 1621 and possibly originally Butchers' Hall.

Hertford, Hertfordshire. TL3212. *Hale's Grammar School*, early C17, brick, with projecting porch matched by staircase at rear.

Heslington Hall, North Yorkshire. SE6250. Heavily remodelled symmetrical house, 1565-8, for Thomas Eames, Secretary to Council of the North. Now part of University of York.

Heydon Hall, Norfolk. TG1127.
Compact, tall, brick house with
projecting porch and flanking bay
windows, 1581-4, for Henry Dynne, one
of the Auditors of the Exchequer.

Highampton, Devon. SS4804. *Burdon*,
house dated 1569 with two projecting
wings defining narrow courtyard.

High Ercall Hall, Salop. SJ5917. (26.)
Detached loggia said to be part of 1608
house for Sir Francis Newport. Difficult
to relate to present C17 gabled house
which adjoins it.

High Legh, Cheshire. SJ6984. *St Mary*,
low, brick chapel with timber piers of c.
1581. Derelict.

Highlow Hall, Derbyshire. SK2180.
C16 crenellated manor house with porch
projection for Eyres family.

Hilgay, Norfolk. TL6298. *Wood Hall*,
brick E-plan house, 1579, with
pedimented windows in wings.

Hilton, Derbyshire. SK2430. *Old Hall*,
C16 timber-framed manor house.

Hinchingbrooke House,
Cambridgeshire. TL2271. Augustinian
nunnery remodelled after 1550. Bow
window on S front dated 1602, moved
from E side in C19 restoration.

Hipswell Hall, North Yorkshire.
SE1698. Early C16 polygonal bay
window and porch dated 1596.

Hoddesdon, Hertfordshire. TL3709.
Rawdon House, brick, 1622, with shaped
gables.

Hodsock Priory, Nottinghamshire.
SK6185. Only early C16 brick gatehouse
with polygonal stair turrets survives of
mansion of Clifton family.

Hoggeston Manor house,
Buckinghamshire. SP8025. Jacobean
brick house with one shaped gable and
giant brick pilaster strips on S and N
sides. Also C16 weather-boarded bell
turret to church.

Hoghton Tower, Lancashire. SD6125.
Double-courtyard house with gate tower
of 1560s for Thomas Hoghton.

Holcombe Rogus, Devon. ST0519.
Holcombe Court, spectacular asymmetrical
front with big buttressed tower over
entrance and broad stair turret to one
side, c. 1520-30. Various internal
decorations, c. 1591.

Holcot, Bedfordshire. SP9439. (114.) *St
Nicholas*, 1590.

Holdenby House, Northamptonshire.
SP6967. (51.) Only 2 archways dated

1583 survive of double-courtyard
mansion for Sir Christopher Hatton.

Hollingbourne, Kent. TQ8455. *All
Saints*, N chapel, c. 1638. *Hollingbourne
Manor*, large incomplete E-plan brick
house with strange gables, c. 1600.
Godfrey House, elaborately decorated
timber-framed house, 1587.

Holme Pierrepont Hall,
Nottinghamshire. SK6239. Remains of
early C16 brick courtyard house of
Pierrepont family.

Hope, Clwyd. SJ2859. *Plas-Teg* (55, 55),
sophisticated compact house of square
plan with extruded ogee-roofed corner
towers and shaped gables, c. 1610 for Sir
John Trevor. *Fferm*, stone gentry house,
1607, comprising hall range with side
wall chimneystack and cross-wing. 2-
storeyed gabled porch added later.

Horden Hall, Durham. NZ4442. Plain
symmetrical manor house, c. 1600, with
central 2-storeyed porch.

Horham Hall, Essex. TL6131. Irregular
brick moated house, c. 1502-20 for Sir
John Cutte, Treasurer of Household to
Henry VIII. Stepped gables and
projecting hall bay window. Formerly
much larger.

Horham, Suffolk. TM2172. *Thorpe
Hall*, compact brick lodge, c. 1560, with
3-storeyed gabled centre projection and
elaborate flanking chimneystacks.
Pedimented windows but still with
arched lights.

Hornby, Lancashire. SD5868. *St
Margaret*, interesting W tower, 1514, for
Lord Mounteagle. Octagonal ground
stage with further octagon above.
Polygonal apse at E end.

Horsley, Gloucestershire. ST8398.
Chavenage House, E-plan, 1576, for
Edward Stephens.

Horton Court, Avon. ST7684.
Detached ambulatory built after 1527
when William Knight had returned from
Rome where he had been prosecuting
Henry VIII's divorce. Perp, but in the
spirit of an Italian loggia. 4 crude stucco
medallion heads of Roman emperors on
inner wall.

Horton-Cum-Studley, Oxfordshire.
SP5912. *Studley Priory*, rambling house
built for John Croke on site of
Benedictine Priory and altered early C17.

Horton Kirby, Kent. TQ5668. *Franks*,
square brick house ranged around small
courtyard, 1591, for Lancelot Bathurst,

London alderman.

Howden, Humberside. SE7428. *Knedlington Old Hall*, early C17 symmetrical brick house with 2 shaped gables.

Howsham Hall, North Yorkshire. SE7362. 2-storeyed stone house, c. 1619, with semicircular cresting to roofline and impressive display of large regular fenestration. Central frontispiece with 2 orders of coupled columns, and terminal canted bays.

Huddington Court, Hereford and Worcester. SO9457. Early C16 timber-framed house remodelled c. 1584 for Wintour family.

Hull, Humberside. TA0929. *Grammar School*, 1583, 2-storeyed, brick, of 4 bays.

Hunsdon, Hertfordshire. TL4114. *St Dunstan*, early C16 N chapel, c. 1600 S chapel, both of brick with brick windows. *Hunsdon House*, gatehouse and few fragments survive of brick palace, built c. 1525 for Henry VIII.

Huntly Castle, Grampian Region. NJ5339. (66.) Mid-C16 rebuilding of medieval castle, further remodelled in richly decorated style, c. 1597-1602 for Marquess of Huntly. Elaborate frontispiece with wealth of heraldic achievements.

Hurst Castle, Hampshire. SZ3189. Henry VIII castle of 1541-4 on complex symmetrical plan.

Hutton John, Cumbria. NY4326. Elizabethan hall range added to earlier pele tower.

Ightham, Kent. TQ5956. *St Peter*, brick N aisle with pointed windows of c. 1639. *Ightham Court*, mid-C16 brick H-plan with taller central block. Frontispiece with 4 orders added 1575. *Ightham Mote*, perfectly preserved medieval manor house with various works of C16.

Ilam, Staffordshire. SK1350. *Holy Cross*, S chapel, 1618, with ogee lights to windows.

Ilkley, West Yorkshire. SE1147. *Old Grammar School*, 1637 and very small.

Ince Castle, Cornwall. SJ4476. Perfect square brick house, 1620s, with 4 corner towers. Originally battlemented throughout and possibly a deliberately sham castle.

Ingatestone, Essex. TQ6499. *St Edmund and St Mary*, Brick S chapel, 1556, for Petre family. *Ingatestone Hall*, the inner court minus hall range survives of double-courtyard brick mansion built for Sir William Petre, Secretary of State to Henry VIII, on site of manor of dissolved nunnery of Barking. c. 1540-8.

Ingestre Hall, Staffordshire. SJ9724. (61.) Large brick mansion on E-plan, early C17, for Sir Walter Chetwynd, with tall bow windows at ends of projecting wings. Hall bay and matching projection in re-entrant angles.

Inverness, Highland Region. NH6645. A few town houses of C16 and C17.

Ipswich, Suffolk. TM1744. *Cardinal College of St Mary* (107), College Street. Only the brick gateway of school founded by Wolsey, 1527, survives. *Christ Church Mansion*, 1548-50 on site of Augustinian priory for Paul Withipoll, London merchant. Brick E plan with far-projecting wings. Altered 1674. Also several timber-framed town houses, especially in Fore Street.

Irnham Hall, Lincolnshire. TF0226. c. 1510-31 for Sir Richard de Thimelby.

Iron Acton Court, Avon. ST6883. Unrestored early C17 L-plan house with stair turret in re-entrant angle and principal rooms on upper floor. Detached entrance gateway.

Isel Hall, Cumbria. NY1533. Medieval pele tower with domestic range added in C16.

Iwerne Courtney, Dorset. ST8513. *St Mary*, remodelled 1610 with triple-stepped lancet windows.

Keevil Manor, Wiltshire. ST9157. Gabled symmetrical house, c. 1580, with porch added 1611.

Kelmscott Manor House, Oxfordshire. SU2498. c. 1570, famous as country home of William Morris.

Kempsey, Hereford and Worcester. SO8549. *The Nash*, brick house, c. 1540.

Kemsing, Kent. TQ5558. *St Clere*, double-pile brick house, c. 1633, for Sir John Sedley. Similar to what is known of Chevening apart from 2 octagonal turrets at corners of entrance front.

Kenardington, Kent. TQ9732. *St Mary*, S aisle reconstructed to replace church struck by lightning, 1559.

Kenilworth Castle, Warwickshire. SP2872. (56, *57*.) Important additions including imposing gatehouse, c. 1563-71, for Robert Dudley, Earl of Leicester.

Keynsham, Avon. ST6568. *St John Baptist*, remarkably Gothic tower built 1634 after a collapse.

Huntly Castle, Grampian Region. Remodelled 1597–1602 with oriel windows based on the work of Francois 1er at Blois applied to a building of conventional tower-house form

Ingestre Hall, Staffordshire, early seventeenth century. The full architectural effect of the E-plan is further emphasised by the bow windows in the wings and the projecting bays in the re-entrant angles

Kilkhampton, Cornwall. SS2511. *St James*, largely rebuilt for John Grenville, rector 1542–80. S porch dated 1567 and initialled.

Killochan, Strathclyde Region. NS2200. L-plan tower-house dated 1586 with stair corbelled-out in re-entrant angle.

King's Lynn, Norfolk. TF6220. Various timber-framed houses in town, especially merchants' houses and warehouses such as *Hampton Court*, Nelson Street, where N range dates from c. 1500.

King's Pyon, Hereford and Worcester. SO4448. *Butthouse*, early C17 gabled timber-framed house with jettied gatehouse dated 1632.

Kingston Maurward, Dorset. ST7191. *Old Manor House*, perfect gabled E-plan house, built 1591 for Christopher Grey.

Kingstone Grange, Hereford and Worcester. SO4234. Gabled symmetrical timber-framed house, c. 1600.

Kington, Hereford and Worcester. SO2956. *Lady Margaret Hawkins Grammar School*, 1625 by John Abel but much altered.

Kinneil House, Lothian Region. NS9880. Ruins of large house, 1542–54, for Earl of Arran, remodelled 1677.

Kinnersley Castle, Hereford and Worcester. SO3449. (78, *78*.) Extraordinary house, c. 1585–1601, for Roger Vaughan with a 5-storeyed embattled tower flanked by 2 lower stone ranges with stepped brick gables on L-plan. Tower contains staircase with 2 chambers above. Castellated entrance porch suggests whole might be fantasy castle.

Kiplin Hall, North Yorkshire. SE2797. Brick oblong house with square projecting towers on each side flanked by gables, c. 1625 for Lord Baltimore.

Kirby Hall, Northamptonshire. SP9292. (51, *52*.) Expressive ruins of large courtyard house begun 1570 for Sir Humphrey Stafford and continued from 1575 for Sir Christopher Hatton simultaneously with his other prodigy house at Holdenby (q.v.). Double bow-fronted wing and great west staircase added at end of century, and gateway range remodelled in Classical form 1638–40.

Kirby Hill, North Yorkshire. NZ1306. *Grammar School*, founded 1556 by John Dakyn.

Kirkandrews, Cumbria. NY3972. Early C16 pele tower of decidedly Scottish nature.

Kirby-In-Ashfield Manor House, Nottinghamshire. SK4956. Asymmetrical house, 1622, with twin gables.

Kirkby Stephen, Cumbria. NY7708. *Smardale Hall*, late C16 house on elongated plan with 4 round corner turrets capped by conical roofs in Scottish manner. *Wharton Hall* partly ruined medieval house enlarged 1540 for Lord Wharton. Gatehouse, 1559.

Kirkcaldy, Fife Region. NT2791. *Sailors' Walk*, early C17 jettied house with crowstep gables.

Kirkcudbright, Dumfries and Galloway Region. NX6851. *Maclellan's Castle*, ruined tower-house, c. 1570–82.

Kirkmaiden, Dumfries and Galloway Region. NX1237. *Church*, 1638 and very plain.

Kirkoswald, Cumbria. NY5541. *St Oswald*, chancel c. 1523.

Kirkstall Abbey, West Yorkshire. SE2635. Central crossing tower heightened 1509-28.

Kirkthorpe, West Yorkshire. SE3520. *Frieston's Hospital Almshouses*, 1595 on square plan with truncated pyramid roof.

Kirkwall, Orkney. HY4410. *Bishop's Palace*, medieval, extended and altered c. 1550 for Bishop Reid and further extended c. 1600 for Earl Patrick Stewart when he linked it to his new *Earl's Palace* (64, *64*), magnificent, richly decorated courtyard house. Complex is now ruined. Also fine series of C16 and C17 burgh houses in town.

Kirstead Hall, Norfolk. TM2998. Brick E-plan house, 1614, with stepped gables and some pedimented windows.

Kirtling, Cambridgeshire. TL6857. (114.) *All Saints*, clerestory c. 1500. Brick S E chapel early C16 for Baron North. Early Renaissance window dated 1564 on N side of chancel.

Kneesall, Nottinghamshire. SK7064. (90.) *Old Hall Farm*, c. 1525 as hunting lodge for Sir John Hussey. Lobby entrance plan in brick with terracotta windows and newel stair.

Knole, Kent. TQ5354. Complicated courtyard palace of Thomas Bourchier, Archbishop of Canterbury, with 1540s additions for Henry VIII. Remodelled 1603-8 for Earl of Dorset and relatively unaltered since.

Knotting, Bedfordshire. TL0063. *St Margaret*, W tower 1615.

Knowle, West Midlands. SP1876. *Grimshaw Hall*, timber-framed house with flanking cross wings and central porch, c. 1560.

Knowlton Court, Kent. TR2853. Tall brick house, 1585, for Sir Thomas Peyton.

Kyre Wyard, Hereford and Worcester. SO6264. *Kyre Park* (22), greatly altered house built 1588–95 and 1611–20 for Sir Edward Pytts. Large brick barn, 1618.

Lacock Abbey, Wiltshire. ST9168. (46.) House of Augustinian canonesses remodelled after 1540 by Sir William Sharington to form courtyard mansion. Octagonal banqueting tower with 2 exquisite Renaissance tables.

Lamphey Palace, Dyfed. SN0100. Medieval palace of Bishops of St Davids with early C16 chapel. Extended in late C16 when granted to Richard Devereaux.

Langley, Salop. SJ5300. *Chapel* (115, 116), simple plain box with weatherboarded belfry, probably 1601. The partly timber-framed gatehouse is only remaining part of *Hall* built for Lee family.

Langley Marish, Buckinghamshire. TQ0079. *St Mary*, N W tower 1609. Brick Kederminster chapel 1613. Brick Kederminster library 1631 and a unique survival. N aisle arcade replaced by wooden arcade with double Tuscan columns in 1630. *Almshouses* founded 1617 by Sir John Kederminster.

Lanhydrock, Cornwall. SX0863. Much altered courtyard mansion begun 1620 for Sir Richard Robartes, Truro tin and wool merchant.

Largs, Strathclyde Region. NS2058. *Skelmorlie Aisle*, added to parish church in 1636–8 to hold remarkable Renaissance tomb of Lord Montgomery. Church demolished 1812 and aisle now stands on its own.

Laugharne Castle, Dyfed. SN3011. Ruins of medieval castle remodelled in late C16 for Sir John Perrot.

Laughton Place, East Sussex. TQ4913. One tall brick tower with Early Renaissance terracotta decoration survives of house built for Sir William Pelham in 1534.

Launceston, Cornwall. SX3384. *St Mary Magdalene*, lavishly rebuilt 1511–24 for Sir Henry Trecarrel.

Launde Abbey, Leicestershire. SK7904. Much altered mansion incorporating parts of Augustinian priory for Thomas Cromwell.

Lavenham, Suffolk. TL9149. *St Peter and St Paul*, N chapel c. 1500. Upper parts of tower c. 1520–5. S chapel 1525. Many timber-framed buildings of the period in town.

Layer Marney, Essex. TL9217. *St Mary the Virgin*, rebuilt in brick c. 1510. *Layer Marney Towers* (44, 44), soaring 8-storeyed brick gatehouse with Early Renaissance terracotta decoration and flanking W range are all that were completed of ambitious house of Lord Marney begun c. 1520.

Ledbury, Hereford and Worcester. SO7037. *Market House* (105), begun after 1617, completed 1650s. Herring-bone framing with open ground floor. *Ledbury Park*, one of the grandest timber-framed mansions in county, c. 1600 for Biddulph family.

Lee Old Hall, Salop. SJ4032. Timber-framed house, 1594.

Leeds, West Yorkshire. SE3034. *St John*, Briggate, church of 1632–4 founded and endowed by wealthy clothier.

Leez Priory, Essex. TL7116. 2 elaborate gatehouses survive of brick courtyard mansion built by Lord Rich after 1536 on site of Augustinian priory.

Leighton Bromswold, Cambridgeshire. TL1275. (117, 118.) *St Mary*, W tower c. 1630 and sophisticated attempt to reconcile Classical theories with a Gothic form.

Leinthall Earls, Hereford and Worcester. SO4467. *Gatley Park*, square, gabled house of 1630s in brick.

Leominster, Hereford and Worcester. SO4959. *Old Town Hall* (103), profusely decorated timber-framed building, 1633, by John Abel, removed to present site and converted into house in 1855. *Wharton Court*, tall, square, Jacobean house with subsequent alterations.

Levens Hall, Cumbria. SD4886. Pele tower remodelled to create the largest Elizabethan house in county after 1578 for James Bellingham. Excellent contemporary interiors.

Leweston, Dorset. ST6312. *Holy Trinity*, 1616 for Sir John Fitzjames with characteristic local triple window.

Lincluden Abbey, Dumfries and Galloway Region. NX9677. (113.) College of secular canons with N lodgings and stair turret, c. 1530.

Lingfield, Surrey. TQ3943. *New Place,* stone house, 1617, on L-plan.

Linhouse, Lothian Region. NT0662. Tower-house extended 1589 and again after 1631.

Linlithgow, Lothian Region. NS9977. *St Michael,* choir 1497–1532 completing rebuilding of church begun in C15. *Palace* (33, 35), medieval courtyard palace with additions of 1534–41, a decorated fountain of c. 1538, and a rebuilt N range of 1618–20 on double-pile plan with Anglo-Flemish decoration.

Little Budworth, Cheshire. SJ5965. *St Peter,* c. 1526.

Littlecote, Wiltshire. SU3070. Large, brick and flint E-plan Elizabethan house added to earlier building for Sir John Popham.

Little Gaddesden, Hertfordshire. SP9913. *Manor House,* stone with stepped gables, 1576.

Little Hadham, Hertfordshire. TL4422. *St Cecilia,* late C16 brick N transept. *Hadham Hall,* entrance range with polygonal towers and pedimented windows survives of brick courtyard house built for the Capels. 1575.

Little Hereford, Hereford and Worcester. SO5566. *Upton Court,* gabled timber-framed house of c. 1600. *Nun Upton,* timber-framed house with brick additions adorned with shaped gables.

Little Moreton Hall, Cheshire. SJ8358. (69, 70.) Possibly best known timber-framed building in country, containing parts constructed for William Moreton in the late C15, additions of 1559 including the 2 large polygonal bay windows for his son, and further alterations of 1570s for his son John.

Littleton, Surrey. TQ0768. *St Mary Magdalene,* early C16 brick tower, porch and clerestory.

Little Wymondley Priory, Hertfordshire. TL2127. Augustinian priory converted into house, early C16 for James Nedeham, Surveyor of the Royal Works, and extended c. 1600.

Liverpool, Merseyside. SJ4383. *Speke Hall,* large, moated, timber-framed courtyard house extended and remodelled late C16 and early C17.

Llanddetty Hall, Powys. SO1220. Early C17 house for Col. Jenkin Jones, altered early C19.

Llanddwywe-Is-Y-Graig, Gwynedd. SH6023. *Church,* S porch 1593. Chapel added c. 1615 for Griffith Vaughan, with splended family monuments. *Corsygedol,* 3-storeyed gabled stone gatehouse with flanking wings erected in 1630 for the Vaughans.

Llandudwen, Gwynedd. SH2736. *Church,* nave rebuilt 1595.

Llandybie, Dyfed. SN6117. *Derwydd,* medieval house remodelled early C17 with good plasterwork and chimney-pieces.

Llanengan, Gwynedd. SH2927. *Church,* remodelled and enlarged with new S aisle 1520–30. Tower 1534.

Llanfaes, Powys. SO0328. (84.) *Newton,* compact, tall, double-pile house dated 1582 for John Games, High Sheriff of Breconshire. The double-height hall still has raised dias and there are fragments of decorated plaster in great chamber above.

Llanfair Talhaearn, Clwyd. SH9076. *Plasnewydd,* stone gentry house of 1585 with side-wall chimneystack.

Llanfihangel Crucorney, Gwent. SO3120. *Pen-y-Clawdd,* C16 stone house with large early C17 wing. *Llanfihangel Court,* late C16 house, altered 1627.

Llangathen, Dyfed. SN5723. *Llethrcadfan,* late C16 hall range with early C17 parlour range incorporating 1st floor great chamber with a plaster ceiling.

Llangattock, Powys. SO2117. *St Catwg,* early C16 W tower and S porch. Late C16 chancel windows.

Llangelynnin, Gwynedd. SH7573. *Old Church,* simple unrestored medieval church with timber porch and large N transept dating from C16.

Llangollen, Clwyd. SJ2641. *Plas-yn-y-pentre,* tall, compact house of 1634 with projecting wings, one of which contains entry.

Llangwnnadl, Gwynedd. SH2033. *Church,* extremely wide, triple-aisled church, that to the N dating from 1520 and to the S c. 1530.

Llanidan, Gwynedd. SH4671. *Plas Berw,* stone house, 1615, with gable-end chimneystacks and rear stair tower.

Llanidloes, Powys. SN9584. *St Idloes,* magnificent hammerbeam roof dated 1542. *Market Hall,* c. 1600 and only timber-framed example surviving in Wales. *Glyn Clywedog,* early C17 gatehouse converted into dwelling.

Llanllechid, Gwynedd. SH6069. *Cochwillan,* stone hall house with hammerbeam roof and side-wall chimneystack. Probably c. 1500 for William Gruffydd.

Llanmartin, Gwent. ST4089. *Pencoed Castle*, ruins of medieval castle remodelled with asymmetrical front and 3-storeyed porch, c. 1600.

Llanmihangel Place, South Glamorgan. SS9871. Complicated mid-C16 stone house for James Thomas, Sheriff of Glamorgan. 1st floor hall with decorated angle turret and defensive-looking tower attached to N.

Llannor, Gwynedd. SH3436. *Bodfel*, early C17 3-storeyed gatehouse with Doric columns for house that was never built due to Civil War.

Llanrhaedr-Yng-Nghinmeirch, Clwyd. SJ0763. *Church*, beautiful Jesse window, 1533.

Llanrwst, Clwyd. SH7961. *Church*, Gwydir chapel on S side of chancel 1633–4. *Almshouse and school*, 1610, for Sir John Wynn. *Bridge*, 1636, improbably attributed to Inigo Jones.

Llanystumdwy, Gwynedd. SH4639. *Talhenbont*, stone, gabled house of 1607 with prominent chimneystacks. T-plan with entrance close to re-entrant angle.

Llyswen, Powys. SO1140. *Llangoed Castle*, small S wing is part of house built 1633 for Sir Henry Williams. Totally swamped by mansion built 1913–14 to design of Clough Williams-Ellis.

Lockinge, Oxfordshire. SU4686. *All Saints*, W tower, 1564.

LONDON

City of London

Inner Temple, gateway on to Fleet Street; 1610–11 (remodelled 1906), stone ground floor and jettied timber-framing above. *Middle Temple* (109), hall with double hammerbeam roof c. 1561–70; restored after war damage. *St Andrew Undershaft*, St Mary Axe, nave, aisles and chancel added 1520–32 to earlier tower. *St Giles*, *Cripplegate*, Barbican, 1545–50; restored after war damage. *St Katherine Cree*, Leadenhall Street, 1628–31 incorporating tower of 1504. Externally Gothic but with Corinthian columns inside. *Tower of London*, timber-framed Queen's House of c. 1540.

City of Westminster

Abbey (28, 28, 111), Henry VII's Chapel, 1503–c. 1512, the supreme late Perp building in the capital. Decorated with

wealth of sculpture and most elaborate system of vaulting. *Banqueting House*, Whitehall (22, 38, 39), begun 1619 to designs of Inigo Jones. Of breathtaking Classical purity for date. Interior contains double-cube saloon with ceiling paintings by Rubens of 1630s. *St James's Palace* (22, 31), gatehouse and chapel survive of Henry VIII's work of c. 1532–40; and *Queen's Chapel* (39), 1623–7 by Inigo Jones and first Classical church in England. *St Margaret*, Westminster, tower 1515, chancel 1518. *St Paul*, Covent Garden (101, 118, 118), 1631–8 by Inigo Jones for Duke of Bedford. Plain box with deep portico and Tuscan columns. Originally brick, but otherwise faithfully rebuilt after fire of 1795. Jones's Piazza has long gone, although Henry Clutton's Bedford Chambers of 1877–9 retains something of its flavour. *York Water Gate*, Embankment Gardens (93), all that remains of Duke of Buckingham's mansion, 1626, demolished 1676. Classical composition with a big broken segmental pediment. Possibly designed by Nicholas Stone with advice of Balthazar Gerbier.

Borough of Barking

Barking. *Eastbury House*, Eastbury Street (68), c. 1560–72 on H-plan with enclosed courtyard at rear. Polygonal staircase towers in rear re-entrant angles (one now ruined). Brick with rendered dressings to give appearance of stone. The plan has affinities to the slightly later Plas Mawr, Conwy (q.v.).

Borough of Barnet

Chipping Barnet. Former *Queen Elizabeth Grammar School*, Wood Street, brick with polygonal angle turrets, c. 1577.

Friern Barnet. *Campe Almshouses*, Friern Barnet Lane, 1612, long rectangular brick range containing 7 tenements.

Borough of Bexley

Bexley. *Hall Place*, Bourne Road, built c. 1538 for Sir John Champeneis, Lord Mayor of London, and extended after 1556 by his son, Justinian. Further extended to the S after 1640 for Sir Robert Austen.

Borough of Camden

Lindsey House, Lincoln's Inn Fields (101, 101), 1640 and recently restored to its orginial brickwork with giant pilasters. *Old Buildings*, Lincoln's Inn, 1490–1520, partly remodelled 1609. Chapel rebuilt c. 1619–23. Court to the W, 1524–34. *Staple Inn*, High Holborn (109), long, tall, jettied timber-framed range of tenements built 1586 and reconstructed 1937. Stands as indication of much that has disappeared from streets of London.

Borough of Chelsea

All Saints, Parish Chapel, Old Church Street, 2 Renaissance capitals, 1528, associated with Sir Thomas More, fortunately survived bomb damage of 1941.

Borough of Croydon

Croydon. *Whitgift's Hospital*, North End, 2-storeyed brick courtyard group of almshouses built in 1596–9 for Archbishop Whitgift. Gabled symmetrical street front and chapel in S E corner.

Borough of Ealing

Southall. *Manor House*, The Green (69), only grand timber-framed house in historic Middlesex. c. 1587 but much remodelled later.

Borough of Enfield

Enfield. *Forty Hall*, 1629–36 for Sir Nicholas Raynton on advanced square plan. *Grammar School*, Market Place, mid-C16 of brick with large school room on ground floor and stair turret giving access to dormered upper storey.

Borough of Greenwich

Charlton House (63, 64), c. 1607–12 for Sir Adam Newton, tutor to Henry, Prince of Wales. Symmetrical H-plan, brick, with flanking towers in centre of each wing. Plain and disciplined design apart from flamboyant frontispiece. See also detached gateway, contemporary stables and charming summer-house of c. 1630, now a public lavatory. *St Luke, Charlton*, Charlton Church Lane, c. 1630 of brick with proto-Gothic details. 66 *Croom's Hill*, exceptionally well-preserved example of smaller brick house of c. 1630. *Queen's House*, Greenwich Park (24, 38, 38), revolutionary Classical villa built astride Dover Road by Inigo Jones, 1616–19 and 1629–37. Modified by John

Eastbury House, Barking, Greater London, c. 1560–72. Brick H-plan house with dressings rendered to give the impression of stone

Webb, 1662. *Well Hall*, Eltham, a range of brick buildings, 1568, survive from moated house once home of Margaret Roper, Sir Thomas More's daughter.

Borough of Hackney
Old St Mary's Church, Stoke Newington Church Street, W tower, S aisle, SE vestry, c. 1560. *St John's Institute*, Sutton Place, early C16 brick H-plan with altered fenestration.

Borough of Haringey
Tottenham. *Bruce Castle*, Lordship Lane, late Elizabethan E-plan house remodelled late C17.

Borough of Harrow
Harrow-on-the-Hill. *The Old School*, the small W wing, 1611
Pinner. Good timber-framed houses in village including converted medieval hall houses at *East End Farm Cottage*, Moss Lane and *Headstone Manor House*, where restored barn dates from c. 1530.

Stanmore. *St John the Evangelist*, Church Road, ruins of simple brick box with embattled tower consecrated by Archbishop Laud, 1632.

Borough of Hillingdon
Harefield, *Almshouses*, 1600 for the Countess of Derby, of brick on H-plan. *St Mary*, early C16 tower, N aisle and N chancel chapel. Splendid collection of monuments.
Hillingdon. *The Cedars*, Uxbridge Road, symmetrical brick compact house of late C16. *St John the Baptist*, W tower 1629.
Ickenham. *St Giles*, N aisle and S porch, c. 1575–80. *Swakeleys*, brick, H-plan Artisan Mannerist house, 1629–38, for Sir Edmund Wright. Shaped gables, pedimented windows, and central porch. Lively design with projecting bay windows at ends of wings.
West Drayton. *Manor House*, Church Road, truncated brick gatehouse is all that survives of 1520s mansion of the Pagets.

Borough of Hounslow
Brentford. *Boston Manor House*, Boston Manor Road, 3-storeyed brick rectangular house of c. 1620 with plain gables and projecting porch. Elaborate internal plasterwork. Pediments to windows and modillion cornice are possibly later embellishments.
Chiswick. *Chiswick House Gateway* with Tuscan columns supporting Doric frieze and pediment, 1621 by Inigo Jones. Originally at Beaufort House, Chelsea.
Isleworth. *Syon House* (46), mid-C16 square courtyard mansion of the Duke of Somerset with square corner turrets. Early C17 loggia on river front and entrance pavilions. Refaced C19.
Osterley Park. The general outline of Sir Thomas Gresham's courtyard house with 4 corner towers is preserved in early C18 rebuilding.

Borough of Islington
The Charterhouse, Charterhouse Square, Carthusian priory converted into mansion after 1545 for Sir Edward North and later, Thomas Howard, Duke of Norfolk. Subsequently remodelled as Hospital of King James with attached boys' school. Badly damaged in World War II but substantial C16 and early C17 work remains. *Cromwell House*, Highgate Hill, medium-sized brick house crowned with cupola, c. 1637–40. *Canonbury House*, Canonbury Place, late C16 brick tower is fragment of large courtyard house of Sir John Spencer.

Royal Borough of Kensington
Holland House (64), remains of house built 1605–6 and extended before 1614 for Sir Walter Cope are incorporated in present youth hostel. Orangery is essentially a remodelling of the sumptuous stables of 1638.

Borough of Kingston upon Thames
Malden. *St John*, Church Road, early C17 in brick for John Goode.

Borough of Merton
Morden. *St Lawrence*, Morden Park, 1636, of brick with stone quoins. Nave and chancel in one, S porch, and embattled W tower.

Borough of Richmond upon Thames
Barnes. *St Mary*, Church Street, early C17 brick tower.
Ham. *Ham House*, H-plan house, 1610 for Sir Thomas Vavassour, extensively altered in 1670s. Interiors of 1637–8.
Hampton. *Hampton Court* (29, *30, 31,* 41, *42,* 44), manor bought by Wolsey in 1514 who built grandest house in

country comprising the present W front (without wings), Base Court, Clock Court (with different buildings on N and S), Master Carpenter's Court and chapel and cloisters to W. Presented to Henry VIII, 1529, who spent more on the building than on any other palace. He built great hall, remodelled Clock Court, built new court (now Fountain Court) and added ranges to the N and E of Chapel Court and 2 wings on W front. Most complete example of a Tudor palace.

Kew. *Kew Palace*, 1631 for Samuel Fortrey, London merchant of Dutch descent. Brick, beautifully laid in Flemish bond, 3 storeys with 3 Dutch gables. Earliest of all Artisan Mannerist houses.

Richmond. *Palace* (27), surviving fragments of Tudor palace, c. 1500, includes brick gateway.

Long Ashton, Avon. ST5470. Long SW wing of c. 1635 is strikingly Classical.

Longford Castle, Wiltshire. SU1726. (20.) c. 1580–91 for Sir Thomas Gorges. Evocative conceit on triangular plan with fat, round corner towers. The NW façade originally had double-storeyed loggia with shaped gables and balustrade (rebuilt in C19 by Salvin).

Longleat House, Wiltshire. ST8043. (15, 22, 25, 26, 47, 47, 55.) Sir John Thynne's obsession with Classical architecture was out of step with the developing spirit of the age, but the final version of the house, built between 1567 and his death in 1580, is a beautifully disciplined imposition of architectural order on rambling fragments retained from his earlier attempts starting in 1540s.

Long Melford, Suffolk. TL8646. *Melford Hall* (60), c. 1545–54 for the lawyer Sir William Cordell. Brick E-plan with long projecting wings and octagonal turrets. Gabled octagonal summer house to one side and conduit house on green. *Kentwell Hall*, brick E-plan, c. 1560, also with long projecting wings and turrets. *Trinity Hospital*, almshouse on green founded by Cordell in 1573, remodelled 1847.

Loseley Park, Surrey. SU9747. 1561–9 for Sir William More. Carefully controlled asymmetrical design with projecting gabled wings, porch and hall bay separated by tall gabled dormers.

Louth, Lincolnshire. TF3287. *St James*, spire 1501–15.

Low Ham, Somerset. ST4329. *Church*, begun 1623 for Sir Edward Hext in spirit of conscious Gothic revival.

Lower Peover, Cheshire. SJ7474. *St Oswald*, tower remodelled 1582, S chancel chapel c. 1610, N chancel chapel 1624.

Lower Whitley, Cheshire. SJ6179. *Church*, early C17. Small and low with hammerbeam roof.

Ludford House, Salop. SO4873. Early C17 house with stone ground floor and timber-framed above.

Ludlow, Salop. SO5175. *Feathers Hotel* Bull Ring (109, 110); 1603 with profusely decorated timber-framing. *Castle*. Ruined range, 1581, for Sir Henry Sidney, President of Council of the Marches. Various other timber-framed buildings of the period in town.

Ludstone Hall, Salop. SO8094. Moated Jacobean brick mansion for John Whitmore, with semicircular bay window in centre and entrance on inner side of one wing.

Lullingstone Castle, Kent. TQ5763. Mid-C16 brick 3-storeyed gatehouse with polygonal projections. *St Botolph*, early C16 brick N chapel.

Lutwyche Hall, Salop. SO5695. Brick E-plan house of 1587, altered C19.

Lydiard Tregoze, Wiltshire. SU1084. *St Mary*, altered c. 1633, including arcade, chancel ceiling and S chapel for Sir John St John. Gothic outside, Classical flavour within.

Lydney, Gloucestershire. SO6203. *Naas House*, c. 1580 for a merchant family.

Lyme Park, Cheshire. SJ9682. N range essentially c. 1570 for Sir Piers Legh with extraordinary frontispiece. House remodelled by Leoni, early C18.

Lytchett Matravers, Dorset. SY9495. *St Mary*, remodelled 1505 for Margaret Clement.

Lytes Cary, Somerset. ST5326. Medieval house extensively altered and extended c. 1515–20. Parlour wing added 1533.

Lyveden, Northamptonshire. SP9885. (18.) *New Build*, begun in 1604 as isolated lodge for Sir Thomas Tresham on plan of Greek Cross as symbol of the Passion. Almost certainly designed by Robert Stickles with advanced window details and a system of floor-framing derived from Serlio. Never completed.

Macclesfield, Cheshire. SJ9173. *St Michael*, Savage chapel 1501–7 for Thomas Savage, Archbishop of York. Sumptuous 3-storeyed porch. Legh chapel rebuilt 1620.

Mackney, Oxfordshire. SU5790. *Small's House*, compact, gabled, stone house, c. 1600.

Madeley Court, Salop. SJ6905. Fragmentary remains of early Elizabethan mansion of Sir Rupert Brooke, Speaker of the House of Commons, including gatehouse with 2 polygonal turrets separated by shaped gable and now converted into cottages.

Madingley Hall, Cambridgeshire. TL3960. Brick mansion, c. 1547, for John Hynde, extended c. 1590 for his son Francis. Subsequently much altered.

Madresfield Court, Hereford and Worcester. SO8047. Very tall brick house with stepped gables of c. 1546–93 for Lygon family, enlarged C19.

Maer, Staffordshire. SJ7938. *St Peter*, remodelled c. 1610. *Maer Hall*. Early C17 with a triple-gabled street front and 2 shaped gables to garden front.

Maidstone, Kent. TQ7656. *Chillington Manor*, St Faith's Street, c. 1561, for Nicholas Barham on a brick E-plan. *Archbishop's Palace*, remodelled as Elizabethan E-plan house for Astley family. Various timber-framed and pargetted town houses.

Mains, Tayside Region. NO4234. *Powrie Castle*, ruined Z-plan tower-house of mid-C16 with 2-storeyed rectangular N range, 1604.

Malpas, Cheshire. SJ4847. *Hampton Old Hall*, large timber framed-house, 1591.

Malton Lodge, North Yorkshire. SE7871. Surviving fragment of large mansion, 1608.

Manchester, Greater Manchester. SJ8398. *Didsbury. St James*, Skinner Lane, W tower 1620 with obelisk pinnacles. *Levenshulme. Slade Hall*, 2-storeyed, gabled, timber-framed house, 1585. *Wythenshawe Park. Wythenshawe Hall*, timber-framed hall range with projecting wings and porch dates from mid-C16.

Mapledurham, Oxfordshire. SU6776. *Mapledurham House*, c. 1581–1612, of brick, for Sir Michael Blount, on H-plan with flanking wings lower than hall range. Remodelled late C18 and 're-Jacobeanised' C19. *Almshouses* (107), single storey brick range founded 1613 by John Lister.

Mapperton, Dorset. SY5099. Mid-C16 house for Robert Morgan remodelled late C17.

Marholm, Northamptonshire. TF1402. *St Mary*, chancel rebuilt for Sir William Fitzwilliam before 1534.

Market Harborough, Leicestershire. SP7387. *Grammar School*, early C17 timber-framed building with open ground floor to serve as market space.

Marske-by-the-Sea, Cleveland. NZ6322. *Marske Hall* (80, 81.). Carefully designed stone house of 1625 for Sir William Pennyman with 3 projecting towers topped with stone domical caps and canted bay windows placed between them.

Marston Hall, Lincolnshire. SK8943. Truncated remains of H-plan house built late C16 for Thorold family.

Mathern, Gwent. ST5290. *Moynes Court*, gabled house, 1609, with tall turretted gatehouse. *St Pierre*, embattled C16 gatehouse with octagonal corner turrets.

Maybole Castle, Strathclyde Region. NS3009. L-plan tower-house, c. 1600,. for Earls of Cassillis.

Meesden, Hertfordshire. TL4432. *St Mary*, delightful brick S porch, c. 1530.

Melbury Sampford, Dorset. ST5706. *Melbury House*, much remodelled house of 1530s for Giles Strangway with remarkable features including hexagonal prospect tower and courtyard corridor (cf. Hengrave Hall). Exact square in plan.

Melcombe Horsey, Dorset. ST7702. *Bingham's Melcombe*, irregular courtyard house of various dates from c. 1500. Hall oriel with Renaissance detail dates from 1550s. *Higher Melcombe*, much altered mid-C16 house for Sir John Horsey. Large private chapel built early C17 for Sir Thomas Freke has triple lancet windows under pointed arch.

Mells, Somerset. ST7249. *St Andrew*, tower and much of church early C16. *Manor House*. Gabled late C16 house much altered c. 1900. Formerly grange of Abbot Selwood of Glastonbury.

Melton Constable, Norfolk. TG0433. Round 5-storeyed hunting tower with pyramid roof. Altered 1721.

Merton Hall, Norfolk. TL9098. Gatehouse, 1620, with steep shaped gables and coupled Tuscan columns framing archway.

Metheringham, Lincolnshire. TF0661. (115.) *St Wilfrid*, rebuilt after fire, 1599, with Tuscan columns instead of piers. John

Tirroll of Northamptonshire was principal mason.

Michaelchurch Escley, Hereford and Worcester. SO3034 *Michaelchurch Court*, single range, 1602, with timber-framing on stone ground floor.

Michaelston-y-Fedw, Mid Glamorgan. ST2284. *Cefn Mably*, medieval house with C16 and early C17 alterations and additions.

Mickleham, Surrey. TQ1753. *Old House*, brick E-shaped house of 1636, with Dutch gables in Artisan Mannerist fashion.

Midcalder, Lothian Region. NT0767. *Church*, choir c. 1540 for rector.

Middle Littleton Manor House, Hereford and Worcester. SP0747. Early C17 small stone manor house with flanking wings, 1 an addition.

Middleton, Greater Manchester. SD8606. Simple, single-storey *Grammar School* founded 1572 and built 1586.

Midhope Castle, Lothian Region. NT0777. Ruined late C16 tower-house for Alexander Drummond.

Midmar, Grampian Region. NJ7005. Z-plan tower-house built by Bell family of masons.

Milton, Cambridgeshire. TL1399. Curious, long, 2-storeyed N front with 7 projecting bay windows and projecting porch. c. 1594 for Sir William Fitzwilliam. Remainder later.

Mitford Manor House, Northumberland. NZ1685. 3-storeyed castellated ruined porch survives of house built 1637 for Mitford family.

Mitton, Lancashire. SD7138. *All Hallows*, Sherburne chapel 1594.

Mobberley, Cheshire. SJ7880. *St Wilfrid*, W tower c. 1533. *Old Hall*, fragment of Jacobean brick house altered late C17. *Dukenfield Hall*, early C17 symmetrical brick E-plan.

Mochrum Old Place, Dumfries and Galloway Region. NX3050. Tower-house, c. 1500, with crow-stepped addition of c. 1580.

Mold, Clwyd. SJ2363. *Church*, early C16 nave. *Gwysaney Hall*, tall, asymmetrical H-plan with double-pile central range, 1603. Extended C19 by J. L. Pearson. *Rhual*, compact double-pile house with symmetrical gabled E front flanked by bow windows. 1634 for Evan Edwards. *Pentrehobyn*, large, stone, asymmetrical half H-planned house, c. 1640, for Edward and Margaret Lloyd.

Monaughty, Powys. SO2468. Large, late C16, stone H-plan house asymmetrically arranged. Built for Price family and refurbished 1636.

Montacute House, Somerset. ST4916. (60.) One of the most immediately attractive of all the great Elizabethan houses. c. 1590–1601 for Sir Edward Phelips, Speaker of House of Commons and Master of the Rolls. Tall H-plan with shaped gables to wings, central projecting porch, staircase turrets in rear re-entrant angles, and proud display of fenestration. Top-floor long gallery is lit at either end by charming little semicircular oriels, and balustraded forecourt garden has ogee-roofed banqueting houses in corners. Porch of c. 1535 on W front was brought from Clifton Maybank, Dorset, in 1786.

Montrose, Tayside Region. NO7157. Few town houses of C17 origin.

Morborne, Cambridgeshire. TL1391. *All Saints*, early C17 squat brick tower.

Morton Corbet, Salop. SJ5623. *St Bartholomew*, W tower begun in 1530s. *Castle*, medieval castle with strange S range, 1579, for Robert Corbet, who had visited Italy. 2 tall storeys of impressive Classical consistency with attached Tuscan and Ionic columns. Mixture of very good and atrocious carving to friezes. Ogee-shaped gables above look almost like an afterthought. Ruined.

Moretonhampstead, Devon. SX7586. *Almshouses*, impressive 2-storeyed range, 1637, with ground floor loggia and architectural emphasis on centre.

Mount Edgcumbe, Cornwall. SX4353. Massive embattled quadrangular block with (originally) 4 round corner towers and hall rising above centre. Built 1547–53 for Sir Richard Edgcumbe and burnt out 1941.

Moyns Park, Essex. TL6940. Early C16 timber-framed and jettied SW wing. Gabled, brick NW façade c. 1575–80 for Thomas Gent.

Muchalls Castle, Grampian Region. NO9091. (71, 72.) L-plan house with enclosed court and decorated gateway c. 1607–27 for Alexander Burnett of Leys.

Muchelney Abbey, Somerset. ST4224. (113.) Early C16 Abbots' lodging with sumptuous fireplaces.

Much Marcle, Hereford and Worcester. SO6531. *Hellens*, fragment of mid-C16 house remodelled in brick in early C17. *Homme House*, partly c. 1500 with low tower, canted oriel window and battlements.

Much Wenlock, Salop. SO6199. *Priory* (113), prior's lodge, c. 1500, on grand scale with continuously glazed gallery on top floor. *Guildhall*, timber-framed with open ground floor, 1577.

Mucklestone, Staffordshire. SJ7438. *Willoughbridge Lodge*. Early C17 hilltop building of 3 embattled storeys with ogee corner turret. Possibly sham castle.

Munterne Magna, Dorset. ST6504. *St Andrew*, c. 1610–20 with typical Dorset triple stepped window.

Murroes House, Tayside Region. NO4635. 2-storeyed rectangular block with circular staircase turret built early C17 for Fotheringhams of Angus.

Mussselburgh, Lothian Region. NT3472. *Pinkie House*, C16 tower-house for abbot of Dumfermline extended on grand scale c. 1613 for Alexander Seton. E range with regular fenestration and 7 tall chimneys. Magnificent well-head in front. Now part of Loretto School. *Tolbooth*, High Street, 1590 with added wing of 1762.

Nantwich, Cheshire. SJ6552. *Wright's Almshouses*, London Road, 1638 for Sir Edward Wright, Lord Mayor of London and builder of Swakeleys (see under London, Borough of Hillingdon). 2-storeyed brick range with Tuscan arch into garden. *Wilbraham's Almshouses*, Welsh Row, derelict timber-framed range, C16. *Churche's Mansion*, Hospital Street, decorated timber-framed house, 1577. Other *timber-framed buildings* dating after the fire of 1583 in the town.

Naworth Castle, Cumbria. NY5662. Medieval castle altered and extended for Thomas Lord Dacre, c. 1520 and further extended c. 1604 for Lord William Howard, son of Duke of Norfolk.

Needham, Norfolk. TM2281. *St Peter*, early C16 brick S porch with polygonal angle shafts and stepped gable.

Nercwys Hall, Clwyd. SJ2460. Stone H-plan with porch and hall bay in re-entrant angles. Side entrance through porch (cf. Chastleton). 1637–8 for John Wynne by Ralph Booth, Chester mason.

Nether Alderley, Cheshire. SJ8275. *Soss Moss Hall*, timber-framed house, 1583, for Thomas Wyche.

Nether Winchendon House, Buckinghamshire. SP7311. Beneath Gothick remodelling of c. 1780 lies medieval stone house altered early C16

Montacute House, Somerset, c. 1590–1601. All the eclectic motifs which give the Elizabethan house such charm are present on the garden elevation – projecting wings, porch and bay windows; a lively skyline; sculptored decoration; and diminishing lines of glittering windows with Early Renaissance decoration of c. 1530 in parlour.

Nettlecombe Court, Somerset. ST0537. Carefully symmetrical S front with 5 gables and projecting 3-storeyed porch matched by hall bay. 1599 for John Trevelyan.

Newark, Nottinghamshire. SK7953. *Castle*, remains of work of c. 1590 for Earl of Rutland on river front. *Old Grammar School*, Appleton Gate, a small stone building, C16.

Newburgh Priory, North Yorkshire. SE5476. Altered fragments, including Jacobean frontispiece, survive of mansion built for Bellasis family on site of Augustinian priory.

Newstead Abbey, Nottinghamshire. SK5453. Sir John Byron adapted buildings of priory of Augustinian canons after 1539 to form house. Extended and altered early C17. Remodelled C19.

Newton Abbot, Devon. SX8671. *Ford House*, ambitious, symmetrical, E front with semicircular gables, 1610, for Sir Richard Reynell.

Newton Nottage, West Glamorgan. SS8278. *Nottage Court*, tall, compact, gabled E-plan house with entrance in W wing, early C17.

Newton Surmaville, Somerset. ST5615. House, 1602–12, with symmetrical gabled N front. 2-storeyed porch topped by balustrade with corner obelisks matched by projecting bay.

Newtown, Powys. SO1392. (70, *71*.) *Penarth*, medieval timber-framed house remodelled c. 1600 with flanking wings.

Nigg, Highland Region. NH8071. *Church*, built 1626 and enlarged C18.

Northampton, Northamptonshire. SP7659. *Delapré Abbey*, Cluniac nunnery incorporated in mid-C16 into house for Tate family of London. c. 1617 W wing remodelled on E-plan with shaped gables (of which only 1 survives) for Zouch Tate.

North Cadbury Court, Somerset. ST6327. Large symmetrical house, c. 1581, for Sir Francis Hastings incorporating earlier C16 W wing.

Northiam, East Sussex. TQ8324. *Brickwall*, large symmetrical timber-framed house with canted bay windows dated 1617 and 1633.

North Lees, Derbyshire. SK2383. Very tall, embattled, small manor house with elaborate internal plasterwork dated

1594 and incorporating arms of Rodes of Barlborough (q.v.). Related to plan in Smythson collection.

North Leverton, Nottinghamshire. SK7882. *Habblethorpe Manor*, small, brick early C17 house.

North Mymms House, Hertfordshire. TL2304. Very carefully designed brick H-plan house, c. 1600, with projecting square porch projection and regular fenestration.

Northop, Clwyd. SJ2468. *School*, 1609, with original fittings.

North Stoneham, Hampshire. SU4417. *St Nicholas*, rebuilt c. 1590–1610 at expense of incumbent.

Northwich, Cheshire. SJ6573. *St Helen*, nave and chancel remodelled with beautiful panelled roof, and W tower added c. 1498–1525.

Norwich, Norfolk. TG2308. *St Stephen*, Rampant Horse Street, chancel 1501–22, clerestory 1550, W tower remodelled 1601. *St Michael*, Coslany Street, c. 1500. *St George*, Colegate, aisles and N chapel 1505, S aisle 1515. *St Andrew*, Broad Street, 1506 (tower earlier). *Guildhall*, Market Place, council chamber of knapped flint and flushwork added 1534–7. *Strangers' Hall*, Charing Cross, street front of 1621 hides complex medieval building with alterations of c. 1530. *Carrow Abbey*, Bracondale (113), sumptuous lodging built early C16 for penultimate prioress. *The Tower House*, Bracondale, late C16. *The Manor House*, Bracondale, dated 1578 with shaped gables and pedimented windows. Also many *timber-framed houses* of the period in city particularly in Elm Hill, Gildencroft, King Street, and Magdalen Street.

Nuneham Courtenay, Oxfordshire. SU5397. Jacobean Conduit from Carfax Oxford was re-erected in gardens as eye-catcher, 1787.

Nursling, Hampshire. SU3616. *Grove Place*, early Elizabethan house for James Paget of brick, with polygonal turrets in re-entrant angles and tunnel-vaulted long gallery on top floor.

Oakham, Leicestershire. SK8608. *School*, founded 1584 by Archdeacon Johnson (cf. Uppingham).

Oatlaw, Tayside Region. NO4956. Fragmentary remains of large early C17 tower-house of Earls of Crawford.

Oborne, Dorset. ST6517. *Old Church*, chancel 1533.

Offerton Hall, Derbyshire. SK2181. C16, extended 1658.

Old Beaupre Castle, South Glamorgan. ST0072. Largely rebuilt in C16 around courtyard for Richard Basset, with gatehouse of 1586 and 3-storeyed porch with attached orders of 1600.

Old Warden, Bedfordshire. TL1343. *Warden Abbey*, fragment of brick house built for Gostwick family after dissolution of Abbey, 1537.

Orchard Wyndham, Somerset. ST0740. Complicated house altered c. 1500 and again c. 1600.

Ormskirk, Lancashire. SD4107. *St Peter and St Paul*, nave 1542, Derby chapel 1572.

Orrell, Lancashire. SD5203. *Bispham Hall*, symmetrical, gabled house of 1573 with porch and hall bay in re-entrant angles of projecting wings.

Oswestry, Salop. SJ2829. *Llwyd Mansion*, jettied timber-framed house, 1604.

Otford, Kent. TQ5359. Fragmentary remains of double courtyard palace built for Archbishop Warham, 1503–18, only 3 miles away from his other palace at Knole (q.v.).

Otley, West Yorkshire. SE2045. *Grammar School*, well-preserved 3-storeyed building founded 1611.

Ottery St Mary, Devon. SY0995. *St Mary*, fan-vaulted outer N aisle, c. 1504–30.

Owlpen Manor, Gloucestershire. ST7998. Medieval manor house, altered and extended c. 1540 and 1616.

Oxborough, Norfolk. TF7401. *St John Evangelist*, Bedingfield Chapel after 1514.

Oxford, Oxfordshire. SP5106. Principal University buildings of the period include: *Bodleian Library* (108), proscholium, 1610–12. Schools Quadrangle with 5-tier frontispiece, 1613–14. Selden End, 1634–7. *Botanic Garden* (108), three Classical gateways by Nicholas Stone, 1632–3.

The main college buildings include: *Brasenose*, founded 1509 by William Smith, Bishop of Lincoln, and Sir Richard Sutton, lawyer. Old Quad (storey added c. 1605–35) and Gate Tower are of the first build. *Christ Church* (107, 108), founded 1525 as Cardinal College by Wolsey. Tom Quad is largest quadrangle in Oxford and hall is largest hall. Intended cloister walks never built. Present cathedral is college chapel. Hall staircase, c. 1640, with convincing fan-vault. *Corpus Christi*, founded 1517 by Bishop Fox of Winchester. Front Quad (battlements added 1625). Sun-dial, 1581, with later alterations. *Exeter*, hall 1618. See also Peryam's Building. *Jesus* (107), founded 1571 by Dr Hugh Price, Treasurer of St David's Cathedral, as

Oriel College, Oxford. Front quadrangle of 1620–42 with symmetrically arranged Gothic decoration to the hall and chapel range, arched lights to the fenestration of the residential sets, and crowning shaped gables

Protestant college, largely rebuilt C19, but hall (c. 1617), Principal's lodgings (c. 1625) and chapel (1621) date from early C17. *Lincoln* (108), chapel and Chapel Quad, 1608–31. *Merton* (108), hall porch, 1579. Merton Street portal, 1599. Fellow's Quad, 1608–10 with 4-tier frontispiece on S side. *Oriel* (108), Front Quad including symmetrically placed hall and chapel, 1620–42. Present college incorporates hall and chapel of St Mary Hall, 1639–40. *Pembroke* (108), founded 1624 but largely rebuilt. *St John's* (107, 108), founded 1555 by Sir Thomas White, a London merchant. Hall, 1555–6. S range of Canterbury Quad, 1596–1601, remainder with Baroque frontispiece and open loggia, 1631–6 for Archbishop Laud. *Trinity* (107), re-founded 1555 by Sir Thomas Pope, Treasurer of Court of Augumentation. Hall, 1618–20. Kettell Hall, 1618–20, originally a private house. *Wadham* (22, 107, 108), founded 1610 by Nicholas and Dorothy Wadham, Somerset landowners, and virtually complete by 1613. Principal mason William Arnold. Very careful concern for symmetry throughout, despite Gothic dress. 4-tier frontispiece to hall range. See also S porch to *St Mary's Church* (116, 118) with twisted columns, 1637 by Nicholas Stone. Among town buildings of the period there are many excellent examples in High Street (96) and Holywell (99, 100.)

Oxhey, Hertfordshire. TQ1192. *Chapel*, plain brick and flint rectangle, 1612, for Sir James Altham.

Oxwich Castle, West Glamorgan. SS4986. Vast building with 6-storeyed tower, c. 1540, for Sir Rice Mansel.

Ozleworth, Gloucestershire. ST7993. *Newark Park*, 4-storeyed E front survives of house said to have been built of stones from demolished Kingswood Abbey, c. 1540. Central bay has fluted columns of Renaissance character.

Painswick, Gloucestershire. SO8609. *St Mary*, spire, 1632.

Papworth St Agnes, Cambridgeshire. TL2664. *Manor House*, early C16 house of brick and stone with interiors (including lavatory complete with seat), 1585, for Sir William Mallory.

Parham, West Sussex. TQ0514. *St Peter*, S chancel chapel, 1545. *House* is plain, gabled E-plan with projections in re-entrant angles, begun in 1577.

Passenham, Northamptonshire.

SP7839. *St Guthlac*, chancel rebuilt 1626 with wagon roof and excellent contemporary furnishings and wall-paintings.

Pebmarsh, Essex. TL8533. *St John the Baptist*, early C16 brick additions include W tower and elaborate S porch with stepped gable.

Pencaitland, Lothian Region. NT4468. *Church*, late C16 long buttressed box with square W tower capped by octagonal top added 1631.

Pendell, Surrey. TQ3250. *Pendell Court*, tall, gabled brick house, 1624. *Pendell House*, built only 12 years later, but a complete contrast. Compact, symmetrical, brick box with hipped roof and central 3-storeyed pedimented porch.

Pendennis Castle, Cornwall. SW8231. (32.) Henry VIII castle, 1544–6, extended late C16.

Pendleton, Lancashire. SD7539. *Little Mearley Hall*, delightful early C16 5-sided bay window in essentially 1590 house.

Penmynydd, Gwynedd. SH5174. *Plas Penmynydd*, stone house, 1576, with side-wall chimneystack, on site of home of Henry VII's grandfather.

Pilmuir, Lothian Region. NT5049. T-plan house, 1624, with well-preserved interiors.

Pitcaple Castle, Grampian Region. NJ7225. Greatly extended Z-plan tower-house c. 1600.

Pitchford Hall, Salop. SJ5204. (12, 70.) Large, timber-framed house for Otley family of Shrewsbury woollen merchants. Late medieval W range extended by stages in C16 and early C17 to form elongated E-plan. Further C19 additions.

Pitreavie, Fife Region. NT1285. (74.) Late C16 symmetrical tower-house with stair turrets in re-entrant angles of 2 projecting wings.

Pittenweem, Fife Region. NO5402. *Church*, tower 1588, belfry stage and spire, c. 1630. *Kellie Lodging*, High Street, tower-house, c. 1600, with crow-stepped gable.

Plaish Hall, Salop. SO5396. (68, 69.) Brick early H-plan house, c. 1540, for Sir William Leighton. Arched lights to windows and some painted Early Renaissance decoration inside.

Pleasington Old Hall, Lancashire. SD6425. Symmetrical with projecting porch and matching bay in re-entrant angles of wings. Dated 1587.

Plowden Hall, Salop. SO3786. Large, Elizabethan timber-framed house for Edmund Plowden, lawyer.

Polesworth, Warwickshire. SK2602. *Pooley Hall*, brick house, c. 1509, for Sir Thomas Cokayne.

Pontrilas Court, Hereford and Worcester. SO3927. Stone, gabled house, c. 1630, with projecting gabled porch.

Porth-Cawl, West Glamorgan. SS7979. *Sker*, large, tall, late C16 stone house with 1st-floor hall. Now sadly abandoned.

Portland Castle, Dorset. SY6972. Well-preserved Henry VIII castle, 1539–40.

Poundisford, Somerset. ST2220. *Poundisford Park*, built shortly before 1546 for William Hill and important as early H-plan house. *Poundisford Lodge*, c. 1540 for William's father, Roger, and on similar plan.

Poxwell Manor House, Dorset. SY7484. Gabled, stone E-plan house (S wing never built) for John Henning, merchant, of 1618. Hexagonal brick gatehouse, 1634.

Prescot, Merseyside. SJ4692. *St Mary*, arcade and nave roof, 1610.

Preston Court, Gloucestershire. SO6933. Large early C17 timber-framed house of 3 storeys.

Preston, Lothian Region. NT5977. *Hamilton House* (75.), half H-plan house with crow-stepped gables and principal rooms on ground floor for John Hamilton, 1626. *Northfield House*, remodelled on L-plan, 1611, for Joseph Marjoribanks. *Preston Tower*, C15 tower-house enlarged on L-plan early C17.

Prestonpans, Lothian Region. NT3874. *Church*, W tower and S door, 1596.

Prinknash Abbey, Gloucestershire. SO8713. Medieval grange and hunting lodge of abbots of Gloucester, enlarged on irregular H-plan, c. 1514 for Abbot Parker.

Probus, Cornwall. SW8947. *St Probus*, magnificent tower, 1520s.

Purley, Berkshire. SU6676. *St Mary*, brick W tower, 1626.

Purse Caundle, Dorset. ST6917. *The Manor House*, medieval house remodelled mid-C16 for William Hannam.

Pyrton Manor House, Oxfordshire. SU6895. Early C17 brick E-plan house remodelled late C18.

Queen Hoo, Hertfordshire. TL2916. Small, brick house with angle projections and corbelled-out gables and finials. Possibly built as hunting lodge.

Quenby Hall, Leicestershire. SK7006. Severe, brick H-plan house of 3 storeys with canted bays and projecting porch as principal decorative features. Begun c. 1615 for George Ashby.

Radclive Manor House, Buckinghamshire. SP6734. Fragment of larger house of 1621 with good staircase.

Raglan Castle, Gwent. SO4108. Medieval castle extensively remodelled c. 1550–70 and again early C17.

Rainthorpe Hall, Norfolk. TM2095. Brick house with partly timber-framed upper storey. Essentially early C16 remodelled c. 1580 for Thomas Baxter, lawyer.

Rampton, Nottinghamshire. SK7978. Lavishly decorated 3-storeyed *gatehouse* with terracotta panels by church is all that survives of early C16 Hall.

Ramsey, Essex. TM2130. *St Michael*, chancel remodelled 1597. *Roydon Hall*, gabled, brick house, c. 1560, with polygonal turrets and pedimented windows.

Renishaw Hall, Derbyshire. SK4577. H-plan manor house, c. 1625, for George Sitwell, greatly extended 1793–1808.

Rhynd, Tayside Region. NO1621. *Elcho Castle*, tower-house, 1560s.

Riber Manor House, Derbyshire. SK3059. Stone, gabled house, 1633.

Ringley, Greater Manchester. SD7605. Tower alone remains of old *church* of 1625.

Ringwould, Kent. TR3648. *St Nicholas*, W tower of flint and brick, 1628, with cupola and pedimented windows, is basically Gothic but with Classical trimmings.

Ripon, North Yorkshire. SE3171. *Cathedral*. Substantial alterations and additions, c. 1510–25, including the rebuilt nave.

Risley, Derbyshire. SK4635. *All Saints*, 1593 but consecrated only in 1632. *Risley Hall*, only late C16 garden gateway survives of residence of Willoughbys, who built the church.

Rivington, Lancashire. SD6214. *Church*, c. 1540. Small, aisle-less, and with a bell-turret.

Rochester, Kent. TQ7467. *St Nicholas*, rebuilt 1624 after fire, with Tuscan columns to arcade but Gothic windows.

Rodd Court, Hereford and Worcester. SO3162. c. 1625 of stone with a brick front and 3-storeyed porch.

Roslin Castle, Lothian Region. NT2663. 3-storeyed E-range with SE corner tower added to medieval castle.

Rotherfield Greys, Oxfordshire. SU7282. *Church*, N chapel with polygonal end, 1605 for William Knollys. *Greys Court*, compact, gabled, brick house with decorative bands of flint. c. 1600 and remodelled C18. Contemporary brick *Donkey Wheel House*.

Rothwell, Northamptonshire. SP8181. (103, *104*.) *Market House*, 1578 for Sir Thomas Tresham, but not completed until 1895.

Rousham Park, Oxfordshire. SP4724. Tall, plain, H-plan house, c. 1635, for Sir Robert Dormer. Sensitively remodelled by William Kent, 1738–40.

Rug, Clwyd. SJ0543. *Chapel*, 1634 for William Salusbury.

Ruperra Castle, Mid Glamorgan. ST2186. (*53, 55.*) 1626 for Sir Thomas Morgan, steward to Earl of Pembroke. Sham castle on square double-pile plan with circular corner towers. Similar dimensions to Lulworth but rather dull in comparison. Regular fenestration apart from the hall. Roof line orginally gabled.

Ruscombe, Berkshire. SU7976. *St James*, remodelled in brick 1638–9.

Rushden Hall, Northamptonshire. SP9566. Jacobean E front with semicircular central bay and matching projections to wings. Shaped gables.

Rushton, Northamptonshire. SP8483. *Rushton Hall*, early C16 courtyard house altered in 1595 for Sir Thomas Tresham and further altered in 1620s for Sir William Cockayne. *Triangular Lodge* (17, *19*), perfect Elizabethan conceit. Enchanting symbol of Tresham's Catholic faith built for his warrener, 1594–7.

Ruthin, Clwyd. SJ1257. (*77.*) Sir Richard Clough's town house in St Peter's Square with tiers of dormer windows set in steep roof echoes his extraordinary Bach-y-Craig.

Rycote Park, Oxfordshire. SP6604. Fragment of Sir John Heron's brick mansion with stepped gables survives. *Chapel* (*115*) has excellent early C17 fittings.

Rye, East Sussex. TQ9220. *Peacock's School*, remarkably advanced brick building with giant pilasters and Dutch gables, 1636. *Camber Castle* (*32*), Henry VIII castle, c. 1540, incorporating work of 1511–14.

Ryme Intrinseca, Dorset. ST5810. *St Hippolyte*, early C17 W tower and two typical stepped triple windows.

St Andrews, Fife Region. NO5016. Some of earliest surviving burgh houses in Scotland including early C16 *71 North Street*. Also *West Port*, fortified gateway, 1589.

St Bride's Wentlooge, Gwent. ST2982. (*111.*) *Church*, ornate early C16 tower with buttresses and rich carving. Stafford manor (cf. Brecon).

St Davids, Dyfed. SM7525. *Cathedral*, Holy Trinity Chapel, upper part of S porch, and upper part of tower, 1509–23 for Bishop Vaughan. *Bishop's Palace*, wing, c. 1500.

St Dogmael's, Dyfed. SN1646. *Abbey*, early C16 N transept.

St Donat's Castle, Mid Glamorgan. SS9368. Medieval castle remodelled early C16 (see especially the inner courtyard). Extensively altered after 1925 by Randolph Hearst. Decorated with terracotta Early Renaissance medallions said to have come from Hampton Court.

St Fagans Castle, South Glamorgan. ST1177. (*60, 61.*) Plain, gabled E-plan house begun c. 1580 for Dr John Gibbon and completed after 1586 by Herberts. Whitewashed in local tradition.

St Germans, Cornwall. SX3557. *Almshouses*, early C17 2-storeyed range with upper balconies.

St Mawes Castle, Cornwall. SW8433. (*32.*) Henry VIII castle, 1540–3, on trefoiled theme.

St Michael's-On-Wyre, Lancashire. SD4640. *St Michael*, W tower c. 1549.

St Nicholas Hurst, Berkshire. SU7972. *St Nicholas*, brick tower, 1612. *Stanlake Park*, late C16 gabled brick house. *Hinton House*, brick house, 1580s, with polygonal bay.

St Osyth, Essex. TM1215. *St Peter and St Paul*, early C16 nave and aisles with brick piers and arches. *Priory* (*113*), magnificent lodgings of brick, c. 1527 for Abbot John Vintoner, including gateway with hall above. Incorporated into mansion for Lord Darcy after 1558, of which fragments survive.

Salisbury, Wiltshire. SU1429. *Timber-*

framed town buildings of the period, including *56–8 St Ann Street.*

Samlesbury Hall, Lancashire. SD5829. One of the most splendid timber-framed halls in county, with additions c. 1545. See also *St Leonard*, enlarged in 1558 with nave and chancel in one.

Sandford Orcas, Dorset. ST6221. *Manor House*, quite irregular house of 1530s for Edward Knoyle with canted bays and gateway set to one side. *Jerrards*, altered house with porch dated 1616.

Sandgate Castle, Kent. TR2035. Remains of the castle built 1539–40 under direction of German engineer, Stephan von Haschenperg.

Sandwich, Kent. TR3358. *Manwood Court*, brick school, c. 1580, for Sir Roger Manwood with stepped gables. Various other buildings of the period in town.

Sawston Hall, Cambridgeshire. TL4849. Stone courtyard house, 1557–84, for Huddlestone family.

Saxlingham Nethergate, Norfolk. TM2397. *Old Hall*, E-plan Elizabethan house.

Scalloway, Shetland. HU4039. Ruins of castellated mansion built in 1600 for Patrick Stewart, Earl of Orkney.

Seckford Hall, Suffolk. TM2248. Long symmetrical brick front with stepped gables, pedimented windows and central 2-storeyed porch. c. 1560.

Selworthy, Somerset. SS9146. *All Saints*, impressive S aisle, 1538.

Sennybridge, Powys. SN9228. *Llwyncyntefin*, much altered house, 1634, for Hugh Penry with 2-storeyed porch.

Shap Abbey, Cumbria. NY5615. W tower early C16.

Shaw House, Berkshire. SU4768. Gabled, brick E-plan with accomplished Classical pedimented porch. Fenestration still emphasises importance of hall. Completed 1581 for Thomas Dolman, wealthy clothier.

Sheffield, South Yorkshire. SK3785. *Manor Lodge*, Manor Lane, late C16 gateway and few ruined walls survive of mansion of Earls of Shrewsbury. *Bishop's House*, Norton Lees Lane, Norton, timber-framed and stone hall house, c. 1500, with rebuilt cross-wing, c. 1550. Remodelled with inserted floor in hall in early C17. *Broom Hall*, Broomhall Road, early C16 timber-framed core beneath later remodelling.

Sheldon Hall, West Midlands. SP1584.

Early C16 brick house extended c. 1600.

Shenley, Hertfordshire. TL1900. *Salisbury Hall*, fragment of early C16 moated brick mansion built for Sir John Cuttes, Henry VIII's Treasurer, survives in remodelled building, c. 1670. 6 stone Early Renaissance medallion heads of Roman Emperors in hall were possibly removed from demolished Sopwell House, St Albans.

Shenton Hall, Leicestershire. SK3800. Large brick symmetrical house, 1629, with gabled semicircular and canted bays. Much altered C19.

Shepperton, Surrey. TQ0766. *St Nicholas*, aisle-less flint church, 1614, with substantial transepts.

Sherborne, Dorset. ST6416. *Abbey*, converted into parish church after dissolution. Chapel of St Mary le Bow remodelled, 1560, to form headmaster's house of *School*, refounded 1550 in part of abbey by Edward VI. School House Dining Hall is original school room of 1606–8. *Sherborne Castle* (55), tall, double-pile rectangular lodge built for Sir Walter Raleigh, 1594. Extended c. 1600 by 4 polygonal corner turrets designed by Simon Basil in sham castle idiom. Further lower, balustraded wings and turrets added for Sir John Digby, c. 1617.

Sherborne St John, Hampshire. SU6255. (114.) *St Andrew*, brick S porch, 1533, with Early Renaissance decoration in spandrels.

Sheriff Hutton Hall, North Yorkshire. SE6566. Brick lodge, c. 1620 for Sir Arthur Ingram of Temple Newsam, survives inside 1732 remodelling. Excellent interior decoration.

Shinfield, Berkshire. SU7368. *St Mary*, S chapel 1596.

Shipton Hall, Salop. SO5591. H-plan house, c. 1587, for Richard Lutwyche with porch in re-entrant angle under dominant 4-storeyed tower. *St James*, chancel rebuilt 1589 with windows reminiscent of Gothic of c. 1300.

Shipton-Under-Wychwood, Oxfordshire. SP2717. *Shipton Court*, c. 1603 for Lacey family. Tall, elegant, gabled, symmetrical entrance front heavily restored in 1903. *Prebendal House*, early C17 remodelling of late medieval upper hall house.

Shorwell, Isle of Wight. SZ4583. *North Court*, symmetrical gabled manor house, 1615. *West Court*, irregular house, 1579 with Jacobean extensions. *Wolverton*

Manor, Elizabethan E-plan with gabled wings.

Shrewsbury, Salop. SJ4912. One of richest towns in kingdom for important buildings of the period. See especially: *Old Market House*, The Square (26), stone market hall with open ground floor, built 1596 by Walter Hancock. *School*, Castle Gates (106), impressively large stone building of 1590s extended by range at right-angles, 1627–30. *Abbot's House, Butcher Row*, (97, 97), early C16 jettied timber-framed building with original shop-fronts. *Ireland's Mansion*, High Street (94, 95), tall, long, timber-framed house for Robert Ireland, wool merchant, c. 1575. *Owen's Mansion*, High Street (94), timber-framed house, 1592, for Richard Owen, wool merchant. *Rowley's House*, Hill's Lane (94), late C16 plain timber-framed house for Roger Rowley, draper and brewer. *Rowley's Mansion*, adjacent, more sophisticated brick house for his son, 1618. *Whitehall*, Whitehall Street (82, 84, 96), compact, square, symmetrical house of red sandstone capped by central wooden octagonal belvedere turret with

ogee cupola and with detached, gabled, gatehouse. 1578–82 for Richard Prince, lawyer, on site belonging to dissolved abbey.

Shrubland Park, Suffolk. TM1252. *Shrubland Old Hall*, important for its two terracotta windows c. 1525 of the Layer Marney type.

Shutford, Oxfordshire. SP3840. *The Manor House*, tall, narrow, compact house, c. 1600, possibly for Fiennes family.

Sissinghurst Castle, Kent. TQ7937. The 4-storeyed brick gatehouse with 2 octagonal side turrets and Classical detailing is the principal remnant of large courtyard house of c. 1560 for Sir Richard Baker.

Siston Court, Avon. ST6875. Large C16 half H-plan house with ogee-roofed octagonal turrets for Dennys family.

Sizergh Castle, Cumbria. SD4988. Medieval pele tower with 2 flanking wings of mid-C16 and the most important early Elizabethan interior woodwork in the country.

Skelsmergh Hall, Cumbria. SD5295. Jacobean house added to C15 pele tower.

Sherborne Castle, Dorset, 1594. Sir Walter Raleigh's compact lodge was extended c. 1600 by the polygonal corner turrets and further enlivened by the projecting wings c. 1617.

Skipton Castle, North Yorkshire. SD9851. Medieval castle with E range, 1535. 2 symmetrically placed polygonal bay windows and polygonal E tower.

Slingsby Castle, North Yorkshire. SE6974. Ruins of mansion, 1620s, for Sir Charles Cavendish with distinctive pedimented cross-mullioned windows. Surviving contemporary drawings by John Smythson.

Slyfield Manor, Surrey. TQ1259. Puzzling remains of Artisan Mannerist house, 1630s, with many interesting details.

Smallfield Place, Surrey. TQ3142. Long, 2-storeyed stone front, c. 1600, with central gabled porch and battlemented bow windows.

Small Hythe, Kent. TQ8930. *St John the Baptist*, 1516–17, of brick with stepped gables and nave and chancel in one.

Snape Castle, North Yorkshire. SE2684. Medieval castle remodelled c. 1585 for Thomas Cecil. Ruined.

Snitterton Hall, Derbyshire. SK2760. Symmetrical gabled Elizabethan house with walled front garden and one surviving corner pavilion.

Snowshill Manor, Gloucestershire. SP0933. Typical Cotswold manor house of early C16 with later alterations.

Solihull, West Midlands. SP1479. *Hillfield Hall*, curious tall brick house, 1576, with embattled, tower-like bay.

Somerhill, Kent. TQ6045. Stone H-plan house with symmetrically restrained elevations and Classical entrance porch. Hall at right-angles. c. 1611 for Earl of Clanricarde, possibly by John Thorpe.

Somersal Herbert, Derbyshire. SK1335. *Somersal Hall*, irregular picturesque timber-framed house, c. 1564, for John Fitzherbert.

Southam, Gloucestershire. SO9725. *Southam Delabere*, large courtyard house, c. 1512–47, for Sir John Huddleston.

Southend-On-Sea, Essex. TQ8885. *Porters*, brick, symmetrical, H-plan house, c. 1600.

South Malling, East Sussex. TQ4211. *St Michael*, 1626–8 incorporating earlier fragments.

South Mimms, Hertfordshire. TL2200. *St Giles*, brick N aisle, c. 1527, for Henry Frowyk, London merchant.

South Ockendon, Essex. TQ5982. *Little Belhus*, late C16 weather-boarded house with flanking wings and detached garden gateway.

South Queensferry, Lothian Region. NT1278. *Church*, 1633, remodelled C19.

Southsea Castle, Hampshire. SZ6498. Altered remains of Henry VIII castle, c. 1539, on square plan within diamond enclosure.

Southwick, Hampshire. SU6208. *St James*, rebuilt 1566 for John Whyte.

South Wraxall Manor, Wiltshire. ST8364. Alterations and extensions to medieval house for Sir Walter Long, c. 1598, including lavishly decorated drawing-room with enormous windows.

Spetchley, Hereford and Worcester. SO8953. *All Saints*, late C16 W tower and S chapel, 1614.

Standish, Greater Manchester. SD5609. (115.) *St Wilfrid*, rebuilt 1582–4 with Tuscan arcading inside. Mason Lawrence Shipway supervised work at Condover Hall (q.v.).

Standon, Hertfordshire. TL3922. *The Lordship*, W wing and part of S wing survive of brick courtyard house, c. 1546, for the Sadliers.

Stanstead Abbots, Hertfordshire. TL3811. *St James*, brick N chancel chapel, 1577, for Sir Edward Baeshe, Surveyor of Victuals to Navy. *Baeshe Almshouses*, gabled, brick 2-storeyed range, early C17. *Old Clock School* (now house), c. 1636 for another Sir Edward Baeshe. *Stanstead Bury*, picturesque house with brick parts of early and late C16.

Stanton, Gloucestershire. SP0634. *Stanton Court*, early C17 with projecting gabled wings for Izod family. *The Manor*, doorway dated 1577.

Stanwardine-In-The-Wood, Salop. SJ4023. *Standwardine Hall*, strange house, c. 1588, possibly for the Corbets, with large gables.

Stanway House, Gloucestershire. SP0532. Unusual elongated L-plan house, late C16, for the Tracy family on site formerly belonging to Tewkesbury Abbey. Well-known gatehouse with shaped gables added c. 1630.

Stanwell, Surrey. TQ0574. *Lord Knyvett's Free School*, comparatively large schoolroom with master's lodging to one side. Brick of 1624.

Stapleford Abbots, Essex. TQ5096. *St Mary*, small brick N chapel, 1638, with un-Gothic round-arched windows.

Stapleford Park, Leicestershire. SK8018. N range is 1633 remodelling with many strange details including statues in niches, reliefs and large, shaped gables.

Staunton-In-The-Vale, Nottinghamshire. SK8043. *Staunton Hall*, c. 1554 but greatly altered.

Staveley, Derbyshire. SK4374. *Hagge Farm*, small, very tall, symmetrical house with square porch projection, 1630, for Sir Peter Frecheville.

Steane, Northamptonshire. SP5539. *St Peter*, private chapel, 1620, possibly re-using medieval materials.

Steeple Bumpstead, Essex. TL6741. *Guildhall*, timber-framed building with school (founded 1592) above open ground storey.

Steyning, West Sussex. TQ1711. *St Andrew*, W tower 1577.

Stibbington Hall, Cambridgeshire. TL0898. (81.) Stone E-plan house with canted bays and detached gateway. Dated 1625 on porch.

Stiffkey Hall, Norfolk. TF9743. (20.) Partly ruined remains of house, 1576–81, for Nathanial Bacon. Laid out in form of precise mathematical conceit, it had circular corner towers with 2 further towers in re-entrant angles of half H-plan.

Stirling, Central Region. NS7993. *Castle*, great hall c. 1500. Palace (34, 34–5,). Exuberantly decorated courtyard building of distinctly French influence, containing the famous 'Stirling Heads', 1540–2. *Chapel Royal* (35, 36), simple rectangular building with crow-stepped gables and restrained Classical S elevation, 1594. *Holy Rude*, crow-stepped and buttressed apse of 1507. *Argyll Lodging* (94), early C17 remodelling of earlier building to form grand courtyard house for Viscount Stirling, completed 1674. Conical towers and tall dormer windows. *Mar's Work*, ruined remains of elaborately decorated town house, 1570. Octagonal towered gatehouse.

Stockton House, Wiltshire. ST9738. (68, 68.) Square, gabled, Elizabethan house built of alternating bands of flint and stone with a 3-storeyed porch for clothier, John Topp.

Stoke Bruerne, Northamptonshire. SP7450. *Stoke Park*, only the tantalising end pavilions and colonnade survive of remarkably Italian villa built for Sir Francis Crane, 1629–35.

Stoke Poges, Buckinghamshire. SU9882. *St Giles*, brick Hastings Chapel, c. 1560 with straight-headed windows.

Stoke-Upon-Tern, Salop. SJ6327.

Petsey, timber-framed house, 1634.

Stonehaven, Grampian Region. NO8685. A few C16 and early C17 houses around harbour.

Stonor Park, Oxfordshire. SU7388. Large medieval house remodelled c. 1600 for Sir Francis Stonor in attempt to introduce symmetry. Further remodelled in mid-C18 to give present appearance.

Stonyhurst, Lancashire. SD6838. Impressive stone courtyard mansion, 1592–c. 1606, for Sir Richard Shireburn. Striking gatehouse with 4 attached orders. Various additons C18 and C19.

Stowell Park, Gloucestershire. SP0813. Large house, c. 1600, for Sir Robert Atkinson, Recorder of Oxford. Embattled W front with projecting end bays and N front with Classical detail.

Stutton Hall, Suffolk. TM1434. Timber-framed house, 1553, for Sir Edward Jermy, encased in brick in C19. Brick gatehouse with semicircular pediment and stucco coupled pilasters.

Sudeley Castle, Gloucestershire. SP0327. Medieval castle extended and altered on grand domestic scale for Lord Chandos after c. 1572.

Sunningwell, Oxfordshire. SP4900. (113, 114.) *St Leonard*, interesting polygonal W porch in full-blooded Classical style, despite Gothic windows added for Bishop Jewel c. 1551.

Sutton Coldfield, West Midlands. SP1296. *Holy Trinity*, chancel aisles added c. 1550 for Bishop Vesey.

Sutton-On-Trent, Nottinghamshire. SK7965. *All Saints*, Mering chapel, c. 1525. Late Perp and splendidly decorated.

Sutton Place, Surrey. TQ0153. (44, 45, 59, 81.) One of the most important houses of its period in England. Built c. 1522 onwards for Sir Richard Weston on deliberately symmetrical courtyard plan (entrance range now demolished). Central entrance to hall and matching projections in re-entrant angles to either side. Decorated with Renaissance terracotta panels but other details conventionally late Perp.

Swanbourne, Buckinghamshire. SP8027. *St Swithin*, S wall to nave rebuilt 1630 with Perp windows. *Manor House*, with large Elizabethan gabled stone house.

Swarkeston, Derbyshire. SK3728. Tall, ruined garden building with bulbous angle towers and open loggia is all that remains of Jacobean mansion of the Harpurs. *Swarkeston Hall*, rectangular, gabled house, c. 1630.

Sydenham, Devon. SX4076. Early C17 E-plan house with unusually far projecting wings for Sir Thomas Wise.

Talgarth, Powys. SO1534. *St Gwendoline*, early C16 tower and S porch. *Great Porthaml*, early C16 crenellated gatehouse to earlier house of Sir William Vaughan.

Tamworth Castle, Staffordshire. SK2003. Medieval castle remodelled in brick in early C17 for Ferrers family.

Tantallon Castle, Lothian Region. NT5985. Ruined medieval castle with various works, c. 1529–39.

Taunton, Somerset. ST2324. *St Mary Magdalene*, tower, 1488–1514, carefully rebuilt in 1862. *St Margaret's Almshouses*, Hamilton Road, leper hospital rebuilt in early C16 and converted into almshouses 1612. *Gray's Almshouses*, East Street, 2-storeyed brick range, 1635. *Grammar School*, Corporation Street, c. 1480, remodelled 1520–30 for Roger Hill, merchant.

Tawstock Court, Devon. SS5529. Gatehouse dated 1574 with 2 polygonal turrets remains of former mansion.

Teddington, Gloucestershire. SO9632. *St Nicholas*, W tower 1567, S nave windows 1624.

Temple Newsam House, West Yorkshire. SE3532. Large, tall, brick open courtyard house begun 1628 for Sir Arthur Ingram, London merchant, and incorporating parts of early C16 house of Lord Darcy. Comparatively plain apart from projecting bay windows and lettered balustrade. Entrance porch with coupled Ionic columns in S wing.

Terpersie Castle, Grampian Region. NJ5420. (71.) Ruined Z-plan tower-house, 1561.

Tewkesbury, Gloucestershire. SO8932. Large number of good timber-framed houses of the period, including early C16 row at *34–50 Church Street* (*98, 99*). *Abbey House*, possibly built as lodgings for Abbot Henry Beoly (1509–31).

Thame, Oxfordshire. SP7006. *Grammar School*, Church Road (106). Large stone building, 1569, for Lord Williams with school room at right-angles to rear and arched lights to windows. Timber-framed *almshouses* adjacent, also for Lord Williams. Various disguised timber-framed buildings in High Street. *Thame Park*. SP7103. Early C16 abbot's lodgings incorporated in present house; including some of earliest Italian Renaissance decoration in England, c. 1530 for Abbot Robert King.

Thelveton Hall, Norfolk. TM1581. Brick E-plan house, c. 1592, with stepped gables, pedimented windows and polygonal angle shafts and pinnacles.

Thetford, Norfolk. TL8783. *Fulmerston Almshouses*, Bury Road, 1612, altered in C19. Various timber-framed buildings.

Theydon Garnon, Essex. TQ4799. *All Saints*, brick W tower 1520.

Theydon Mount, Essex. TQ4999. *St Michael*, small brick church of 1611–14. *Hill Hall* (48, *48*), sad ruins of very important house begun c. 1575 for Sir Thomas Smith. Although exterior has been much altered, courtyard elevations with 2 orders of attached columns are remarkably Classical for the date.

Thornbury, Avon. ST6590. *St Mary* (112, *113*), rebuilt early C16 with lavish tower. *Castle* (15, 41, *41*), remains of grand courtyard mansion with huge bay windows, built c. 1511–21 for Edward Stafford, Duke of Buckingham.

Thorney, Cambridgeshire. TF2804. *St Mary and St Botolph*, ruined abbey church restored in Perp fashion as parish church in 1638. *Abbey*, house partly late C16 with gables and shallow canted bay-window, remainder of 1660.

Thorpe, Surrey. TQ0268. *St Mary*, early C17 brick tower.

Thorpe Salvin, South Yorkshire. SK5281. Ruined manor house, 1570s, for Henry Sandford.

Thorpland Hall, Norfolk. TF9130. Surviving range is excellent example of decorated brick architecture with polygonal angle buttresses, lavish chimneyshafts and projecting porch.

Throwley Hall, Staffordshire. SK1152. Imposing ruin of early C16 house with 3-storeyed tower and arched window lights.

Thrumpton Hall, Nottinghamshire. SK5031. Symmetrical brick H-plan house with shaped gables and loggia on garden front, c. 1608.

Tibbermore, Tayside Region. NO0825. *Church*, 1632, enlarged 1810. *Huntingtower*, medieval tower-house with stepped L-plan block added mid-C16 and separated from E tower by 'the maiden's leap'. Linking section added

C17.

Tillington, West Sussex. SU9621.
Manor, stone house, c. 1600, with one
large gable and a small 2-storeyed porch.
Dean House, plain, symmetrical house,
1613.

Tissington Hall, Derbyshire. SK1752.
Plain, square, medium-sized Jacobean
house with walled garden.

Titchfield Abbey, Hampshire.
SU5406. (42.) Surviving gatehouse of
mansion created from dissolved abbey by
Earl of Southampton, c. 1538–42.

Tiverton, Devon. SS9512. *St Peter*,
sumptuous S porch and chapel for John
Greenway, merchant. 1517. *Blundell's
School*, symmetrical school room, 1604.
Chilcot School, modest foundation, 1611,
by nephew of Peter Blundell. *Greenway's
Almshouses*, Fore Street, only the chapel
remains of foundation, 1529. *Waldron
Almshouses*, Well Brook Street, c. 1579
with wooden gallery and Perp
decoration. *Slee Alsmhouses*, St Peter's
Street, low range, 1610, also with
wooden gallery.

Tixall, Staffordshire. SJ9722. (56, 58.)
Magnificent isolated 3-storeyed
gatehouse with 4 ogee-capped polygonal
angle turrets. Balustraded roof and
glittering fenestration suggest dual
function as lodge or stand. c. 1575 for Sir
Walter Aston.

Tolleshunt D'Arcy Hall, Essex.
TL9312. Moated house, c. 1500, with
brick and stone bridge dated 1585 and
Early Renaissance panelling in W wing.

Tolquhon Castle, Grampian Region.
NJ8728. Ruined late C16 courtyard
house.

Torksey Castle, Lincolnshire. SK8378.
Ruins of Sir Robert Jermyn's brick
mansion, c. 1560, with octagonal
projecting towers.

Torwoodhead Castle, Central Region.
NS8484. Ruined tower-house, 1566,
with elongated main range and plain
gabled roof.

Toseland Hall, Cambridgeshire.
TL2362. (79.) Beautifully contrived
compact brick house, c. 1600, with
projecting canted bays and embattled
chimneystacks.

Totnes, Devon. SX8060. (114.) Various
town houses of period.

Trefnant, Clwyd. SJ0671. *Perthewig*,
timber-framed house, 1594, with gable-
end stack and through-passage.

Toseland Hall, Cambridgeshire, c. 1600. A disciplined and symmetrical gentry house
enlivened by canted projections and fanciful chimneystacks

Trecarrel, Cornwall. SX3382. Remains of Sir Henry Trecarrel's early C16 manor house, now incorporated in barn.

Trefeglwys, Powys. SN9590. *Rhydycarw*, early C17 timber-framed lobby-entrance house with storeyed porch, converted to gable-end stacks C19.

Tregarden, Cornwall. SX0373. E-plan house, 1631, still with small, mullioned windows.

Trelawne, Cornwall. SX2055. Late C16 remodelling of medieval house for Sir Jonathan Trelawny.

Tremeirchion, Clwyd. SJ0771. (76.) *Bach-y-Craig*, 1567, Sir Richard Clough, Gresham's agent in Netherlands, built himself a uniquely Flemish house of brick consisting of compact cube with steeply pitched roof surmounted by cupola and adorned with tiers of dormers. This was linked to a large gatehouse by arcaded range. It is only the latter two elements (including the date) which have survived by incorporation into later farmhouse.

Trerice, Cornwall. SW8256. Symmetrical E-plan house with shaped gables and vast windows to hall, built 1570s for the Arundells.

Tretower Court, Powys. SO1821. Courtyard elevation of medieval mansion

of Vaughans, remodelled c. 1630 in modishly symmetrical fashion.

Trevalyn Hall, Clwyd. SJ3656. (60, 61.) Sophisticated H-plan house, 1576, for John Trevor with pedimented windows and finials to gables. Originally brick, but now rendered. Curious matching, separate rear range linked by miniature lodge seems to have been part of original composition.

Trewern, Powys. SJ2611. Large, ornate timber-framed addition, 1610, to earlier house.

Trewydir, Gwynedd. SH7961. *Gwydir Castle*, much altered house of Wynn family with 4-storeyed early C16 tower and later gatehouse.

Tullibole Castle, Tayside Region. NO0202. T-plan tower-house, 1608, with upper part of stair corbelled-out.

Turvey Abbey, Bedfordshire. SP9452. Gabled and irregular house of first decade of C17.

Tutbury Castle, Staffordshire. SK2029. King's Lodging added to medieval castle, 1631–5.

Ufton Nervet, Berkshire. SU6367. *Ufton Court*, large jettied timber-framed house, 1570s.

Ulverston, Cumbria. SD2878. *St Mary*, W tower c. 1540, replacing earlier tower destroyed in gale.

Upper Swell, Gloucestershire. SP1726.

Old Gwernyfed, Velindre, Powys. Early seventeenth-century Welsh E-plan house. The small windows are in complete contrast to contemporary English practice

(92.) *Manor House*, small, early C17 manor house of through-passage plan with added porch of considerable sophistication decorated with segmental pediment and Tuscan columns. Chimneypiece based on Serlio in upper room.

Uppingham, Leicestershire. SP8699. Small rectangular *school* to SE of church, founded late C16 by Archdeacon Johnson (cf. Oakham).

Upton, Cambridgeshire. TF1000. *St John Baptist*, N aisle rebuilt 1633 to receive monument to Sir William Dove. Gothic windows but Classical internal balustrade.

Upton Cressett, Salop. SO6592. *Upton Hall*, isolated brick house, c. 1540, with detached, turretted gatehouse of 1580.

Upton Lovell, Wiltshire. ST9440. *Church*, tower 1633.

Velindre, Powys. SO1836. (78.) *Old Gwernyfed*, early C17 E-plan house with ruined SW wing and 2 circular pavilions in forecourt, for Sir David Williams, MP for Brecon.

Vowchurch, Hereford and Worcester. SO3636. *St Bartholomew*, timber bell turret, c. 1522. Re-roofed and refurnished, 1613, by John Abel.

The Vyne, Hampshire. SU6356. Large, brick courtyard house, 1518–27, for Lord Sandys, remodelled after c. 1655.

Wallasey, Merseyside. SJ2992. *Leasowe Castle*, octagonal hunting tower, 1593, for Earl of Derby and greatly extended C19.

Wallingford, Oxfordshire. SU6089. Well-preserved town with important buildings of C16 and C17, including timber-framed Castle Street range of former *Lamb Inn*, High Street elevation of *Flint House*, and 3 tenements at *16–18 High Street*.

Walmer Castle, Kent. TR3750. Henry VIII castle, c. 1539, on quatrefoil plan.

Waltham Holy Cross, Essex. TL3800. *Abbey*, W tower 1556–8 after collapse of crossing tower, 1552.

Walton-in-Gordano, Avon. ST4273. Octagonal embattled tower surrounded by octagonal wall. Built, possibly as sham castle, c. 1615–20 for Lord Poulett.

Walworth Castle, Durham. NZ2218. (55.) Very plain house of c. 1600 with semicircular corner towers and spectacular frontispiece with 3 superimposed orders.

Warblington Castle, Hampshire.

SU7205. (42.) Ruined remains of moated brick courtyard house built for Countess of Salisbury, 1514–26.

Wardour, Wiltshire. ST9326. *Old Castle*, alterations and additions, c. 1570–8, to medieval castle for Sir Matthew Arundell, possibly by Robert Smythson. Significant intermingling of Classical and self-consciously Gothic motifs.

Wargrave, Berkshire. SU7878. *St Mary*, brick W tower c. 1635.

Warleigh House, Devon. SX4761. Irregular E-plan to S front, late C16.

Warmington, Warwickshire. SP4147. *Manor House*, late C16, flanking gabled wings and prominent side-wall chimneystack to hall range.

Warmwell House, Dorset. SY7585. Y-planned house, c. 1618, for Sir John Trenchard with central loggia.

Warwick, Warwickshire. SP2865. *St John's*, Smith Street, symmetrical town house, c. 1626, with 3 shaped gables and central porch. *Marble House*, Theatre Street, tall, Jacobean stone house with 3 shaped gables, central porch and canted bay windows. *Leycester's Hospital*, High Street, courtyard almshouse founded by Earl of Leicester in 1571 and incorporating medieval buildings of guilds of Holy Trinity and St George. Various other timber-framed buildings of the period in the town.

Walreddon, Devon. SX4774. Fragment of manor house with projecting porch dated 1596.

Water Eaton, Oxfordshire. SP5112. *Chapel*, 1610 with contemporary fittings. Also remains of early C17 manor house.

Watford, Hertfordshire. TQ1196. *St Mary*, N chancel chapel, 1597, with Tuscan column to nave arcade.

Welbeck Abbey, Nottinghamshire. SK5674. (58.) Riding house and stables, 1623–5, for Duke of Newcastle by Huntingdon Smythson.

Welshpool, Powys. SJ2207. *St Mary*, C16 arcades with Tudor arches and slim piers. *Powis Castle*, long gallery with originally open loggia beneath and contemporary decoration, c. 1590 for Sir Edward Herbert. *Sylfaen*, timber-framed lobby-entrance house with storeyed porch and service wing at the rear.

Welton Hall, Northumberland. NZ0667. Addition of 1614 to medieval tower.

Weobley, Hereford and Worcester.

SO3951. *The Ley*, multi-gabled timber-framed house, 1589, with off-set porch. *Fenhampton*, Jacobean E front with gabled porch.

Westbourne, West Sussex. SU7507. *St John the Baptist*, early C16 tower.

West Bromwich, West Midlands. SP0091. *Manor House*, Hall Green, medieval timber-framed house remodelled C16 with Elizabethan gatehouse. *Oak House*, Oak Road, C16 timber-framed house partly encased in brick and extended by curious gabled tower in early C17.

West Burton, West Sussex. TQ0113. *Coke's House*, plain, stone house, c. 1580, with added porch and pedimented garden gate, 1610.

West Coker Manor House, Somerset. ST5113. C15 house altered c. 1600.

West Deeping, Lincolnshire. TF1009. *The Manor House*, stone H-plan house, 1634, with central 2-storeyed porch.

West Hoathly, West Sussex. TQ3632. *Manor House*, stone, gabled house of 1627. *Gravetye Manor*, late Elizabethan gabled house with single-storeyed porch for iron-master, Richard Infield.

West Horsley Place, Surrey. TQ0753. Large medieval house remodelled in Artisan Mannerist style, 1630s.

Weston-Upon-Trent, Derbyshire. SK4028. *Weston Hall*, impressive remains of great H-plan mansion commenced c. 1633 for Roper family and never completed.

West Stafford, Dorset. SY7290. *Stafford House*, stone E-plan house, 1633, with 2-storeyed entrance porch.

West Stow Hall, Suffolk. TL8170. 3-storeyed brick gatehouse with polygonal turrets, 1520s, for house built for Sir John Crofts.

West Wittering, West Sussex. SZ7999. *Cakeham Manor House*, medieval palace of Bishops of Chichester with brick tower of c. 1520.

Westwood, Wiltshire. ST8158. *St Mary*, W tower early C16 for Thomas Horton, clothier. *Manor*, medieval house altered and extended for Horton c. 1515–30 and again after 1616.

Westwood Park, Hereford and Worcester. SO8764. Exceptionally tall, square, brick hunting lodge built on site of Benedictine nunnery c. 1598 for Sir John Pakington. Extended c. 1660 in triadic form.

Weymouth, Dorset. SY6779.

Sandsfoot Castle. Ruins of Henry VIII castle completed in 1541.

Wheathampstead, Hertfordshire. TL1713. *Water End Farm*, compact, gabled, brick manor house of Jennings family, c. 1610.

Wheatley, Oxfordshire. SP5905. *The Manor House*, C16 core with added E wing dated 1601. Remodelled in C20.

Whiston, Northamptonshire. SP8560. *St Mary*, complete church finished 1534 for Anthony Catesby.

Whitchurch, Oxfordshire. SU6377. *Hardwick Court*, gabled, brick, irregular house, c. 1530 for Richard Lybbe, extended in C17 and early C18.

Whiteparish, Wiltshire. *Newhouse*, Redlynch. SU2121. (20, 21.) Very stark brick hexagon with 3 projecting wings built as hunting lodge for Sir Thomas Gorges (of Longford Castle), c. 1619. *Eyte's Folly*. SU2423. Octagonal brick tower with pyramid roof. Built 1606, possibly as a stand.

Whitmore Hall, Staffordshire. SJ8141. Stables, 1620s, with perfectly preserved decorated stalls.

Whitton Court, Salop. SO5773. Medieval house altered in brick in C16 and again 1621.

Wigan, Greater Manchester. SD5805. *Winstanley Hall*, Elizabethan house with projecting wings and square projections in re-entrant angles. Altered early C19.

Wilderhope Manor, Salop. SO5492. Late C16 gabled stone house with circular stair turret on rear elevation.

Willaston Hall, Cheshire. SJ3277. Tall, compact, brick symmetrical house, c. 1600, with square projecting bays.

Willington, Bedfordshire. TL1150. *St Lawrence*, N chapel and possibly remainder of church, c. 1530 for Sir John Gostwick, Master of the Horse to Wolsey. *Dovecote and Stable*, all that survives of his house where he entertained Henry VIII in 1541. Exaggerated stepped gables.

Wilne, Derbyshire. SK4431. *St Chad*, Willoughby chapel, 1622.

Wilsford, Wiltshire. SU1339. *Lake House*, flint and stone house with 5-gabled front and embattled 2-storeyed porch, c. 1580 for George Duke, clothier.

Wilton House, Wiltshire. SU0931. Of courtyard house, c. 1560, for Earl of Pembroke on site of Benedictine nunnery, the porch survives. S front

rebuilt after fire, 1647–8, by John Webb.
Wimborne St Giles, Dorset. SU0312.
Brick *almshouses* attached to NW corner
of church, 1624 for Sir Anthony Ashley.
2-storeyed centre with short loggia.
Winchcombe, Gloucestershire.
SP0228. *George Hotel*, galleried courtyard
inn, c. 1525, for pilgrims to abbey.
Winchester, Hampshire. SU4829.
Cathedral, upper parts of the chancel
early C16. Fox chantry chapel c. 1528.
Gardener chantry (114)c. 1555 with
Renaissance detail.
Windsor, Berkshire. SU9676. (27, 29.)
St George's Chapel, wooden oriel to
chancel for Henry VIII, 1520s. Panelling
with Renaissance detail.
Wingham, Kent. TR2457. *St Mary the
Virgin*, legacies for rebuilding nave and S
aisle, 1541–62. Timber arcade possibly
result of embezzlement of funds in 1555.
Winkfield, Berkshire. SU9072. *St
Mary*, nave remodelled 1592. Brick SW
tower 1629.
Winsford, Cheshire. SJ6566. *St Chad*,
Over. Remodelled c. 1543.
Winterborne Clenston, Dorset.
ST8403. *The Manor House*, compact
symmetrical house, 1530s, with right-
angled service range at rear and unusual
octagonal central porch.
Winton House, Lothian Region.
NT4468. Earlier house enlarged and
embellished, 1620–7, by William
Wallace for Earl of Winton. Roughly
symmetrical with corner towers. Altered
in C19.
Winwick Manor House,
Northamptonshire. SP6273. Partial
remains of brick half H-plan house with
porch and hall bay in re-entrant angles, c.
1560. Tripartite gateway with Roman
Doric columns.
Wisbech, Cambridgeshire. TF4609. *St
Peter and St Paul*, sumptuously decorated
detached tower and SE vestry, c. 1520.
Wiston Park, West Sussex. TQ1512.
Symmetrical house with shaped gables
and central porch, c. 1575, for Sir
Thomas Shirley. Much altered in C19.
Witchampton, Dorset. ST9806. (81.)
Abbey House, large early C16 rectangular
brick house, probably for parson,
William Rolle.
Withcote, Leicestershire. SK7905.
Chapel, rare survival of early C16
detached private manor chapel with angle
pinnacles.
Wollaton Hall, Nottinghamshire.

SK5339. (24, 25, 52, 55.) One of the
most fantastic of all Elizabethan fantasy
houses. Symmetrical square plan with
extruded corner towers and prospect
chamber above hall towering over centre
of house. Richly modelled silhouette
appears like nothing so much as fairy-tale
castle. Built 1580–88 for Sir Francis
Willoughby, almost certainly to the
designs of Robert Smythson.
Wombourne, West Midlands.
SO8893. *The Wodehouse*, Jacobean E-
plan house with fanciful shaped gables.
Wonastow, Gwent. SO4611. *Treowen*,
tall, stone, gabled double-pile house,
1627, with slightly later Classical porch.
Woodbridge, Suffolk. TM2749. *Shire
Hall*, brick, originally with open ground
floor. Given by Thomas Seckford and
said to be of 1575. *The Abbey*, Church
Street, 3-storeyed brick porch, 1564,
from Seckford's house built on site of
Augustinian priory.
Woodham Walter, Essex. TL8006. *St
Michael*, 1563–4, brick with stepped
gables. Built for Earl of Sussex because
old church ruinous and too far away.
Wool, Dorset. SY8487. (81.) *Woolbridge
Manor*, stone and brick rectangular block
with later rear wing. Large 'gabled'
chimneystacks on rear wall and niches
flanking 1st floor windows on main
front. Early C17.
Wootton Lodge, Staffordshire.
SK0943. (56.) tall, compact house with
raised ground floor and regular
projections. Stylistic affinity with
Barlborough Hall (q.v.). c. 1580 for Sir
Richard Fleetwood.
Wormleighton Manor House,
Warwickshire. SP4453. Battlemented
brick remains of large house of Spencers,
c. 1512, with stone gatehouse dated
1613.
Worsborough, South Yorkshire.
SE3404. *Houndhill*, late C16 or early
C17 timber-framed E wing with central
chimneystack for Elmhirst family.
Remainder rebuilt late C17. *Worsborough
Mill*, c. 1625 of stone with overshot
wheel. Extended 1843.
Wothorpe House, Cambridgeshire.
TF0205. (56.) Ruined lodge on Greek
Cross plan with 4 tall octagonal towers in
re-entrant angles. Built early C17 for
Thomas Cecil.
Wotton-Under-Edge, Gloucestershire.
ST7593. *Hugh Perry's Almshouses*, 1632.
Bradley Court, irregular gabled house,

1567, with 2 projecting 3-storeyed staircase towers.

Wraxall Manor House, Dorset. ST5601. (84, 85.) Compact stone house, c. 1630, of regular, gabled design with central porch.

Wrexham, Clwyd. SJ3349. *St Giles*, early C16 tower.

Wrotham, Kent. TQ6159. *Wrotham Place*, part of Elizabethan brick mansion much altered in C19. *Ford Place*, one wing of large early C17 brick mansion with stepped and shaped gables.

Wroxham Manor House, Norfolk. TG2917. Irregular brick house, 1623, with stepped gables and pedimented windows.

Wroxton Abbey, Oxfordshire. SP4141. Remains of Augustinian priory incorporated in house begun in early C17 for Sir William Pope and incomplete at his death, 1631. 'Finished' in 1858.

Wothorpe House, Cambridgeshire; early seventeenth century. Thomas Cecil's lodge in the form of a Greek cross to which he retired for privacy away from Burghley House

Wyddial, Hertfordshire. TL3731. *St Giles*, brick N aisle and chancel chapel, 1532.

Wyke Champflower, Somerset. ST6634. *Holy Trinity*, 1623–4.

Wymondham, Norfolk. TG1101. *Abbey*, S aisle, 1544–60. Various timber-framed buildings in town include octagonal *Market Cross*, 1617.

Wynford Eagle, Dorset. SY5896. *Manor Farm*. Rectangular double-pile house with central 3-storeyed porch and axial chimneystack.

Yarmouth, Isle of Wight. SZ3589. Henry VIII *castle*, 1547, with single pointed bastion.

Yarnton, Oxfordshire. SP4711. *St Bartholomew*, chapel at E end of S aisle and SW tower, 1611. S porch, 1616.

Yaverland Manor House, Isle of Wight. SZ6185. H-plan, gabled symmetrical front. Dated 1620.

Yeaveley, Derbyshire. SK1840. *Stydd Hall*, strange 3-storeyed double-pile building erected in early C17 on site of preceptory of Knights Hospitallers, possibly as lodge in sham castle idiom.

York, North Yorkshire. SE6052. *St Michael-le-Belfry*, Minster Yard, rebuilt 1525–c. 36. *The King's Manor*, Exhibition Square, residence of President of Council of the North created from Abbot's House of St Mary's Abbey. Entrance range 1560–70 with doorway of c. 1625. Courtyard range c. 1610–15. Large number of timber-framed buildings of the period in the city.

BIBLIOGRAPHY

ENGLAND

Airs, Malcolm, *The Making of the English
Country House, 1500-1640*, London, 1975
Colvin, H. M. (Ed), *The History of the King's
Works, Vol. III, 1485-1660* (Part 1), London,
1975
Girouard, Mark, *Robert Smythson and the
Architecture of the Elizabethan Era*, London,
1966
Life in the English Country House, New
Haven and London, 1978
Mercer, Eric, *English Art, 1553-1625*,
Oxford, 1962
English Vernacular Houses, London, 1975
Pevsner, Nikolaus, *The Buildings of England*,
Harmondsworth, 1951-74
Summerson, John, *Architecture in Britain,
1530-1830*, Harmondsworth, 1953, 1st
paperback ed. 1970
Inigo Jones, Harmondsworth, 1966

SCOTLAND

Cruden, Stewart, *The Scottish Castle*,
Edinburgh, 1960
Dunbar, J. G., *The Historic Architecture of
Scotland*, London, 1966
Hay, G., *The Architecture of Scottish Post-
Reformation Churches, 1560-1843*, Oxford,
1957
McWilliam, Colin, *The Buildings of Scotland:
Lothian*, Harmondsworth, 1978

WALES

Beazley, Elisabeth, & Howell, Peter, *The
Companion Guide to North Wales*, London,
1975
The Companion Guide to South Wales,
London, 1977
Haslam, Richard, *The Buildings of Wales:
Powys*, Harmondsworth, 1979
Hilling, John B., *The Historical Architecture of
Wales*, Cardiff, 1976
Smith, Peter, *Houses of the Welsh Countryside*,
London, 1975

For houses open to the public see:
Armstrong, J.R., *Traditional Buildings
Accessible to the Public*, Wakefield, 1979
Burton, Neil, *Historic Houses Handbook*,
London, 1981

INDEX OF CRAFTSMEN

ILLUSTRATION ACKNOWLEDGEMENTS

Acknowledgement is made to the following for permission to reproduce copyright photographs on the pages specified:

Country Life, 148; Greater London Council, 101; A. F. Kersting, 142; National Monuments Record, London, 8–9, 42, 50–1, 54, 76; Megan Parry, 13, 18, 19, 41, 52 (b.), 62, 80 (t.), 83, 92, 99, 104, 112 (t.), 113 (b.), 172; E. M. Price, 23, 33; Anthony Quiney, 30, 31, 32, 38, 60, 63, 82 (b.). 106, 118, 167; Scottish Development Department (Crown Copyright Reserved), 64; Scottish Department of the Environment (Crown Copyright Reserved), 162 (t.); Scottish Royal Commission on the Ancient and Historical Monuments of Scotland, 74; Mary and Roddy Smith, 49, 109; Chris Tyson, 52 (t.); Richard Whitlock, 107.

The plans are reproduced, by permission, from the following sources: plans at All Souls' College, Oxford, 30; The Archaeological Journal, cxxviii, 1971 (Royal Archaeological Institute, London), 43; Garner and Stratton, Domestic Architecture of England during the Tudor Period, B.T. Batsford, London, 45; Sir John Summerson, Architecture in Britain, 1530–1830, Penguin, 1963, 60; Royal Commission on Historical Monuments, 63, 83; Scottish Development Dept (Crown Copyright), 73; original drawings by R. S. Mant, 91, 92